UNDERSTANDING SEMICONDUCTORS

A TECHNICAL GUIDE FOR NON-TECHNICAL PEOPLE

Corey Richard

Apress®

Understanding Semiconductors: A Technical Guide for Non-Technical People

Corey Richard
San Francisco, CA, USA

ISBN-13 (pbk): 978-1-4842-8846-7   ISBN-13 (electronic): 978-1-4842-8847-4
https://doi.org/10.1007/978-1-4842-8847-4

Managing Director, Apress Media LLC: Welmoed Spahr
Acquisitions Editor: Jessica Vakili
Development Editor: James Markham
Coordinating Editor: Susan McDermott

Cover designed by eStudioCalamar

Cover image designed by Freepik (www.freepik.com)

Distributed to the book trade worldwide by Springer Science+Business Media New York, 1 New York Plaza, Suite 4600, New York, NY 10004-1562, USA. Phone 1-800-SPRINGER, fax (201) 348-4505, e-mail orders-ny@springer-sbm.com, or visit www.springeronline.com. Apress Media, LLC is a California LLC and the sole member (owner) is Springer Science + Business Media Finance Inc (SSBM Finance Inc). SSBM Finance Inc is a **Delaware** corporation.

For information on translations, please e-mail booktranslations@springernature.com; for reprint, paperback, or audio rights, please e-mail bookpermissions@springernature.com.

Apress titles may be purchased in bulk for academic, corporate, or promotional use. eBook versions and licenses are also available for most titles. For more information, reference our Print and eBook Bulk Sales web page at http://www.apress.com/bulk-sales.

Any source code or other supplementary material referenced by the author in this book is available to readers on GitHub via the book's product page, located at www.apress.com/. For more detailed information, please visit http://www.apress.com/source-code.

Printed on acid-free paper

Contents

About the Author

Corey Richard helps lead the Executive Search and Developer Recruiting practice at SignalFire, an SF-based $2B Venture Capital Fund with notable investments in Grammarly, Uber, Ro, and Color Genomics. He supports over 150 seed and growth stage startups, helping founders attract and hire key talent across Engineering, Product, and GTM. Before coming to SignalFire, Corey supported Apple's Silicon Engineering Group for four years, where he built next-generation engineering organizations across all facets of silicon design – supporting both the Analog-Mixed-Signal (AMS) Design and IC Packaging Orgs. Prior to Apple, he consulted for a wide array of hardware technology giants including Harman International, Cirrus Logic, and Xilinx FPGA. Corey completed his MBA in Organizational Development and Entrepreneurship at the University of Pennsylvania's Wharton School of Business and was valedictorian of his undergraduate class at SDSU, where he studied finance, sustainability, and organizational psychology.

About the Technical Reviewer

Brian Trotter is CEO and Founder of Bishop Rock, an Austin-based technical research and intellectual property (IP) consultancy. Prior to founding Bishop Rock, he spent 10 years at Maxim Integrated, climbing the ranks to Executive Director of IC Design, where he led design teams to develop cutting-edge audio processors. Brian also spent 13 years at Cirrus Logic as a digital design engineer specializing in RTL implementation, synthesis, layout, and debug for advanced analog-to-digital and digital-to-analog converters.

Brian holds 12 US patents in areas of converter design, delta-sigma modulation, and digital interfaces. He is published by the IEEE and Audio Engineering Society (AES) and is a Registered Patent Agent with the United States Patent and Trademark Office (USPTO).

He received a BS degree in Electrical Engineering from Columbia University, and an MS degree in Electrical Engineering from the University of Texas at Austin.

Acknowledgments

I have to start by thanking my old boss and mentor, Bob Liebesman, who gave me my start in the recruiting industry and spent countless hours painstakingly teaching me the ins and outs of semiconductor technology. We've come a long way since those long afternoons off Opal St. in Pacific Beach. My three years with you and Troy at BSI have opened doors that have changed my life in such profoundly positive ways. Thank you so much for your guidance and friendship.

I'd like to thank Hina Azam, Charlie Zhai, Reggie Cabael, Martin Thrasher, John Griego, and the Packaging & SIPI and Hardware Tech Recruiting teams at Apple. Thank you for giving me the opportunity to work with such a driven group of people and challenging me every day for four years to learn and improve.

Thank you to the many contributors that made this project possible including Prof. Jan Van Der Spiegel who helped vet the technical content and Craig Heller who helped review style and craft compelling publisher applications just to name a few. A big thank you as well to my foreword author, Brian Santo. Your willingness to help a complete stranger on their passion project was a heartwarming act of altruism. I truly appreciate your time and generosity.

A special shout-out to my technical reviewer, Brian Trotter. You've read *Understanding Semiconductors* almost as many times as I have now and that's saying something. Really appreciate the attention to detail and the color your on-the-ground perspective added to each chapter.

A big hug to my family and the educators in my life including my parents Rhonda and Glen, my sister Eliza, and my grandparents Arnold, Janice, Hal, Elaine, and Howie. Your support and example have inspired me to help others grow too. Love you all to the moon and back.

Foreword

Through my entire career mostly as a journalist (with stints at an analysis firm and a PR agency), I have written exclusively about semiconductor technology and the electronics industry. I've met many people who could have benefited by having read something like this book — if only it had existed.

In fact, I could use this book. I'm a non-technical person.

The semiconductor industry is now one of the biggest, most valuable businesses in the world. Semiconductor technology is furthermore the driving force for advancements in a growing number of other enormous industries, everything from automotive manufacturing to financial services to medicine. Product differentiation is largely dependent on semiconductor technology, whether the products are smartphones, industrial robots, or pacemakers. Understanding this stuff is crucial to the jobs of so very many people.

Who, exactly? The people who sell, market, and publicize the semiconductors themselves. The people who sell, market, and publicize the products that incorporate semiconductors. The people who write about semiconductors, and the people who write about the products that incorporate semiconductors. For consumers, knowledge of semiconductor technology can be useful, and for some it has become critical — talk to almost any serious gamer and they're almost as familiar with the chips that are inside their PCs as the PC makers themselves.

And then there are those who need at least a basic grasp of the technology not for its own sake, but because it is important for understanding the business of semiconductors, as well as all the many businesses that depend on them. They include financial analysts, investors, and policy makers.

The number of non-technical people around the world who would benefit from having a basic understanding of semiconductor technology easily numbers in the hundreds of thousands, and possibly the millions.

It's a tough subject to learn as you go. I know this because that's what I did. In college I took courses mostly in the humanities. I graduated with a journalism degree and an expectation that I'd be writing about all sorts of subjects, not one of which was electronics. And then I got a job working at a newspaper that covered the semiconductor industry. Perhaps I was smart enough to learn as I went, but there is no question that I was fortunate. My mentors and people in the industry were all kind about sharing their knowledge. Patchwork learning can be serviceable – it has been for me, mostly – but I'm always discovering gaps in my knowledge. As I said, I can use this book today.

And I know it's not just me. Every day I work with and talk to other non-technical people – other journalists, PR people, salesmen, policy wonks – who must also deal with semiconductors and who similarly lack any relevant background in the field. Experience demonstrates to me almost every day that something like this book would be really handy for a lot of people.

Ah! But there's this thing called the Internet! Why not just look up this stuff online when you need to?

I spent most of my career reading engineering information on the Internet (not all of my career because I had to wait a few years for the World Wide Web to be introduced and then get populated with pertinent information). Much of what can be found online is written by techies assuming they are talking to other techies. The ability to communicate clearly is not as widely distributed a skill as one might hope, and even when engineers do write well, their meaning is apt to be obscured by jargon certain to be unintelligible to the uninitiated. If you're non-technical, and you need to understand semiconductors, here is a comprehensive volume, with comprehensible explanations, all ready to hand. This book is useful and necessary.

Brian Santo

ΛSPENCORE

Global Managing Editor

EETimes

Editor-in-Chief

Introduction

To the non-engineer, modern computing can seem supernatural. In the words of science fiction author Arthur C. Clarke, "Any sufficiently advanced technology is indistinguishable from magic."

So how did human beings figure out how to take the rocks you might find on an everyday hike and transform them into powerful machines, capable of revolutionizing the way we work, the way we communicate, the way we live?

From the towering mainframe computers of the 1960s to the powerful microscopic computers running society today, humanity's ability to process, store and manipulate data has advanced at an astonishing pace. In 1965, Gordon Moore, renowned technologist and founder of Intel, posited what came to be known as Moore's Law, which predicted the doubling of the number of transistors, and resulting computing power, a given chip could hold every two years. Since the first hand-sized transistor developed by William Shockley, John Bardeen, and Walter Brattain at Bell Labs in 1947 to the 3-**nanometer** (one-billionth of a meter) transistors in development today, engineering leaders have continued to prove Moore's prediction correct, doubling the number of components we can fit on a chip approximately every 18 months (Yellin, 2019) (Moore, 1965).

This exponential growth in computing power has led to what many have deemed the **Digital Revolution** and has been responsible for the abundance of technologies we enjoy and depend on today. From cell phones to artificial intelligence, semiconductor technology has enabled the explosion of countless industries and innovations.

The semiconductor industry is in and of itself massive; it recorded roughly $440 billion in revenue in 2020 and reached $559 billion in 2021, with an expected growth to over $600 billion by the end of 2022 (SIA Factbook, 2021). In the United States alone, 250,000 people are directly employed by the semiconductor industry in addition to an estimated 1 million indirect jobs (SIA, 2021). Industry leaders and politicians are trying to increase these numbers even further and bring more semiconductor jobs to the United States.

The original version of this book was revised. A correction to this book is available at https://doi.org/10.1007/978-1-4842-8847-4_11

Semiconductors are the United States' third largest export behind oil and aircraft, comprising an outsized portion of GDP (Platzer, Sargent, & Sutter, 2020). Without semiconductors, we wouldn't have any of the things that have come to define modern life - no cell phones, no computers, no microwaves, no video games - I'm sure anyone who tried buying a car during the pandemic understands what it means when there aren't enough of them. In short, semiconductors are a big deal.

So, wouldn't it be a good idea to learn something about them?

It's easy to see why those whose livelihood depends on semiconductors would want to read this book. But even for someone with no connection to the industry, understanding what semiconductors are, how they are made, what the future holds, and why they are so important to our everyday lives, will be a rewarding experience. Ideally, it will shine a light of comprehension on what can often be a complicated and foreboding subject. It will help you make connections to other areas of technology. It will give you a working technical vocabulary you can eventually master. You might even impress your friends at your next dinner party.

And, if those reasons aren't enough, reading *Understanding Semiconductors*, charging into the unfamiliar technological fray determined to emerge with new insights about the world around us, might even make you feel proud.

Semiconductor Basics

Semiconductors are all about harnessing the power of electricity to do amazing things. When you think about it, human advancement has always been characterized by our ability to harness and control powerful natural forces. Sunlight was harnessed to grow crops, gravity was harnessed to move water from rivers to cities, and wind was harnessed to sail across the oceans. In the last 100 years, semiconductors have been the key to harnessing the amazing power of a special natural force – electrical energy. To understand exactly how this works, we first need to learn a bit of the basics of electricity and conductivity.

Don't worry, there's no math. Well, maybe just a little…

Electricity and Conductivity

Electricity is used to describe a bunch of different things, but isn't really a "thing" at all. More accurately, electricity describes the relationship between **charge** and **current** (BBC, n.d.).

© Corey Richard 2023
C. Richard, *Understanding Semiconductors*, Maker Innovations Series,
https://doi.org/10.1007/978-1-4842-8847-4_1

Electric charge is a fundamental property of matter born by two of the particles that make up the basic building blocks of matter – **protons** and **electrons** (Encyclopedia Britannica, 2021). To understand how protons and electrons interact with one another, let's harken back to middle school physics and remember the solar system–like structure of an atom. In our model, each atom has a nucleus made up of positively charged protons and neutral **neutrons** stuck together in a ball. Surrounding the nucleus are a bunch of negatively charged electrons whizzing about. Atomic structure is held together by the balance between two forces – electromagnetic force and strong force, which we can see from the electron cloud model in Figure 1-1. While many physics textbooks depict electrons orbiting the nucleus of an atom along neat concentric lines, in real life they are much more disorganized and are better pictured as a field or cloud (Williams, 2016).

Electromagnetic force causes opposite charges to attract and similar charges to repel one another. It is the force responsible for keeping electrons close to the nucleus and moving between atoms. **Strong force** is what holds the neutrons and protons together despite protons having similar charges. In some elements, electrons stay close to the atom's nucleus, but in other elements, electrons are constantly bouncing around to other nearby atoms. Elements with these more active electrons are called **conductors**.

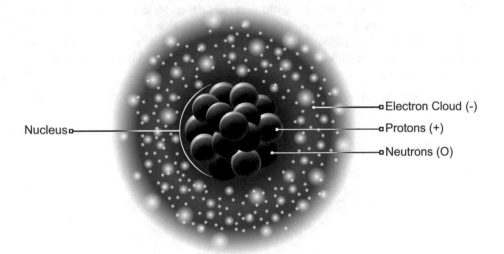

Figure 1-1. Electron Cloud Model of an Atom

In a conductor like copper, electrons are constantly jumping from atom to atom. Every time an electron in one copper atom jumps to a neighboring copper atom, the transmitting atom and receiving atom each receive a charge – the transmitting atom with one fewer electron (atom 1) now has a positive charge and the receiving atom with one greater electron (atom 2) now has a negative charge. Once atom 1 has a positive charge, the electromagnetic force that causes opposite charges to attract will draw a nearby electron from atom 3, which will quickly jump in to fill the void. Atom 1 will now be neutral while atom 3 is now positive, thus attracting yet another electron from atom 4. We can see this process play out in Figure 1-2.

This process continues constantly in everything you see; we just can't tell because these movements are happening randomly in all directions and in aggregate cancel each other out. This canceling out effect is why everyday objects don't have a negative or a positive charge – each thing we encounter may contain billions of positively and negatively charged atoms at any given time, but collectively, each object as a whole is neutral with no charge at all. This is why your couch doesn't electrocute you every time you sit down! In a neutral state, electrons may jump from atom to atom at random, but what happens if instead of randomly moving from place to place, these electrons were given some guidance?

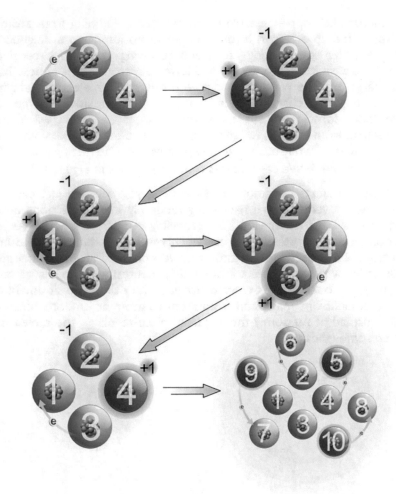

Figure 1-2. Charges and Electron Movement Between Atoms

Electric current is what results when electrons flow in the same direction (Science World, n.d.). "Flow" does not mean that electrons themselves are moving along at the speed of the current – this is a common misconception. What is really happening is the process we described previously, with electrons leaving their home atom to join a neighboring atom, which subsequently loses an electron to a 3rd neighboring atom, which loses an electron to a 4th atom, and so on and so forth. The collective effect of these movements is the transmission of electric current along a wire at nearly the speed of light, even though individual electrons travel only a few millimeters a second (Mitchell, n.d.).

To illustrate this process, we can zoom in to see how current is transmitted along a wire (see Figure 1-3). Remember that electromagnetic force causes opposite charges to attract. If we apply a positive charge to one end of the wire (to the left of Atom 1), Atom 1 will lose an electron, which is drawn to the positive charge. Atom 1 is now missing an electron and has a net positive charge. An electron in neighboring Atom 2 is now drawn to the positive charge and jumps to Atom 1, leaving Atom 2 with a positive charge. An electron from Atom 3 now jumps to Atom 2 and the chain goes on and on. Positive charge is "transferred" along the wire from one atom to the next, even though the electrons are moving in the opposite direction. The same basic process is happening with random electron movement in neutral objects like we saw in Figure 1-2, the only difference is that we've now given it direction.

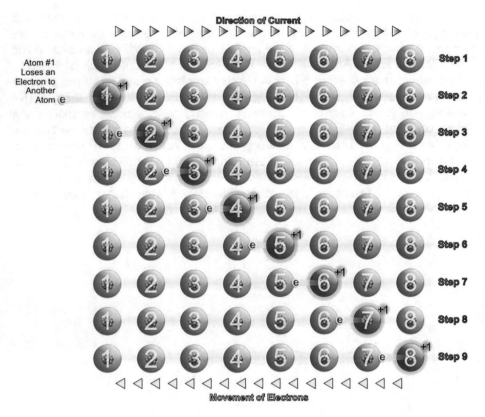

Figure 1-3. Electronic Current

You can picture this process by imagining a line of pool balls on a table (see Figure 1-4). If you hit the ball on one end of the line, the ball at the other end will move as though it was hit by you directly. In the same way that the **kinetic energy** (energy of motion) was transferred from the number 1 ball at the front of the line to the number 15 ball at the back, the energy from the atoms at the front of a copper wire can be transferred to the atoms at the back of the metal wire through an electric current (Beaty, 1999). The strength of an electric current is expressed in units called **amperes (amp or A)**, which measures how many electrons flow past a given point in a single second (Ada, 2013).

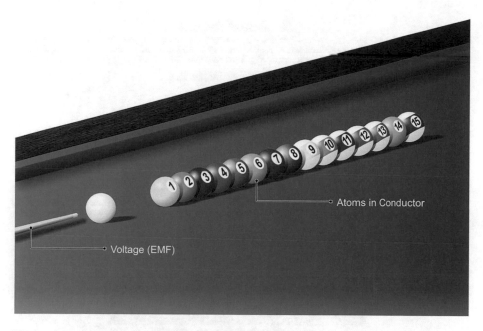

Figure 1-4. Playing Pool with Electromagnetic Force

Figures 1-3 and 1-4 help us picture what's happening within a wire at an atomic level. If we zoom out a bit and see what's happening along the wire as a whole, we can see that current and the electrons flow in opposite directions (see Figure 1-5). If this is confusing, a useful heuristic is to remember that conventional current flows from positive charge to negative charge. We know that electrons (-) are attracted to the positive charge (+) and thus flow from negative to positive, so the current must flow in the opposite direction. By creating a charge differential, we've initiated the chain reaction of electron movement between atoms that allows current to flow along a wire. The difference in charges between two objects is called **electric potential** and is responsible for the flow of charge through a circuit.

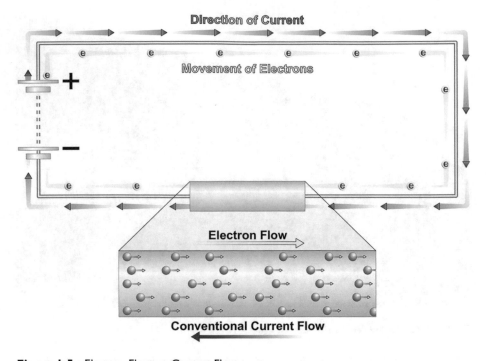

Figure 1-5. Electron Flow vs. Current Flow

So how exactly do we get electrons to form a current from one point to another? The answer lies in **voltage (V)**, also called **electromotive force (EMF or E)** (Nave, 2000). You can think of voltage like the water pressure in a hose, except that instead of pushing water out onto your lawn, it is pushing electrons to move from point A to point B (Nussey, 2019). Technically speaking, voltage exists wherever there is a difference in charge between any two places.

If your cell phone has a negative charge and your charger has a positive charge, a voltage exists between them. If your dog has a positive charge and your cat has a negative charge, a voltage exists between them. If your boss has a negative charge and your car has a positive charge, a voltage exists between them. Though it is highly unlikely that your boss or your dog has a net positive or negative charge, what's important is the charge differential. If we connect your cell phone to your charger, dog to cat, or boss to car with a conductor like a copper wire, an electric circuit will form through which electric current can flow.

A **circuit** is any closed loop between a source of voltage like a battery, a conductive wire, and other electrical elements (Rice University, 2013). Don't let the fancy terminology scare you – if you shuffle across the carpet in winter and touch your friend, you are forming a circuit. Current flows (in the form of charges) from you, through your friend, and to the ground. Ouch!

Another name for voltage is **potential difference**, which describes the amount of work required to bring a positive charge from one point to another (Electrical Potential, 2020). An object's **electric potential** is determined by its charge condition at a given point in time. A positively charged object is considered to have a higher potential than one that is negatively charged. If we connect an object with a higher potential to an object with a lower potential using a conductor, the electrons will flow from the low potential body to the high potential one, while current flows from high potential to low. The greater the difference in charges between the two objects, the greater the voltage. We can see potential difference illustrated in Figure 1-6.

Remember how current flows along a wire – with a positive charge moving along from one end to the other as electrons are transferred between neighboring atoms in the opposite direction. To start this chain reaction and transfer positive charge along the wire, we need an initial difference in charges between two parts of the circuit. Why else would the electron from Atom 1 in our diagram shift to the left and keep the current moving in the same direction? Electric current cannot flow without voltage – it is this potential difference that allows electricity to light our homes, heat our water, and do the work we need to power our lives.

No Potential Difference vs. Potential Difference

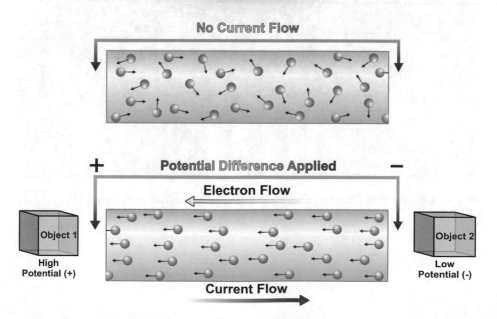

Figure 1-6. No Potential Difference vs. Potential Difference

If we imagine any two bodies with a difference in charges, whether they be the two ends of a battery powering a light bulb or between the key and the thunder clouds in Benjamin Franklin's famous kite experiment, a potential difference exists between them. We can activate this potential difference by connecting them with some sort of conducting material or a direct connection between the objects themselves, thus forming a circuit. For a circuit, this might mean connecting one end of the battery with the other, which causes current to flow from one end of the circuit to the other and turns on the light. For Ben Franklin, this could be a connection between a cloud and the key at the end of his string. In both cases, positive charge flows from the object with higher potential (positive end of the battery or the thunder cloud) to the object with lower potential (negative end of the battery or the key).

Franklin was trying to prove that lightning was an electrical discharge that can be redirected safely into the ground and away from flammable structures. We can see a famous drawing of his daring work published in 1876 by one of America's most prolific printmaking firms Currier & Ives in Figure 1-7. The experiment led to the invention of lightning rods that have protected buildings and people to this day (Currier & Ives, 2009).

Figure 1-7. Benjamin Franklin's 1752 Electricity Experiment (Currier & Ives, 2009)

Rather than depending on potential difference in the natural environment, **batteries** work by lifting the charge and therefore potential of one end of the circuit (+) relative to the other end (-). Current will not stop flowing until all of the surplus negative charges on the negative part of the circuit have flowed to the positive side of the circuit and the battery is empty. We can see this illustrated in Figure 1-8.

If you've ever wondered why there's a positive (+) and negative (-) side to a household battery, it marks each end necessary to form a potential difference and power whatever appliance you're using it for. The materials that make up a battery enable it to create this electronic potential – a **cathode** made of a material "in need" of electrons forms the positive (+) side of the battery (where the current leaves or electrons enter) and an **anode** made of a material "with excess" electrons forms the negative (-) side of the battery (where the current enters or electrons leave) (US Department of Energy, n.d.). The potential difference between each end is stored as **chemical energy**, which is then converted into **electrical energy** as the battery is used.

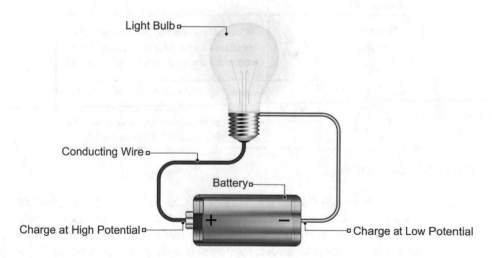

Figure 1-8. Battery – Powered Light Bulb Circuit

Current and voltage tell us how electricity works in principle, but to understand what electricity can really do, we need to talk about Power. **Power** describes the work done by an electric circuit when an electric current is converted into some form of useful energy. This useful energy could be a plethora of things – motion, light, heat, sound, satellite signal, etc. When your speaker plays your favorite song or your bedside lamp helps you read before bed, they are turning electrical power into useful energy. Power is measured in **watts (W)**. One watt measures the amount of work executed by an electronic circuit in which one amp of current is "pushed" by one volt (Electronics Tutorials, 2021).

Remember, **amps** measure the number of electrons flowing across a given point over time (current), while **volts** measure the amount of pent-up electrical pressure between two points due to potential difference (voltage). You can see a summary of these three forces, as well as electrical resistance, in Figure 1-9.

	UNIT	DEFINITION
Current	Ampere (A)	Flow of electrons moving in the same direction. Specifically measures how many electrons flow past a given point in a single second.
Voltage	Volt (V)	Pent up electrical pressure between two points of unequal charge. Also called Potential Difference.
Power	Watt (W)	Work done by an electric circuit. Specifically measures the amount of work executed by a circuit in which one amp is "pushed" by one volt.
Resistance	Ohm (Ω)	Amount of opposition to the flow of current in an electric circuit. Specifically measures the resistance level when one ampere is produced by applying one volt between two points.

Figure 1-9. Units of Electricity

The relationship between Power (P), Voltage (E), and Current (I) is reflected in **Joule's Law**, which was named after the English physicist James Prescott Joule who discovered it in 1840 (Shamieh, n.d.). You don't need to memorize this equation, it's just good to understand how the three are related and how voltage and current can work together to create something we can use (power). If you do plan on using this equation, it's important to use the correct units for power (watts), voltage (volts), and current (amperes).

Joule's Law: Power (P) = Voltage (E) x Current (I)

We can think of power, voltage, and current like the flow of water from a water heater to a shower head. Charge, in our analogy, is like the water itself – it's what moves through the system to get stuff done. We can pretend voltage is like water pressure and current is the flow of water (or charge) throughout the system. If we multiply the water pressure (voltage) by the flow of water (current), we deliver the power that comes out the other end – the more power, the better the shower. We can see this analogy visualized in Figure 1-10.

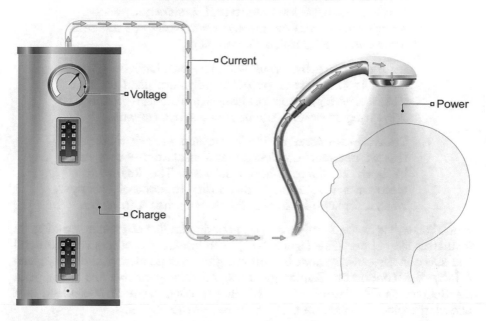

Voltage (E) x Current (I) = Power (P)
Water Pressure x Water Flow = Shower Power

Figure 1-10. Joule's Law and a Good Shower

Electricity describes the relationship illustrated by Joule's Law. It is the phenomena in which voltage is applied to drive current, which happens when electrons are pushed to flow in the same direction. This happens at large scale in your local utility company that ships power to your home. But let's face it, that's not really the interesting part to everyday consumers. The challenge is to figure out how to harness this current to do something useful. For that, we need a way to control the current we have created. All these flowing electrons (current) must be channeled through a material of some kind to make them useful as electricity. We need materials with conductivity.

Conductivity is a measure of how easily electric current can pass through a material. The key to performing useful work with electricity is to control conductivity – allowing current to flow in some cases and restricting it in others. That overhead light in your room would be much less useful if it was just on all the time or off all the time. Turning the current on and off is critical.

Different materials have different conductivity, which can be grouped into three main types – conductors, insulators, and semiconductors. Here are some concise definitions:

- **Conductors** are materials with high conductivity (think metallic materials like copper and aluminum, which are the most common conductors used in electronics). Conductors have low **electrical resistance**, allowing electric current to flow through them easily. Resistance is measured in units called **Ohms (Ω)**.

- **Insulators** are materials with low conductivity (think materials like plastics or other polymers used to coat electrical wiring). Insulators have high electrical resistance, preventing or slowing the flow of electric current.

- **Semiconductors**, as the name implies, are materials that sit between conductors and insulators – they can be both conductors and insulators. The key to the electronics revolution is the ability to control exactly when a semiconductor conducts, and when it insulates.

Electrical wiring is commonly made of a conductor, like copper, encased by an insulator, like rubber (See Figure 1-11). The insulator protects the wire and the surrounding environment by absorbing the excess electrical energy given off by the conductor. Semiconductors, containing properties from both conductors and insulators, are better able to control the flow of electricity, allowing engineers to create smaller, more intricate systems.

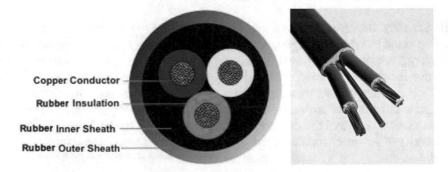

Figure 1-11. Electrical Wiring Left: Rubber Insulated Rubber Sheathed Red, Yellow, and Blue Three Core Round Cable (Jainsoncables, 2007) Right: "Twin and Earth" Electrical Cable, Commonly Used in the United Kingdom and Other Countries (Allistair1978, 2020)

By harnessing the properties of each of these types of materials, engineers can build elaborate systems that store and send information, solve complex problems, and perform all kinds of tasks that make modern technology possible.

Since the semiconductor is the key to this technology, let's learn a little more about what a semiconductor is and how they are built.

Silicon – The Crucial Semiconductor

There exists a large variety of semiconductor materials, each with varying levels of conductivity. Though other semiconductors, like **germanium** and **gallium arsenide (GaAs)**, are also used in electronic devices, the vast majority of electronics are made using an element called Silicon (Si14 for all you periodic table enthusiasts out there). **Silicon** has numerous advantages that make it an ideal material for building computer chips – in addition to useful mechanical and thermal properties, it is inexpensive and abundant. Comprising roughly 30% of the Earth's crust, silicon is the second most abundant element in Earth's crust after oxygen and can be found in sand, rocks, clays, and soils (Templeton, 2015). We can see a picture of purified silicon in Figure 1-12.

Figure 1-12. A Piece of Purified Silicon (Enricoros, 2007)

A Quick Semiconductor History

Before we dive deep into the details of the semiconductor design and manufacturing technology, it can be helpful to know just a little bit about its history and key inventors. Once scientists discovered the semiconductor properties of silicon, they were able to build simple **transistors**, which are basically switches that prevent current from moving forward or allow it to pass. By arranging transistors in intricate patterns, they realized they could selectively guide current along a path of their choosing and make it do some useful work along the way. For about a decade after the first transistor was invented in 1947, semiconductor design and manufacturing were slow, cumbersome, and costly.

Individual transistors and other components had to be manufactured independently, then fit together manually using **"flywire" connections**, which are basically metal wires connecting transistors to one another one at a time. A complete transistor circuit could literally fill an entire room. This was not going to be the basis for any kind of world-altering technological revolution.

All this changed in 1959, which can be officially observed as the beginning of the semiconductor revolution (doubtful we can get a national holiday and a day off out of it, but still worth noting). This was due to two key events. First, the invention of the **integrated circuit** by Jack Kilby at Texas Instruments, and Robert Noyce at Fairchild Semiconductor allowed hardware designers to fit a bunch of transistors together on a single chip (Nobel Media, 2000) (Kilby, 1964). Second, the invention of **planar manufacturing** by Jean Hoerni at Fairchild Semiconductor allowed chip companies to fabricate multitudes of components at the same time and on the same **substrate** (semiconductor base material, kind of like the foundation of a house but for computer chips) (Nobel Media, 2000) (Hoerni, 1962). Kilby received a Nobel Prize for Physics in 2000 for his work. Hoerni (deceased, 1924–1997) never received a Nobel Prize, but is widely recognized for his contributions. The importance of these core innovations – the integrated circuit (IC) and planar manufacturing process – cannot be overstated. They serve as the foundation of the design and manufacturing-based value chain that semiconductors and computers are built with to this day. We will cover each in detail in Chapters 3 and 4.

Semiconductor Value Chain – Our Roadmap

In trying to discuss a complex technical topic like semiconductors, it can be a real challenge to decide how exactly to tell the story. Should we start with "Once upon a time..." and proceed chronologically up to today? Should we start with the smallest elements like atoms and electrons, and work our way up to huge systems like computers and cars?

In *Understanding Semiconductors*, we've decided to tell the story just like a semiconductor company operates – from deciding what products to build, to designing and manufacturing them, to packaging and integrating them into the system.

We call this sequence the **Semiconductor Value Chain**, and it will serve as our roadmap for our entire journey. We'll go on a few detours to discuss some fundamentals and a couple of special topics, but for the most part, everything that follows in this book can be tied back to a part of this core sequence and can serve as a mental foundation on which to build your understanding of the industry as a whole.

Starting from a product concept, the value chain in the semiconductor industry can be broken down into six main components:

1. **Customer need and market demand:** First, the need for a "system" or product must be established. A new system could be anything from a rocket ship control panel to the next iPhone. What is important here is that there is a market need — without a customer, why build a new system in the first place? But remember, customers may not always tell you what they need. Recall the classic quote from Henry Ford, "If I had asked people what they wanted, they would have said faster horses."

2. **Chip design:** Second, a firm must consider a product and design a chip that will fit that product accordingly. This design process is broken down into front- and back-end design. To make sure this is clear, here's what happens at each step:

    Front-end design: System requirements are gathered, and a detailed schematic is developed to create a design concept. This design concept is tested and verified before moving to back-end design.

    Back-end design: A detailed list of instructions, called a **netlist,** is converted into a physical layout, which can then be tested and validated before being sent to a factory called a semiconductor fabrication plant, or **fab**, for manufacturing.

3. **Fabrication and manufacturing:** Third, a design must be manufactured at a **wafer fab**. In this step of the process, numerous integrated circuits, also known as **die** or **IC's**, are printed onto a sheet of silicon called a **wafer** through a process called **photolithography**.

4.   **Packaging and assembly:** Fourth, once the die have been cut apart from one another, they are individually packaged in plastic or ceramic packages called **IC packaging** in a process called **assembly**. These **package-die assemblies** are tested one last time before being sent to end systems or product companies.

5.   **System integration:** Once the system or product company has received the final die-package assembly, they can solder it onto a larger **circuit board** or **substrate** with other components or ICs and integrate it into the end, consumer-ready product.

6.   **Product delivery:** The product is shipped to customers, where it is ready to be used.

For all you visual learners out there, Figure 1-13 features a step-by-step conceptual framework of the Semiconductor Value Chain, from design to delivery.

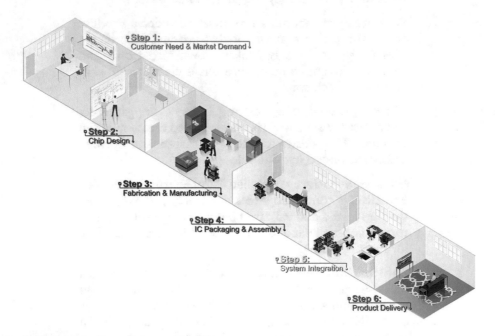

Figure 1-13. Semiconductor Value Chain

For the most part, semiconductor companies concentrate on Steps 2–5. And, in fact, some companies (called 'fabless' companies) really only do step 2. They design the chip, and then outsource most of the other steps. Companies start by forecasting market demand or collecting orders from downstream device companies and focus their energy on building chips that can satisfy the needs of their customers. Since the industry's inception in the 1940s, this value chain has remained, conceptually, relatively stable. At the same time, however, the organization and business strategies of how each step is done have been incredibly dynamic, driven by innovative companies competing to provide the best performing chips and highest quality products. We will use this value chain to guide our discussion of key sub-processes and anchor our understanding of each step to the bigger picture.

Performance, Power, Area, and Cost (PPAC)

For semiconductor companies focused on the design, manufacturing, assembly, and integration portions of the value chain (steps 2, 3, 4, and 5), the goal is to achieve the **Highest Performance**, using the **Lowest Power** and the **Smallest Area** possible. These three key design metrics are typically measured in **clock frequency (Hz)**, **watts**, and **nanometers (nm)**, respectively. Each semiconductor design may trade off one of these for the others, depending on the application. For example, a team designing a chip for a server in a data center with plenty of space and an industrial grade power source may focus on performance, while not caring as much about size or power. A team designing a chip for a battery-powered cell phone, however, may be concerned more about power and size than performance. For any given application, the goal is to optimize a chip design along these three constraints at the **Lowest Cost** and in the **Shortest Time** frame possible. We can better picture how these factors relate to one another in Figure 1-14.

Each chip must balance PPAC constraints to provide an optimal solution. Design teams must keep in mind the problem they are trying to solve and the application the circuit they are building is meant to address. For example, plugged-in devices like desktop computers may not have to optimize for power consumption as much as battery-powered laptops. Laptops, in turn, may have greater flexibility on area than smaller, hand-held devices like cell phones. It is important not to forget time as a key constraint as well – it may be worth lower performance if you can cut your design cycle short and beat your competitors to market. There are virtually limitless applications of circuits, all with unique performance, power, area, cost, and time constraints – the important thing is to understand the trade-offs.

In the back-and-forth of semiconductor product development, the marketing and business teams always want the best of all three metrics: highest performance, lowest power, and smallest area. In making trade-offs, the engineering teams frequently respond with, "You pick two, we get to pick the other one." While this is a bit snarky from the engineering teams, it does highlight the trade-offs required. For example, if you really must have the highest performance and smallest area, the laws of physics will limit your efficiency on power.

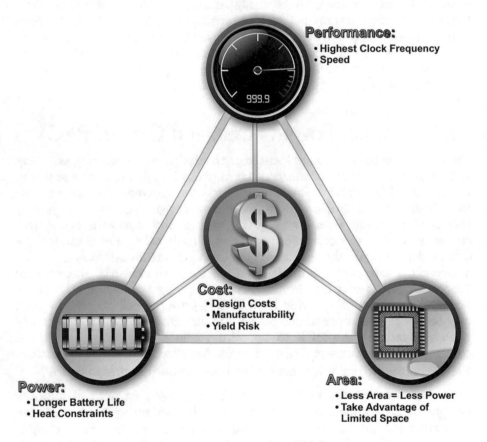

Performance:
• Highest Clock Frequency
• Speed

Cost:
• Design Costs
• Manufacturability
• Yield Risk

Power:
• Longer Battery Life
• Heat Constraints

Area:
• Less Area = Less Power
• Take Advantage of Limited Space

Figure 1-14. Power vs. Performance vs. Area vs. Cost (PPAC)

Who Uses Semiconductors?

Before we move into the more technical details of how chips are designed and fabricated, it's important we don't lose sight of why we're building them in the first place. The **Semiconductor Industry Association** is one of the key trade groups in the semiconductor industry, and they define six different categories for end-use applications (see Table 1-1).

Table 1-1. SIA Framework – End-Use Applications

MARKET	SPECIFIC APPLICATIONS
Consumer	TV, Video, Audio, Household Appliances, Other Consumer Goods like Cameras, Games, Smart Watches, Fitness Monitors, Alarm Clocks, etc.
Automotive	In-Vehicle Entertainment and Information Systems, Power Train, Control Systems, Infotainment, etc.
Computing	Personal Computers, Office Equipment and Peripherals, Handheld Computing Devices, Servers, etc.
Industrial	Power Supplies, Commercial Internet of Things (IoT) Devices, Manufacturing Test, Control, and Measuring Equipment, etc.
Communications	Cell Phones and Wireless Handsets, Networking and Remote Access Devices, Base Stations, Broadcasting Equipment, etc.
Government	Military and Aerospace Electronics

Within these categories, the most recent 2021 report by the **World Semiconductor Trade Statistics (WSTS)** and Semiconductor Industry Association (SIA, 2021), states that "Communications" and "Computer & Office" accounted for the greatest proportion of semiconductor sales, combining for nearly two thirds of industry revenues. But as cars become more electrified, and as industrial operations become more and more automated, analysts expect the Automotive and Industrial and Instrument categories to grow in the future. We can see a breakdown of what end-use applications semiconductors are used for in Figure 1-15.

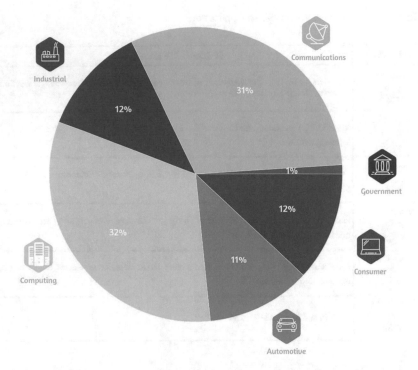

Figure 1-15. 2020 Semiconductor Market by End Use Application (SIA and WSTS) Power vs. Performance vs. Area vs. Cost (PPAC)

Each of these applications has different PPAC requirements and drivers based on their unique purpose, which impacts each stage of the design, manufacturing, and assembly processes.

Summary

In this chapter, we examined how electricity and conductivity work together to make semiconductor technology possible. We discovered what semiconductors are, what they do, and why silicon is the most useful one. We introduced the Semiconductor Value Chain that converts ideas and raw materials into chips and finished products. Finally, we reviewed the key PPAC parameters that shape how chips are optimized for their intended purpose and what those real-world applications actually are.

The ideal chip is high performance, requires low power, and takes up little space. Accomplishing all three would be ideal, but cost and time force us to make tough choices. Each step of the value chain is essential to get a chip from concept to customer – at every stage, companies fight for profits and market share by balancing these factors more effectively than their competitors.

Your Personal SAT (Semiconductor Awareness Test)

To be sure that your knowledge builds on itself as we move through each subject here are five questions relating to the previous chapter. It's "open book" so please feel free to go back and reread any material that will be helpful.

1. Define electricity and conductivity. How do they relate to current and charge?

2. What is the most important semiconductor and why?

3. Which two inventions are responsible for the modern semiconductor industry? Why were these innovations so important?

4. After fabrication and manufacturing, what step in the semiconductor value chain is necessary before system integration? Can you name all six?

5. What does PPAC stand for? Can you name which key design factor is missing?

Circuit Building Blocks

Before anyone could carry a powerful computer in their pocket, electronic circuits were made up of lots of little components on a circuit board. If you ever opened up an old stereo or television, you've probably seen some of these little green rectangles covered with black, brown, and silver boxes and cylinders. Those circuits were built with what's called "discrete components." The story of electronic circuits begins there...

Discrete Components – The Building Blocks of Circuits

All electronic devices are built using some combination of **discrete components** – the smallest building blocks of an electronic device.

Although there are numerous component "LEGO blocks" with which modern electronics are built, these are the most important to remember and understand:

© Corey Richard 2023
C. Richard, *Understanding Semiconductors*, Maker Innovations Series,
https://doi.org/10.1007/978-1-4842-8847-4_2

1. **Transistor:** Transistors function like electronic switches – they stop electricity from passing or allow current to flow through. By stringing many transistors together, off (0) and on (1) transistor switches can form patterns that can represent and manipulate information.

2. **Resistor:** A resistor is a device made of a material that impedes the flow of electricity through a circuit, controlling voltage and current.

3. **Capacitor:** A capacitor is a device that stores electrical energy.

4. **Inductor:** An inductor is a device that uses magnetic fields to control the flow of electricity; these are found as discrete components in power supplies that convert a battery or **Alternating Current AC** wall power supply into low-voltage **Direct Current (DC)** power supply for computers and mobile devices (Murata, 2010). **Capacitors** and **inductors** regulate or stabilize **voltage**, so that there's never too little or too much voltage in any given place. Too little voltage and the system can't do its job; too much voltage and the system could be damaged.

5. **Diode:** Diodes are somewhat like transistors, except that instead of allowing the flow of electricity to be controlled like a switch, they only allow the flow of electricity in one direction. They essentially act as a one-way gate, or valve, for electricity. You are likely familiar with **light emitting diodes (LEDs)**, which are a specific kind of diode that help you read at night and make parties more fun.

These five major components are used to manipulate the flow of electricity. They can be either discrete (manufactured separately) or integrated (manufactured on the same substrate) and vary widely in size and dimension. We can see each component illustrated in Figure 2-1.

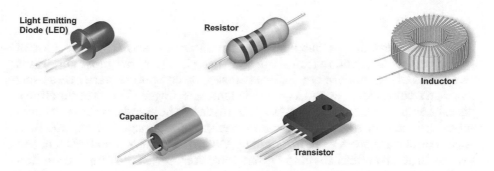

Figure 2-1. Discrete Components

Non-integrated discrete components are called "discrete" because they are manufactured separately from one another, as opposed to all on a single **wafer**. **Integrated circuits**, on the other hand, are made up of many "functional" components integrated onto a single **substrate**, the base semiconductor material on which integrated circuits are built, kind of like a house foundation, but at microscopic scale (Saint & Saint, 1999). Instead of manufacturing a given number of transistors, resistors, capacitors, and diodes separately and connecting them afterward, patterns can be etched together on the same **chip**, or die, using specialized manufacturing technologies like photolithography.

A single advanced **die** can literally have billions of individual **functional components** performing the same activities as **discrete components** manufactured separately from the IC. The important distinction here is that they are integrated and fabricated on the same substrate as the rest of the circuit. In addition, integrated circuits can be fabricated by the thousands, or even tens of thousands, on a single wafer. By tightly integrating these functional components on the same chip and manufacturing thousands at the same time, power is saved (smaller system), speed is increased (greater density), and area is reduced, which further lowers manufacturing unit costs (less materials and fewer process runs) (New World Encyclopedia, 2014).

The reason a smaller system requires less power is simple – it takes more power to drive current along a longer wire than a shorter one. The more tightly integrated a given chip, the closer the functional components are to one another, which means the interconnects and wires that tie everything together are closer to one another as well. Although all these discrete components are important, we will pay special attention to the transistor.

Transistors

When discussing the various kinds of components, **transistors** get a lot of attention, and for good reason – the transistor is one of the most important inventions of the modern era. Before transistors, computers were made using **vacuum tubes** that were large, inefficient, and fragile. The first functional digital computer, called the ENIAC, was made of thousands of these vacuum tubes, in addition to **capacitors** and **resistors** (Hashagen et al., 2002). It wasn't until transistors were invented by William Shockley, John Bardeen, and Walter Brattain at Bell Labs in 1947 that computers began their rapid evolution to the microelectronics we see today. These scientists received the 1956 Nobel Prize in Physics for their work (Nobel Prize Outreach AB, 1956).

We can see the differences in vacuum tubes and transistors illustrated by the pictures in Figure 2-2. The vacuum tube (left) looks like a light bulb and is visibly fragile as compared to the transistor (middle) made of metal and enclosed in a protective plastic package. The **ENIAC**, invented by J. Presper Eckert and John Mauchly at the University of Pennsylvania in 1946, was basically a giant room full of vacuum tubes taking up almost 1,800 square feet and weighing nearly 50 tons (U.S. Army, 1947). We can see it pictured in Figure 2-3 (left) next to a picture of the ENIAC-on-a-Chip implemented (right) (1996). The chip which measures 7.44x5.29 square mm is placed next to a coin for reference, illustrating the progress made by the semiconductor industry in shrinking computer sizes over the course of several decades (Hashagen et al., 2002). Vacuum tubes are still used in select applications like microwave ovens and audio equipment, but transistors have taken over as the main building block of modern electronics. The transistor block diagram in Figure 2-2 (right) depicts the **base, emitter**, and **collector** that make up an early **bipolar transistor**. You can refer back to Figure 2-2 if you need help visualizing transistor structure, which we will discuss shortly.

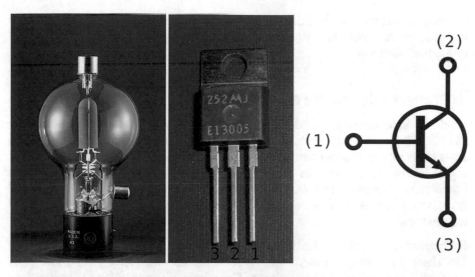

Figure 2-2. Vacuum Tube vs. Transistor (Ikeda, 2007) (Reinhold, 2020)

Figure 2-3. ENIAC vs. ENIAC-on-a-Chip (U.S. Army, 1947) (Hashagen et al. 2002)

A transistor is a semiconductor device that, in its simplest form, acts like a switch. Using voltage from a battery or other power source, transistors control something called a **gate**, allowing them to stop a current in its tracks or allow it to pass through. The pattern of "on" transistors with flowing current and "off" transistors with halted current are the basis for **binary computer language** used in **digital electronics**. Computers are able to interpret these patterns of 1's and 0's as information (called **signals**) which they can then manipulate, process, and store. Like a telegraph operator sending a message with different pulses of Morse code, transistors enable computers to process and store information by controlling the flow of individual electrons.

Transistor Structure

Modern **transistors** (called **Metal-Oxide Field Effect Device**s, or **MOSFETs**) have three main parts – the source, the gate, and the drain. The **source** is where the current, or signal, comes from. The **drain** is where the signal leaves. The **gate** sits between them and decides whether to let the signal pass through (Riordan, 1998). The source, gate, and drain in MOSFET transistors are akin to the emitter, base, and collector in earlier bipolar transistors.

Each of these blocks is made of silicon or another semiconductor material. On their own, they wouldn't be very useful, as electricity would just pass through if we applied enough voltage. The magic happens when we manipulate these blocks in a process called **doping**. In this process, each neutral block is injected with a material (called **dopants** or **impurities**) that either has an extra electron or is missing one (Honsberg & Bowden, 2019). The resulting blocks with an extra electron are called **n-type (negative) semiconductors**, while the blocks missing an electron are called **p-type (positive) semiconductors** (Sand & Aasvik, 2019). Transistors can be made of an n-type semiconductor sandwiched between two p-type semiconductors (**PMOS transistor**) or vice versa (**NMOS transistor**); the important thing to note is that the gate is a different charge from the source and the drain. Either way, the resulting apparatus is now ready for action.

How Transistors Work

For the purposes of demonstration, imagine a PMOS transistor made of a p-type semiconductor sandwiched between two n-type semiconductor blocks. Though the source, gate, and drain are each lacking an electron or carrying an extra, the resulting combination is effectively neutral. Without power or voltage, the transistor is stagnant, and no electrons can flow through the system. Lucky for us, electromagnetic force causes opposites to attract, so if we apply positive voltage to the gate, the negative electrons from the source and drain are drawn to this voltage, while the positive charge in the gate is pushed away. This establishes an opening called a **channel** through which the electrons can flow, allowing current to pass through (Channel MOSFET Basics, 2018). We can see how this process works in Figure 2-4.

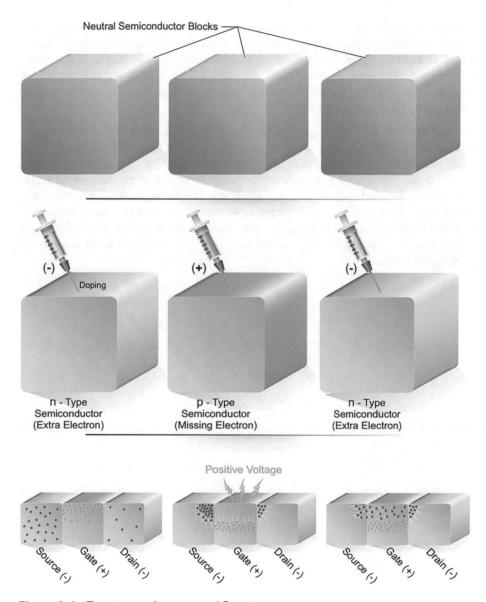

Figure 2-4. Transistors – Structure and Function

How Transistors Work – A Water Analogy

A little confused? Don't worry. Let's use something we're all familiar with to help explain how this works. Think of charge as water, and the current, or flow, of electricity as the movement of water down a pipe. In theory, we could control the amount of electricity running through a gate by varying the degree of voltage, like twisting a knob to open or shut a valve. This is done in some analog circuits, where voltages and currents are tightly controlled. But in more common digital applications, the transistor simply acts like a switch, blocking electrons or allowing them to pass. This is where we get the binary computer language with which most of us are familiar. Each bit consists of an open gate (1) or a closed gate (0).

We can see this analogy played out in Figure 2-5. Individual "valve transistors" can be combined to make higher level **logic gates** like "AND" and "OR," which can then be used to program more sophisticated logic (more on logic gates soon). By opening or closing thousands, millions, or billions of these pipes, the flow of water can be used to create elaborate patterns and sequences. The "brains" of the computer can then read different sequences and use these instructions to save a file, send an email, or take a selfie. Swap out valves for transistors and water for electrons, and you have a complex electronic system!

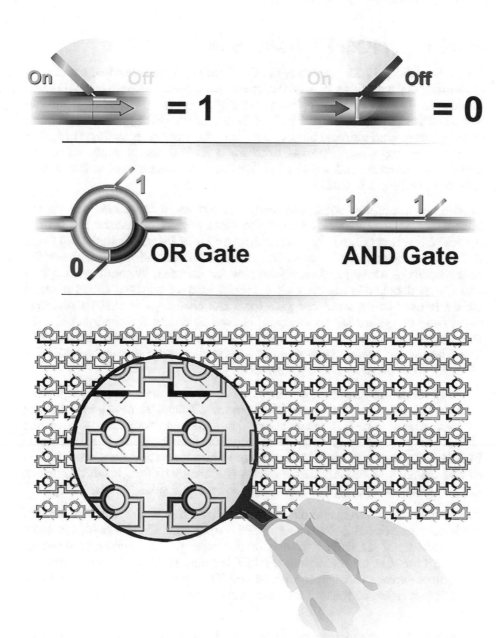

Figure 2-5. Transistors – Water Flow Analogy

FinFET vs. MOSFET Transistors

From the hulking 1960s transistors at Bell Labs to the microscopic transistors in modern electronics, transistor structures have been on a path of continuous evolution. There are two primary transistor types – **Bipolar Junction Transistors (BJT)** and **Field Effect Transistors (FET)**. For illustration's sake, we described a simple bipolar transistor for our water analogy. In reality, bipolar transistors are primarily used for a limited set of applications like power management and signal amplification for wireless and audio devices (Electronics Tutorials, 2021).

Outside of this limited set of use cases, most modern computing devices are built using FETs. Of the FET family, the most popular transistor type is the **MOSFET (Metal Oxide Semiconductor Field Effect Transistor)** (Teja, 2021). Developed at Bell Labs in the 1970s, it has served as the bedrock for microelectronic design and manufacturing for decades. Without getting into too much detail, this means that a special kind of material called a metal **oxide** is used to separate the gate from the channel, and that an **electric field** (via voltage applied to the gate) is used to create the channel between the source and drain. You don't need to understand the physics behind why this is important, just that there are structural differences that make MOSFETs different from other types of transistors.

As semiconductor technology continues to evolve, engineers have devised new and creative ways to make them more efficient. A new generation of devices called **FinFET transistors** have helped mitigate performance challenges as transistors reach their physical limitations. While traditional **MOSFET** transistors are 2-D structures where the gate covers only the top of the channel, FinFET transistors raise the channel through which current can travel, allowing the gate to surround it on three sides (Cross, 2016).

We can see these structural differences illustrated in Figure 2-6. On the left, we have a traditional 2-D planar MOSFET transistor. On the right, we see a more advanced 3D FinFET transistor. By raising the source and drain to surround the gate on three sides, FinFET transistors allow for more efficient control of current through the transistor. The term FinFET isn't a technical term, it just refers to the fact that the gate is flipped on its side and looks like a "fin."

Though FinFET transistors are more difficult to manufacture, they allow for greater control over the flow of current, consume less power, and reduce the amount of **current leakage** (Cross, 2016). Currently, FinFET and MOSFET transistors are the primary transistors in production, although there are new developments on the horizon. Two of these in particular – **Gate All Around (GAA)** and **Nanosheet transistors** – will enable greater control and significant performance advantages. We discuss these in our final chapter on the *Future of Semiconductors and Electronic Systems*.

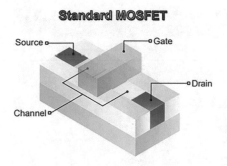
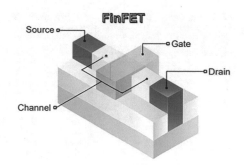

Figure 2-6. MOSFET vs. FinFET

CMOS

Making high-performance ICs at scale is challenging and expensive, especially as transistors shrink to ever smaller geometries. Most chips today use advanced **CMOS (complementary metal-oxide semiconductor)** technology to get the job done. CMOS may be used to refer to the circuitry itself, but can also refer to the design methodology and processes that are used to manufacture Integrated Circuits. The "complementary" part of CMOS just means that both p-channel and n-channel transistors are used – believe it or not, early technologies used only n-channel or p-channel transistors, so CMOS was a major development. CMOS has long been the dominant IC design and fabrication technology and enjoys a competitive advantage in power consumption, area requirements, and cost over more specialized alternatives like **bipolar semiconductor manufacturing**.

Each successive generation of CMOS technology has accomplished these advantages by shrinking transistors and other components through a process called **geometric scaling**. The key metric in geometric scaling is the **gate length** – effectively the distance between source and drain. The smaller that length, the smaller your overall circuit and the less distance current needs to travel between components. When you hear people talking about "seven nanometer technology," seven nanometers is referring to the gate length. When the founder of Intel, Gordon Moore, made his famous prediction, formerly known as **Moore's Law**, that computer processing power will double every two years as a result of shrinking transistor sizes, he was referring to geometric scaling. We can see this dynamic at play in Figure 2-7, which charts the transistor counts of major processors released from 1970 to 2020.

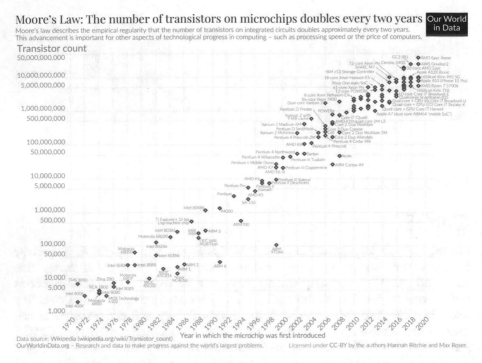

Figure 2-7. Moore's Law (Roser & Ritchie, 2020)

As transistors shrink, they require less electricity (power), take up less space (area and cost), and enable faster signal processing (performance) (Schafer & Buchalter, 2017). For decades, geometric scaling of transistors has driven **functional scaling**, which measures meaningful, real-world performance improvements. Because geometric scaling has continued unabated for so long, the engineering community has not had to squeeze as much efficiency out of their designs at each process node. By the time they were ready to roll out a next generation design at a given node or gate length, the next generation of smaller and more powerful transistors were ready for production. In recent years, however, the pace of geometric innovation has slowed as researchers have approached the physical and practical boundaries of transistor sizes. The smaller transistors get, the more expensive it becomes to manufacture them and the harder it is to accurately etch circuit patterns on chip substrates. After all, you can't build things out of atoms that are smaller than the atoms themselves!

We can see the differences between geometric and functional scaling in Figure 2-8 across generations of transistor technology. Each successive generation of semiconductor manufacturing technology is called a **technology node**, or **process node**. These technologies are made of a mix of improved equipment, new materials, and process improvements that enable chip makers to make chips with smaller transistors (measured in nm). The smaller the node, the smaller the transistors and the more powerful the chip. Geometric scaling aims to increase performance by shrinking transistor sizes across the board – the smaller we make transistors, the greater the performance we will receive for next generation chips. An IC made with 3nm transistor technology, for example, can operate much faster, consume less power, and take up less area than one made with 90nm transistor technology. Functional scaling, on the other hand, aims to increase performance by maximizing utilization at existing transistor sizes. It accomplishes this through things like application-specific design, tighter system integration, and developing new packaging and interconnect technologies. We'll discuss each of these developments in later chapters.

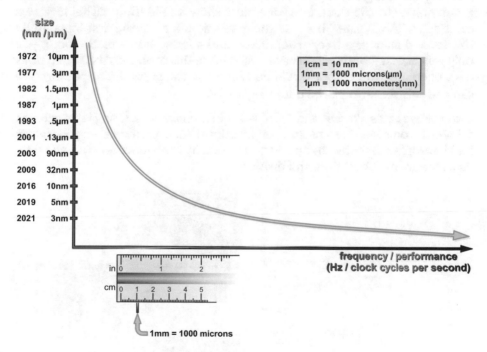

Figure 2-8. Geometric vs. Functional Scaling

How Transistors Are Used

We now understand how transistors are made and how they work, but how exactly are they *used*? A lone transistor can only do one thing – turn an electrical path on or off. But together, transistors can form the building blocks of computer engineering – logic gates.

Logic Gates

Logic gates are simple circuits that use **Boolean logic** to enable simple computations (Fox, n.d.). They are built from as few as two transistors and perform Boolean operators like "and," "or," and "not." In Boolean logic, values can be only true or false, or in the case of transistor-based digital electronics, ON (1) or OFF (0). **Logic gates** can receive multiple input data signals, which they can compare to one another before spitting out an output signal to the next gate in the system.

You can think of logic gates like a bouncer who only lets people enter the bar if they show a valid ID. Taking our analogy a step further, let's say the bouncer is acting like a logic gate who has been given strict instructions that when a group comes to the door, everyone must show a valid ID. In digital logic, we call this an "AND gate," because the gate outputs a 1 if the first input AND the second input are 1 (or true). If you and a friend come to the door, you only gain access if both of you have a valid ID. In this case, the AND conditions have been met, the output would be 1, and you can party the night away. We can see this scenario played out in Figure 2-9.

Other logic gates like OR and NOT work in a similar way. Using logic gates as a lowest common denominator or functional unit, hardware engineers can build complex systems that perform important base functions like addition, subtraction, multiplication, and division.

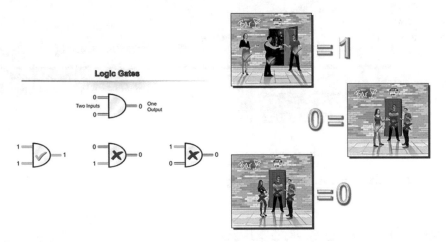

Figure 2-9. Logic Gates

The information era would not be possible without transistors. Moore's rosy 1965 prediction that computing power would double every two years has made it a lengthy 55 years, though there are signs that this pace of innovation is slowing. Arguably the most important invention of the 20th century, the transistor is responsible for the world as we know it today.

We've covered a lot of ground in the last two chapters. Don't worry if you feel a knot in your stomach – silicon engineering is complicated, but we've got your back. Everything in semiconductors is strongly interrelated – the further you read, the more the things we've covered will make sense. In the next chapter, we'll cover Step 2 in the semiconductor value chain – Design – and begin to tie all these various elements together.

Summary

In this chapter, we explored the major kinds of discrete components and functional building blocks used to construct electronic systems. We learned what makes discrete and integrated circuits different and the advantages of tighter integration. Using a water analogy, we took a deeper dive into a special type of component – transistors – examining their structure and how they function. We analyzed CMOS technology and two of the most popular transistors in production today – MOSFET and FinFET. Finally, we broke down how transistors fit together to form logic gates and build a more complex system.

Integrated circuits are really just collections of functional components all fit together on a single piece of silicon. Transistors – the most important building block – combine to form the most basic operational unit – logic gates – that run software and keep our computers cranking day after day.

Your Personal SAT (Semiconductor Awareness Test)

To be sure that your knowledge builds throughout the book, here are five questions relating to the previous chapter.

1. Name the five types of discrete components we covered in this chapter. What function does each one perform? What are their differences?

2. Describe how a transistor is structured. What are its major components and how do they work?

3. What is the difference between a MOSFET and a FinFET Transistor?

4. What is CMOS and what can it refer to?

5. How do logic gates work? What kind of logic do they use?

Building a System

Transistors and other key components have driven the digital revolution of the last four decades, fueling innovation across all scientific disciplines and industries. If we really sit down and think about it though, transistors are rather unremarkable on their own. A source, a gate, and drain by themselves perform no useful function. It is only strung together, with trillions in investment and the herculean efforts of millions of humanity's brightest minds focused on building ever more complex designs, that transistors can do what they do today. The most advanced IC's in production require as many as two *trillion* transistors on a single chip (Hutson, 2021) – imagine if your job required you to get two trillion things right! To accomplish this feat, hardware designers must group and organize electronic systems across ever higher levels of abstraction . In this chapter, we'll explore how such advanced IC's are designed, but first we must understand how these levels fit together.

© Corey Richard 2023
C. Richard, *Understanding Semiconductors*, Maker Innovations Series,
https://doi.org/10.1007/978-1-4842-8847-4_3

Different Levels of Electronics – How the System Fits Together

To understand how individual components fit together to form a final product, we can visualize a system hierarchy, where each level is the sum of the levels below it (see Figure 3-1).

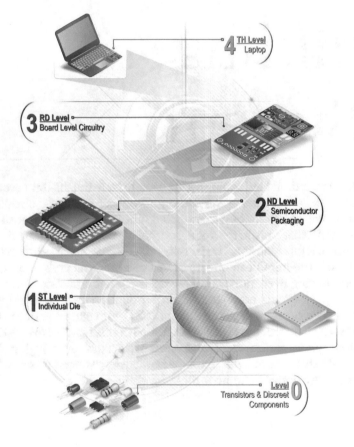

Figure 3-1. Different Levels of an Electronic System

The ground floor of an electronic system is made of a combination of (1) separate **discrete components** soldered directly to a **Printed Circuit Board (PCB)** or **(2) functional components** integrated onto a single die.

Some components like transistors lend themselves to die-level integration while other components like larger capacitors and inductors that make up a system's power circuitry lend themselves to integration at the package or PCB levels. Whether die-level or PCB level integration, these transistors and components comprise the basic building blocks that form the foundation on which all higher levels are built. We can see them illustrated in Figure 3-1 as **level 0**.

At the **IC** or integrated **circuit level 1**, entire chips are developed and designed using a combination of smaller discrete or functional components. These designs could be extraordinarily complex circuits with billions of transistors, like the CPU that runs your laptop, or smaller, specialized circuits like the memory that the CPU might use to store information or access data and instructions.

At the **package level 2**, individual (and sometimes multiple) ICs are wrapped in a protective enclosure to ensure they do not experience interference from neighboring components. Multiple components may be grouped into something referred to as a **module**, which describes a bundle of smaller circuits and components that work together in a unit to perform a task.

At the **PCB (printed circuit board) level 3**, smaller components at "lower" levels are soldered onto a board, where they are connected to one another to form a larger system. The packages and modules from level 2 can be seen on the PCB as (usually) square black components on a circuit board. A PCB mechanically supports and serves as a foundation by which electronic components are connected to one another using conductive **tracks**, **pads**, and other features etched on to its surface (Printed-Circuit-Board Glossary Definition, n.d.).

Modern boards have multiple layers, so wires traverse up and down inside the board to get from one component to the other. If you've ever taken apart an electronic gadget, the PCB is the green piece of plastic with all these little black squares and rectangles stuck to it. Different system components are often soldered to the PCB itself. If an electronic system is Australia, the PCB is the continent, the cities are different chips, the buildings are functional and discrete components, and the roads are the **interconnects** that tie everything together. We can see a real PCB pictured in Figure 3-2.

Figure 3-2. A PCB (Tronicszone, 2017)

At the **system level 4**, everything is tied together to create a fully functional system or product. It is important to note that the term "system" can be used at different levels to describe a fully functional and discrete structure as it relates to the task it is designed to do at that level. In other words, a **system architect** at a semiconductor company could be working on the overall design and integration of numerous parts of a single chip, while a system architect in a different part of the company could be integrating multiple chips into a larger system. If you've ever had to do any minor repairs on an electronic device, like replacing a cracked screen on your mobile phone, you'll see that inside the phone there are many different little PCBs connected together by plastic cables and connectors. These multiple boards and components (like the LCD screen and the headphone jack) must all work together at the overall system level.

Integrated Circuit Design Flow

We can break down the semiconductor design flow into six major steps. In a similar fashion to the Semiconductor Value Chain, understanding the design process from end to end can serve as an anchor on which to build a deeper understanding of each of its constituent parts.

We will use a construction analogy to better visualize what's going on at each step and assume that we are designing a standard digital circuit, though similar steps would be followed for analog and mixed signal devices as well. We can see this analogy played out in Figure 3-4.

Table 3-1. Chip Design vs. Construction Process

Chip Design	Construction Process
System Level Architecture	Building Architecture
Front End Design	Detailed Schematics
Design Verification	Verify Building Schematics
Physical Design	Build a Prototypical Unit
Back End Validation	Validate Structural Integrity
Manufacturing	Build a Housing Community

The Design Process

The design process is composed of six discrete steps (see Table 3-1), including:

1. System Level Architecture – To start off the design process, a **system architect** develops an idea of what chip their team is trying to design. This process frequently starts with input from the business and marketing team indicating a market or customer need. The system architect needs to decide specifically what the chip will do, what technologies, materials, and components will be used to build the chip, and how the team will evaluate whether a chip is a success. This is like what a real estate developer and an architect would do in the construction industry. At the beginning of a project, they would start by deciding what to build (A movie theater? A gym? A house?). Once this decision has been made, they'll need to answer questions like how many rooms should this building have? How big should each room be? How many floors? What materials will be used? Ultimately, the developer and architect need to ensure that what they are building will accomplish the task it was built for and fall within budgetary constraints. Like an architect in the construction industry, a system architect doesn't just make a list of what they want, send their requirements to other teams, and call it a day; they will continue to monitor the progress throughout the design process and guide their team as they move through each step of the way. The system architect isn't simply working with the engineering teams, they also have to interface with the business and marketing teams to be sure their product meets the demands of the market and falls within budget.

2. Front End Design – After hammering out higher level details and before construction can begin, engineers will need to create detailed models of the system. This starts with a high-level model of overall behavior and graduates to more specific models and detailed schematics. Where will the plumbing go? How will the electrical wiring connect to the grid? What materials will be used for the ceiling and the floors? In silicon engineering, this is the stage where **logic design engineers** buckle down and fill in the details. For digital systems or components, you may hear this called **logic design** or **RTL Design (register transfer level)**. In the early days of the semiconductor industry, designers would manually position individual transistors to create individual Boolean logic gates.

Today, design engineers use **Hardware Description Languages (HDL)** like **VHDL** or **Verilog/SystemVerilog RTL** to describe what they want the circuit to do (RTL Register Transfer Level, 2021). HDL's are specialized computer "programming" languages used to describe the physical structure of ICs and electronic systems (Tucker, 1994). Physical design tools translate these languages into the individual gates and transistors for a given function. At the conclusion of this stage, designers should have completed a virtual version of a chip that should, in theory, serve its purpose flawlessly in the real world.

3. Design Verification – As with construction, silicon design is a capital-intensive industry. You would not want to have an architect hammer out some schematics on the back of a napkin and just start building, especially if you were building multiple units. To ensure a successful project, you would want to verify that, if built, these schematics will translate into a fully functional structure(s). In semiconductors, a single chip design may be used for thousands or millions of units that must be manufactured, shipped, assembled, and integrated into a larger system. It is at this stage that engineers verify what the design team has built.

Verifying a complex design is a difficult task, so difficult, in fact, that it takes up over half of the total design time for an average **SoC** – 56% of labor time by some 2020 estimates (Foster, 2021). Verification is critical because chip manufacturing is so expensive - design teams have to know they got it right. **SoCs (system on chip)** are a type of IC that includes an entire system on a single substrate. Instead of building a main processor and peripheral chips like memory ICs and GPUs separately before connecting them to one another, SoCs contain all of the necessary circuitry on the same chip – we'll cover them in greater detail later on.

Because there are so many potential test cases, or ways the device might be used, it is nearly impossible to verify a design for every possible scenario. There are numerous techniques, however, that are effective in different cases.

By and large, the most common verification methodology is **functional verification**, which simulates a design using **SystemVerilog** HDL code (Wile, Goss, & Roesner, 2005). The same HDL language that physical design tools can translate into physical gates and wires can be used by front-end verification tools to simulate the exact behavior of the circuit.

Functional verification is, quite simply, verifying the design does what it is supposed to do in any possible condition. For a simple AND gate, this is almost trivial. But for a billion-gate processor chip, it's not so simple. How can you possibly test every condition? To help manage this complexity, verification engineers created a new way to do verification, called **UVM (Universal Verification Methodology)**. In this methodology, **verification engineers** build a model of each part of the system. Outputs of the design are then compared against this model to determine if the circuit is behaving as expected. UVM even has the capability to collect statistics on which portions of the design have been verified, and which have not.

Any flaws in the design should result in an incorrect output from a given **testbench** input, which can then be identified and corrected through **debugging** (Wile, Goss, & Roesner, 2005). As you can imagine, this is a very time- and resource-intensive process. In one sense, you have to build your chip twice – once to create the "golden model" you're comparing against, and again for the actual implementation that you'll manufacture.

An alternative, or supplemental, verification methodology, **emulation** uses **FPGAs** (more on this in later chapters) to program a design and observe a circuit in the real world (Chang et al., 2009). This can be especially useful for applications that are dealing with real physical signals. For example, if you're designing an audio processor, functional verification tools can tell you that you should expect a 24-bit number as the correct output for a given set of inputs. This is great if your end customer is a Mathematics Professor at MIT, but what you really want to know is "How does it sound?" To do this, an FPGA emulator can be "programmed" with the newly designed audio processor so you can listen directly through your headphones or speaker.

FPGA stands for **Field Programmable Gate Array** – the key word here being "programmable." Because an emulator has a bunch of non-essential circuitry your end chip won't need, it will almost certainly be slower and consume more power than the final product. The point is not to build something ready for market, but rather a testable prototype as close to the real deal as possible. The emulation process is clunky and expensive, but the results are more tangible.

Another verification method, **formal verification**, uses mathematical reasoning and proofs in lieu of a simulation to verify that an RTL design will perform its desired function without directly testing any input-output scenarios. While simulation-based verification techniques apply a trial-and-error approach, guessing and testing as many scenarios as possible, formal verification tries to test a design using algorithms that theoretically cover all possible input-output combinations (Sanghavi, 2010). In formal verification, you establish the rules that govern proper behavior of the design (i.e., signal A is always the inverse of signal B, or clock X is always twice the frequency of clock Y), and the tool checks that the design abides by all these rules. With greater design complexity, however, this type of verification becomes prohibitively difficult, limiting its usage at higher ends of the market (Sanghavi, 2010).

Part of the design process includes choosing the right verification strategy for different parts of the chip. Some simple input/output relationships may be effectively verified with formal verification, while a real-time video engine may require a complex emulation platform.

4. Physical Design – This is the stage at which the chip is physically built. You have constructed a high-level model, written your RTL code and verified that it operates as expected. Chips are ultimately made of millions of transistors and other electrical components. How exactly does that RTL code turn into wires and transistors?

Advanced **EDA (electronic design automation) tools** bring what your front-end design team has built into the real world. This is an incredibly complex process, and can sometimes take as long as the front-end design phase. We can break physical design into five constituent steps:

> **High Level Synthesis (HLS)** – This is the stage that marks the end of **front-end design** and the beginning of **back-end design**. At this stage, the chip has been described in an RTL language (like VHDL or Verilog), and you've simulated that it should work as intended. **physical design engineers** are now ready to convert that RTL code into transistors and wires using **Synthesis**. For a billion-gate design, synthesis is an incredibly complex process. It can take many hours

or even days to complete the process. Take Synopsys (SNPS), a leading developer of synthesis tools - with a $50 billion market cap as of January 2021, you know this is a difficult and costly problem to solve. By converting from one language to another, physical, or "back-end," design engineers can manipulate the front-end design team's work and complete the next stage of the design process.

Design Netlist – The product of high-level synthesis is a **netlist,** a list of the electronic components in a circuit and all the nodes to which they are connected. Keeping our list of semiconductor vernacular up-to-date, **circuit nodes** are any individual element that an electrical signal can be sent to, whether they be interconnects, transistors, or other components that make up the circuit. These are not to be confused with **technology nodes**, which describe successive generations of manufacturing technology required to manufacture smaller ICs and transistors. If a chip exists as a two-dimensional network of electronic components strategically placed in an IC or on a circuit board, the netlist is a written description of which components are connected to which, like a list of driving directions without "left" or "right." Unlike a design schematic that would show the relative position of each component relative to one another, a netlist's main purpose is to describe information about connectivity (Holt, n.d.).

Floorplanning – At this stage of the physical design process, Physical Design Engineers decide where everything should be located. A given design may include blocks of memory and large logic blocks that need to read and write data to those memories. Floorplanning ensures that those blocks are placed near each other. The physical design engineer must figure out which components should be clustered or placed apart and which combinations will result in the least area and the most speed (remember PPAC!). If the netlist is a list of all the things we need inside a building, floorplanning is where we decide where to put the furniture, the TV, the desk, etc. to maximize the efficient use of our limited space.

Place-and-Route – First, during **placement**, engineers decide exactly where to put all the electronic components and circuitry. Once they've decided that a large logic block needs to reside in a particular area of the chip, a placement tool is used to allocate specific locations for each and every logic gate. If you could break up your furniture into smaller constituent parts, this is the step where you would decide where each of these subcomponents would go. Placement is followed by **routing**, where **CAD tools** integrate all the wiring required to connect the placed components. Some critical wiring like power supplies or high precision signals may actually be routed by hand. Recall that the netlist specifies every gate in the design and how it is connected, so routing merely implements all of those connections with physical wires.

So now we're done, right? Everything is hooked up and matches the netlist, so what is left to do? While the functional components that make up our chip have been positioned and connected to one another, we have yet to analyze a critical aspect of our new design – its timing.

Clock-tree Synthesis (CTS) – During Clock-Tree Synthesis, engineers make sure that the electrical signaling that delivers information around the circuit "clocks" evenly, or as intended, throughout the chip (VLSI Guide, 2018). **Clock frequency**, or **clock rate**, a common measurement of processor speed and performance, assesses how quickly a signal travels through an IC, which determines how quickly it can execute instructions (Howe, 1994). Processors are such complicated circuit designs that engineers have come up with techniques to manage that complexity. One of those techniques is called synchronous design. **Synchronous design** uses a common "clock" across all circuits. It is important that signals do not reach the different components of a chip at the incorrect times, or the chip may be slow or fail to perform as intended. The clock ensures that this happens and that all parts of the system receive the **clock signal** at the same time. If one side of a chip thinks it is computing a result for one **clock cycle**, but another side of the chip has already completed that same clock cycle, computation errors can result.

You can visualize this process as a line of firefighters trying to put out a fire with pails of water, as depicted in Figure 3-3. The line works most optimally if everyone hands their pail of water at the same time. The line starts with a firefighter who scoops water out of a tank and into a pail, then passes it to the second firefighter in line. This first firefighter then grabs another pail and hands it to the second firefighter as the second firefighter hands the first pail to a third firefighter and prepares to receive the second pail. Each pail gets passed to the next firefighter in line along the "critical path," until it gets to the last firefighter who is positioned next to the fire. That firefighter throws the water "signal" onto the fire. If one firefighter takes too long to pass a pail to the next person in line, they will not have enough time to turn around and receive the next pail. As the speed of the pail passing ramps up, the firefighters are more likely to drop water or be forced to slow down the chain. In a similar fashion, if the timing for part of the chip is "offbeat" from the clock that sets the processing cadence for the rest of the device, instructions may not complete in time for the next **clock edge** (also known as **capture edge**). Failure is not necessarily an inevitable outcome here – just because a firefighter slows down or can't get their pacing right doesn't mean they can't put out the fire. Rather, the system will slow down as more quickly executed instructions are forced to wait for those that were delayed. Though failure may not result, such timing issues can have a significantly detrimental effect on system performance and are a critical consideration in chip design.

Instructions and Data — Signal — Signal — Critical Patch — Timing Issue — Signal — Signal

Figure 3-3. Clock Cycles and System Timing—Firefighting Analogy

A common simulation method to compute and verify the expected timing of digital circuits is called **static timing analysis (STA)**. STA ensures that all logic paths are properly timed relative to each other so there is never a chance of a timing error.

We will discuss signals and clock frequency in greater detail in the upcoming chapters *Analog, Memory,* and *Common Chip Architectures.*

5. Validation (also called Physical Verification or Back-End Verification) – Once a circuit is ready for manufacture, as a GDS Design file is generated that includes all the necessary information required by the fab, including transistor configuration, interconnect network, and other functional components that will be etched onto the silicon substrate. Before generating a GDS file to send to a semiconductor factory, or **fab, validation engineers** need to double check that a chip is manufacturable. They do this using **EDA (Electronic Design Automation)** software tools like **Design Rule Checkers (DRC)** to verify that the chip complies with all the rules of the chosen foundry. Constraints can vary from chip size to how closely wires and transistors can be placed to each other. You can think of these validation engineers like an Inspector checking your "prototype" housing unit before building the rest of the housing community.

6. GDS II Generation – GDS II is a standardized format that is used to send a finished design to the fab at the end of the IC design cycle (Rubin, 1993). Think of it like a Word or Excel file you might send to your manager when you're done with a project, except that the file includes the culmination of millions of dollars of engineering ingenuity and a final chip design ready to be manufactured. Physical design engineers working on digital projects will often use the phrase "RTL-to-GDS" to describe what they do. This is referring to the physical design process that turns front end RTL design into ready-for-manufacture GDS. In many companies, this process of creating the **GDS file** and sending it to the foundry is still called **tapeout**. This term has its origins back in the early days of the semiconductor industry, when a final GDS file was put onto a big magnetic tape and shipped to the foundry or perhaps just walked across the street in Silicon Valley from the engineering building to the fab. Thankfully, today those files are sent via FTP across the world in minutes.

Please note that in Figure 3-4 illustrating our chip design construction analogy, we've depicted steps 4 and 5 as fully packaged with leads for the sake of illustration. In the real world, the physical design process would result in a chip layout, not a fully completed and packaged IC.

Manufacturing – The i's are dotted, t's are crossed, your team sent the finished GDS II file to the fab and it is time to build an IC. When it comes to microelectronics, this is no small task. Billions of interconnected transistors and other electrical components can fit onto a single chip, and the manufacturing process is neither simple, nor cheap. It can also take an incredibly long time. Modern processes may take over 12–16 weeks from when you send the GDS file until you have finished wafers. We will cover many of these processes and technologies in the following chapter *Semiconductor Manufacturing Process*.

I recognize this is a lot of information to absorb so, to review briefly, the six steps of the semiconductor design process are

1. System level architecture.
2. Front end design.
3. Design verification.
4. Physical design.
5. Validation.
6. GDS design file sent to fab for manufacturing.

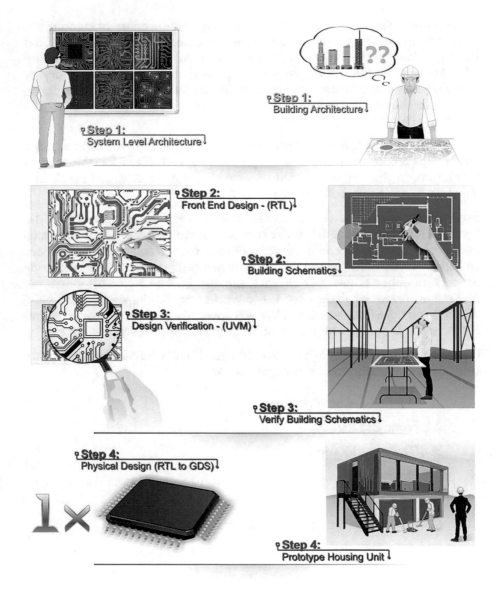

Figure 3-4. Semiconductor Design Flow—Constructing a Circuit

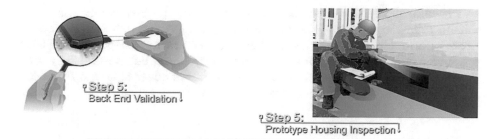

Figure 3-4. (continued)

EDA Tools

EDA stands for **electronic design automation**, also referred to as **e-CAD** (**electronic computer-aided design**). With up to billions of components on a single chip, architects and designers cannot just sketch out a chip design on a piece of paper. EDA tools are used throughout the design process to help hardware engineers and chip designers build electronics systems. Prior to EDA, ICs were manually laid out by hand, a slow and grueling process. When designs were only a few hundred transistors, this was manageable. But not today. To tackle challenges throughout the design flow, EDA providers began developing tools to automate and streamline everything from functional verification to high level synthesis (Nenni & McLellan, 2014). EDA companies helped develop and spread **VLSI HDLs** like Verilog and VHDL, which automated the design flow and enabled further technology development (Nenni & McLellan, 2014).

The EDA tool market was worth about $11 billion dollars in 2020 and is expected to grow to over $21 billion by 2026 (Mordor Intelligence, 2021). The three biggest EDA tool companies are Cadence, Synopsys, and Mentor Graphics.

We've thoroughly explored the second stage in the Semiconductor Value Chain, following a chip's journey from a System Architect's imagination to production-ready blueprints. A good design on its own is no more useful than a drawing of your dream home – we're halfway there, but we are still a long way away from walking in the front door. Next we cover Step 3 in the Value Chain – let's see how the semi-sausage gets made.

Summary

In this chapter, we broke down an electronic system into five different levels – Device, PCB, Package, Die, and Component – each built upon the smaller abstractions of the level beneath. From here, we dug into the silicon design flow. Starting from system level architecture, we made our way through front-end RTL design and verification, before passing through high level synthesis to arrive at the back-end physical design and validation process. Each of the five major physical design steps – HLS, design netlist, floorplanning, place-and-route, and clock tree synthesis – culminated in an end GDS II file ready to be sent to the wafer fab for manufacturing. Finally, we learned how EDA tools have reduced the cost and difficulty of an arduous and complicated design cycle!

Your Personal SAT (Semiconductor Awareness Test)

To be sure that your knowledge builds on itself throughout the book, here are five questions relating to the previous chapter.

1. What five levels of electronics did we cover? On which level are all higher levels built?

2. Can you name each stage of the IC design flow? How does each step relate to a construction analogy?

3. What are the differences between emulation, functional and formal verification? Pros and cons for each?

4. Which stage of the silicon design flow represents the transition between front- and back-end design? What happens at this stage?

5. How do EDA tools help hardware designers build better systems?

Semiconductor Manufacturing

We've followed the journey of a new chip from high-level system architecture through a mosaic of concurrent design steps and subprocesses and are finally ready to bring our new chip to life. Semiconductor manufacturing is no cakewalk though – fabricating ICs containing billions of transistors with feature lengths only a handful of atoms thick is an incredibly ambitious undertaking that must be done with surgeon-like precision at scale. In this chapter, we'll explore each step of the recipe from front-end manufacturing through to final assembly and testing. Before we start cooking though, it's important that we understand some basic terminology.

Manufacturing Overview

Semiconductor manufacturing is a highly complex and ultra-precise process that requires specialized chip factories called **wafer fabs** filled with hundreds of millions or billions of dollars of cutting-edge equipment. The product of this complex process can be a few dozen to several hundred to several thousand finished ICs per wafer, depending on the **die area** and **batch yield**.

© Corey Richard 2023
C. Richard, *Understanding Semiconductors*, Maker Innovations Series,
https://doi.org/10.1007/978-1-4842-8847-4_4

Unique processes are used to manufacture different types of semiconductor devices. You can think of these as the "recipes" for successful manufacturing. Each recipe is made up of steps leveraging a combination of technologies to successfully take a design from GDS to reality. Within the industry, these process recipes are called **technology nodes**, **process nodes**, or just **nodes**. The term **node** refers to the minimum feature size for a given generation of process technology. Feature sizes are measured in **nanometers (nm)**, or one billionth of a meter. To put that in perspective, a sheet of paper or a strand of human hair is about 100,000 nanometers thick (NNI, n.d.). A wafer fab running an advanced 3nm node, for example, can produce chips with many more transistors than one running a 90nm node, since each transistor is significantly smaller (PCMag, n.d.).

Each time a process technology enables a smaller transistor size, a new node is born. If you hear an engineer or a news anchor discuss Intel's old "14nm node" vs. TSMC's groundbreaking "5nm node," what they are discussing is TSMC's ability to make transistors with dimensions as small as 5nm, while Intel can only fabricate ICs with feature sizes as small as 14nm. The industry naming system for advanced technology based on gate lengths is deceiving and does not reflect true feature dimensions, which are many nm behind. For simplicity, however, and perhaps to avoid any outraged emails from the marketing departments at TSMC or GlobalFoundries, we will assume that these measurements are accurate (IRDS, 2020). The most advanced technology node in development is the 2nm process node, which Samsung plans to put into production in 2025 (Shilov, 2021).

Figure 4-1 breaks down 2019 SIA and BCG data describing which generations of manufacturing technologies (nodes) are being used to create which types of semiconductor devices. Memory chips with smaller feature sizes, repetitive feature sets, and simpler architectures are manufactured using the most advanced nodes, while discrete, analog, optoelectronics, and sensors (DAO) devices are made using older, less advanced technologies (Varas et al., 2021). Listed next to each process node along the x-axis is the percentage of wafer runs currently running at that node. Less than 2% of all wafer runs in 2019 were running on 10nm equipment and process technology, 37% of all nodes were running 10–22nm manufacturing technology, and so on and so forth. Notice that while the most advanced nodes get all the notoriety, lots of chips are manufactured in decades-old nodes larger than 90nm. A **wafer run** is a single run-through of the semiconductor manufacturing process, from initial **wafer fabrication** to when the individual die are cut apart from each other during **wafer dicing**, we'll discuss these processes in detail in the coming sections.

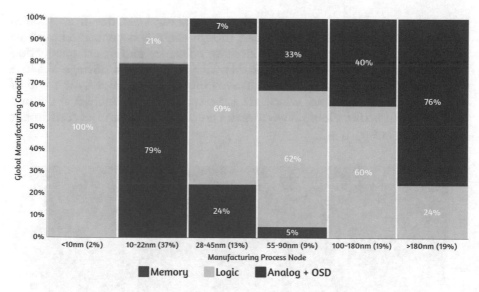

Figure 4-1. 2019 Utilization of Semiconductor Manufacturing Capacity by Node and Component Type (SIA and BCG)

The manufacturing process is divided into two subsections – front-end manufacturing and back-end manufacturing. Taken very simplistically, front-end manufacturing puts your desired circuit onto a silicon wafer, and back-end manufacturing gets the individual chips on that wafer ready for a customer's system. We'll explore each in detail in the coming sections.

Front-End Manufacturing

The first step in front-end manufacturing is called **wafer fabrication**. A **wafer** is a thin slice of semiconductor or **substrate** on which any number of chips are built. Silicon wafers are created by first melting a combination of **silica** and carbon down and shaping them into cylindrical objects called **ingots** (Stahlkocher, 2004). Ingots are then sliced into thin, unfinished wafers, ready to be used for manufacturing. Wafers used in manufacturing are typically round with a flat edge, allowing engineers and equipment to handle the wafer more easily. We can see ingots (left) and wafers (right) on display in Figure 4-2.

Wafers have doubled in diameter over the last several decades, from 150mm in the 1980s to 300mm in use today, though there is a concerted push to adopt 450mm wafers as a way to increase efficiency and boost production (more die per wafer) (AnySilicon, 2021). Like stamps on a postage sheet, a single wafer can contain hundreds or even thousands of chips by the end of the manufacturing process, which are later cut apart into individual die in a process called **wafer dicing**. We can see a processed wafer and its constituent die pictured in Figure 4-3.

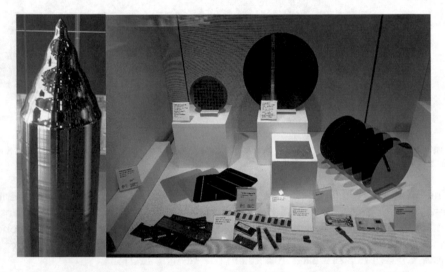

Figure 4-2. Ingot vs. Silicon Wafer (Stahlkocher, 2004) (Mineralogy Museum, 2017)

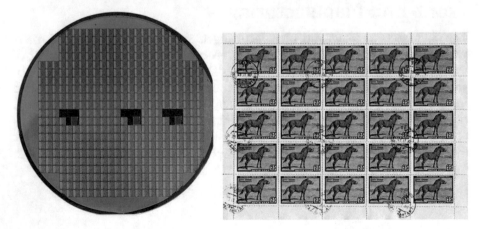

Figure 4-3. Processed Wafer vs. Stamp Sheet (Silicon Wafer, 2010) (STAMPRUS, 1959)

In general terms, the wafer fabrication process can be thought of as like building a layer cake one layer at a time. This is oversimplifying things, but in essence, the different steps of the front-end manufacturing process are meant to build intricate combinations of substrates, circuitry, and other materials one on top of the other with the precision and accuracy needed to make a fully functioning chip.

We could spend volumes breaking down the steps of front-end wafer fabrication into countless processes, subprocesses, and technologies (don't worry, that wasn't a threat), but for our purposes, we can group most major front-end wafer fabrication processes into four major categories:

1. Deposition: This category encompasses a set of processes that adds materials called **thin films** onto a wafer's surface (STMicroelectronics, 2000). This is accomplished by employing a multitude of technologies such as **atomic layer deposition (ALD)**, **molecular beam epitaxy (MBE)**, **physical vapor deposition (PVD)**, and **electrochemical deposition (ECD)**, to name a few. You don't need to know each of these processes, just understand that there are a lot of them. To properly deposit material layers onto the wafer's surface, the wafer is heated in a furnace filled with oxide gas through a process called **oxidation**. In our cake analogy, deposition is where we add successive layers of pastry or frosting.

We can see ALD, MBE, and ECD machines pictured left to right in Figure 4-4. It doesn't take a PhD in Engineering to tell that such equipment is intricate and expensive. Filled with hundreds of these machines, you can also start to see how a modern manufacturing facility can cost billions of dollars.

Figure 4-4. ALD, MBE, and ECD Deposition Machines (Potrowl, 2012) (Paumier, 2007) (Argonne National Laboratory, 2008)

To better illustrate what is going on in deposition, we can zoom and analyze what is happening in a common process called **Physical Vapor Deposition (PVD)**, which is pictured in Figure 4-5. In this process, the wafer substrate is placed in a **vacuum chamber** across from a piece of material called a

sputtering target. Sputtering gas is pushed into the chamber and aimed at the sputtering target. Atoms from the sputter target are subsequently knocked off the sputtering target and are directed at the surface of the wafer substrate, where a coat of materials called thin films are formed. Other deposition processes may use liquids or other materials for "layer-building", but this is a great example of the mechanisms by which deposition processes work in general.

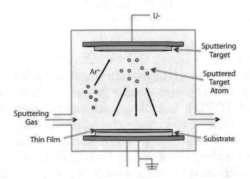

Figure 4-5. Physical Vapor Deposition (PVD) Process (Aldrich, 2018)

2. Patterning/Lithography: This step encompasses any process that shapes or alters the material on the wafer. During the **photolithography** process, illustrated in Figures 4-6 and 4-7, the wafer and its constituent materials first are coated with a chemical called **photoresist**, which breaks down in reaction to light (Valentine, 2019). From there, a giant machine called a **stepper** aligns a **photomask** over the wafer. This photomask is specific to a single layer of the process for a given chip design. The stepper then passes light at a unique wavelength (commonly deep Ultraviolet) through the photomask and onto the wafer. The presence of the photomask creates a desired pattern on the wafer which softens the photoresist in regions exposed to this light. Similarly, during **electron beam (e-beam) lithography**, a beam of electrons – instead of light – is shined through a mask and leaves an imprint on the wafer (Rai-Choudhury, 1997). We can see pictures of both a stepper and a photomask in Figure 4-8.

This pattern-etching process can happen dozens of times, with some advanced runs requiring over 75 different masks to produce a single design. Once the photoresist has been removed, metal or other materials can be deposited into the remaining areas to form wires connecting individual transistors and functional features to one another. You can think of patterning or lithographic processes like drawing a picture using a stencil, except here the stencil is the **mask** and the pen is a beam of light or electrons.

This may sound like boring manufacturing details, but lithography is a critical bottleneck technology that's enabled geometric scaling to keep pace with Moore's prediction over the last several decades. Each generation of lithographic equipment enables fabs to etch smaller substrate features and pack more transistors on each chip, which improves speed, lowers costs, and boosts power efficiency across the board. In order to successfully implement the most advanced process nodes, lithographic equipment suppliers have had to continually find new and creative ways to make ever smaller patterns and transistors. One of the ways has been to use shorter **light wavelengths** as with **EUV lithography**, which has been in development since the 1980s and has only recently gone into production for high volume manufacturing (Samsung, 2020).

To grasp why lithography is so critical, it's important to understand the wavelength of the light that is typically used. For many years, the main light source for lithography had a wavelength of 193 nanometers. Light can only directly etch features as large as its own wavelength, which became a serious issue as foundries moved below the 250nm node (Samuel, 2018). Optical workarounds and the use of multiples of photomasks have allowed fabs to etch smaller patterns than the 193nm light wavelength would directly allow, but as semiconductor feature sizes dropped lower and lower, performing lithography with light at a wavelength of 193 nm became increasingly difficult (Samuel, 2018). This necessitated the need for EUV, which operates at a much smaller wavelength of 13.5nm (ASML, 2022).

As this technology has advanced, lithography equipment has become incredibly expensive, with individual EUV systems integrating components from a global network of more than 5,000 specialized suppliers and costing as much as $150 million apiece (Varas et al., 2021)!

As manufacturers pursue smaller and smaller nodes, you can expect continued innovation in lithographic technology. I'm sure SEUV (Super Extreme Ultraviolet Lithography) is just around the corner.

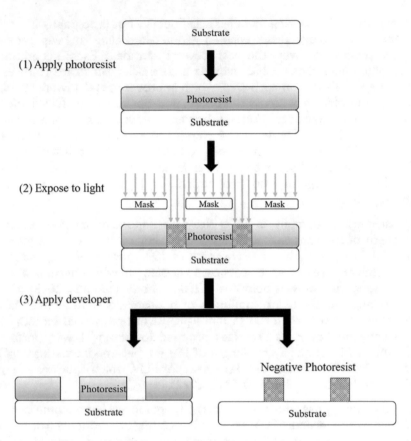

Figure 4-6. The Photolithographic Process (lam, 2017)

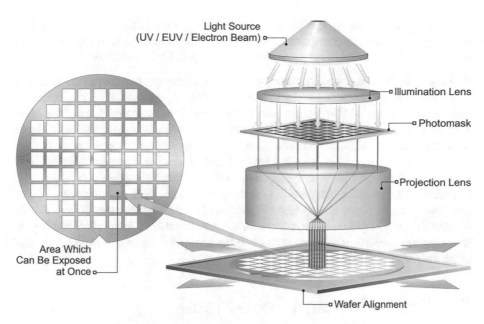

Figure 4-7. Patterning and photolithography – inside a stepper

Figure 4-8. Stepper and Photomask (A13ean, 2012). (Peellden, 2011)

3. Removal: While deposition adds thin film materials to the wafer, removal, you guessed it, removes them. Once a "picture" of the circuitry is imprinted onto the deposited and patterned photoresist and underlying thin film layer, a removal process like **wet etching** or **dry etching** and **chemical-mechanical planarization (CMP)** are used to wash away the photoresist material that is no longer needed, leaving an area that can be later filled with the desired metals, oxides, transistors, or passive components on the underlying wafer material. Wet etching uses liquid compounds, while dry etching uses gaseous compounds to dissolve unprotected thin film materials and "etch" a pattern of the underlying circuitry (STMicroelectronics, 2000).

4. Physical Property Alteration: This encompasses processes that modify the electrical or physical properties of the wafer responsible for the behavior and performance of transistors and other functional components. Processes like this include **doping**, **rapid thermal annealing**, **ultraviolet light processing** (**UVP**), and others. During doping, materials creatively named dopants are shot under the surface of the wafer in a process called **ion implantation** or **ion introduction**. These materials create positive and negative charges that are used to facilitate control and conductivity of the overlaying transistors and other circuitry (STMicroelectronics, 2000). As we discussed in Chapter 2, **dopants** are vital to the healthy functioning of transistors, which require a charge differential to operate their gate and control their channel.

Cycling – Pre- and Post-Metal

Each of these four process types are repeated many times before enough layers are properly fabricated in our wafer "layer cake." The four steps may not always be performed in the same order, and some steps (like Physical Property Alteration) are performed much less than others (like deposition and patterning). For example, a typical cycle may look like

1. Doping the wafer with ionic materials.

2. Deposition of oxide material on the wafer surface.

3. Lithographic patterning through wafer mask(s).

4. Dissolving exposed photoresist in a chemical bath through a wet etching process.

This cycle then repeats as many times as required, with some high-end chips requiring hundreds of steps for a single production run. Figure 4-9 summarizes the front-end manufacturing process in six major steps, which can be used across both FEOL pre-metal and BEOL post-metal processes.

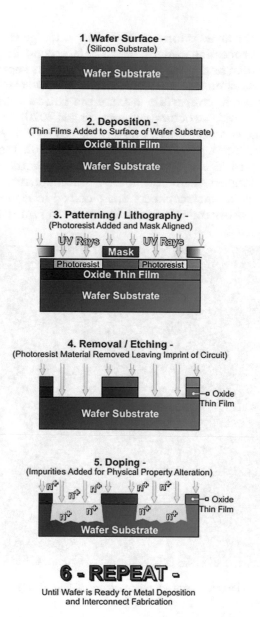

Figure 4-9. Front-End Manufacturing Cycle

In the early stages of front-end manufacturing, transistors are directly etched into the wafer in the "pre-metal" **Front-end of the Line (FEOL)** portions of the wafer fabrication process.

After the transistor array is formed, the wafer undergoes **Back-end of the Line (BEOL)** processing, where metallic interconnect materials, usually made from aluminum or copper, are deposited in layers separated by dielectric materials using the same four processes used for FEOL manufacturing (Singer, 2020). The **dielectric materials** insulate the **metal interconnects** from one another and provide structural support (Singer, 2020). These interconnects connect individual components to one another to form logic gates and other circuitry that ties the system together (Singer, 2020). Modern devices can have as many as 15 layers, with upper layers connected using vertical **via structures** to connect them to underlying components. Lower-level local and upper-level global interconnects are pictured in Figures 4-10 and 4-11, while the BEOL post-metal process is illustrated in Figure 4-12.

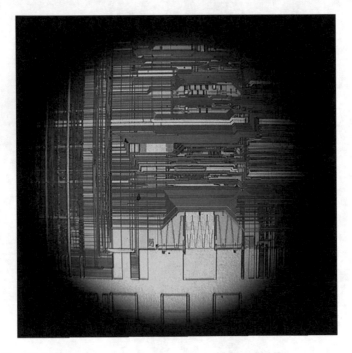

Figure 4-10. Global interconnects – Intel processor (Gibbs, 2006)

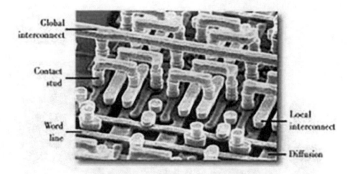

Figure 4-11. Global and Local Interconnects - IBM SRAM Memory Chip (IBM, n.d.)

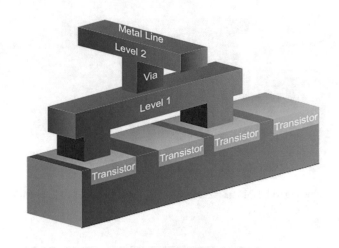

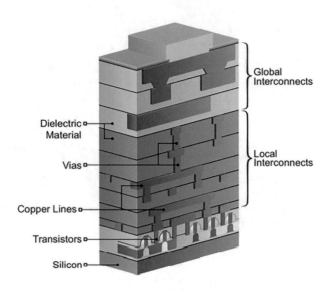

Figure 4-12. Back-End-of-the Line (BEOL) Manufacturing Process – Metal Deposition and Interconnect Formation

The entire front-end manufacturing process for a complex wafer can require several dozen mask layers and take weeks to finish. These challenges are reflected in the industry's cost distribution, with front-end manufacturing machinery comprising 60% of the $62 billion in 2020 spent on semiconductor production equipment as a whole (Precedence Research, 2021). Each successive node brings an added layer of complexity which makes wafer probing, yield, and failure analysis even more crucial to meeting production goals and keeping unit costs low. We cover these in the next section.

Wafer Probing, Yield, and Failure Analysis

At the conclusion of the front-end manufacturing process and before the back-end manufacturing process can begin, a process called **wafer probing** may be implemented. In simple terms, you have this wafer, packed with hundreds or thousands of die of your latest design. But does it actually work?

Wafer probing uses a device called a **wafer prober** to electrically test wafer die before final packaging, assembly, and testing is done. In some cases, the back-end process is so lengthy and expensive, manufacturers want to test the wafer beforehand, so they only send tested and functional die through the back-end process. In other types of wafer processing such as **Chip-Scale Packaging**, the entire wafer is packaged, and testing is done afterwards.

When initial probing is done, two types of tests are performed – **parametric testing** of the fabrication processes and **wafer testing** to ensure each individual die is defect-free and fully functional (STMicroelectronics, 2000). At such a small scale, a single particle landing on the surface of an unprotected die, a tiny vibration near fab machinery that misaligns a wafer, flaws in a chip design, or any number of issues can ruin the functionality of a die or even an entire wafer.

Parametric testing measures several key circuit parameters on a test circuit structure to ensure the process is performing as expected. The manufacturer needs to ensure that all the basic parameters like resistances and device thresholds are within their standard tolerances. Foundries typically add small circuit structures in between each die which are measured during this parametric testing phase. This in-between space is called the **scribe line**. When the wafer is diced into individual chips, the scribe line provides the space for sawing, and its test structures are destroyed. But the structures have served their purpose, and the customer is none the wiser.

Even if everything is done correctly, at least some of the die on a wafer will not work. **Wafer testing** enables fabs to identify dysfunctional die for disposal, measure performance, and track recurring errors so that processes can be improved. As one example, it is not uncommon for failures to be clustered in either the center of a wafer, or near the edges. This can help identify issues with fab equipment which may be contributing to these failures.

Testing enables **failure analysis engineers** to derive and analyze **yield**, an important statistic of which there are two types – line yield and die yield. **Line yield**, also known as **wafer yield**, measures the number of wafers that successfully make it to wafer probing without being thrown out. If there's a major issue in the line, a manufacturer may have to scrap an entire wafer. For example, during testing of the structures in the scribe line, it may be determined that a fundamental parameter is way off. **Die yield** measures the number of functional die divided by the total number of potential die that make it to wafer probing (Backer et al., 2018). Together, they measure **end-to-end yield**, which holistically accounts for the efficacy of the entire front-end manufacturing process (Backer et al., 2018). For a new manufacturing line of chips, yield will generally start lower and gradually increase as the equipment is properly calibrated and manufacturing engineers have time to adjust processing steps. For the most advanced processes, initial yield may be less than 50%. **Yield optimization** has long been considered one of the most critical performance objectives – yield increases, even small ones, can drive down unit manufacturing costs and boost margins (Integrated Circuit Engineering Corporation, n.d.). End-to-end yield optimization across both line yield and die yield can be a strong competitive advantage (Backer et al., 2018).

Why is yield improvement so important? Take a hypothetical case where your chip is manufactured on wafers that cost $1000 each, and you can sell each chip for $3 (sorry, this section will involve a bit of math...). Let's assume at 100% yield, you can get 1000 functional chips out of each wafer. Then, you would collect $3000 in revenue assuming all the die could be sold. That's $2000 in profit off your $1000 wafer cost. But at a die yield of 80%, you're left with just 800 chips at $3 a piece, or $2400 in revenue, yielding $1400 in profit and 58% growth profit margin (after the $1000 cost of the wafers). If we can increase die yield to 95%, which is achievable for more mature processes, our revenue increases to $2850, profit is $1850, and gross margin increases to 65%. That may not seem like a lot, but gross margin is one of the critical financial metrics in the semiconductor industry, and a 7% increase in gross margin is a massive improvement that can have a big impact on a company's profitability and stock market valuation.

In Figure 4-13, we can see wafers with progressively smaller die and their respective yields. Because tiny contaminants or slight movements can permanently ruin a given die, smaller die sizes typically result in higher yields, since failure is more likely to be contained in a smaller portion of the overall wafer area. Defective die are often marked with a black dot so they can be tossed out or sold at a discounted price if still semi-functional (this is called **inking**).

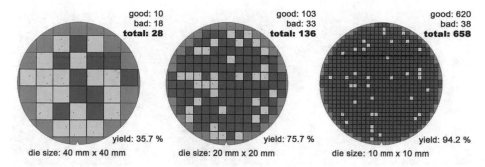

Figure 4-13. Wafer Sizes and Die Yields (Shigeru23, 2011)

With such complex manufacturing processes at nanometer scales, wafer fabrication must be ultraprecise. The process is so sensitive that almost all fab manufacturing is done in **clean rooms** with air filtration that shrinks the number of airborne particles to 1,000 times fewer than a sterile hospital operating room (Intel, 2018). If you ever see photos or video of semiconductor workers in the head-to-toe white "bunny suits," that's a clean room. Fabs are mostly housed in single-floor structures or near to the ground in order to prevent the impact of footsteps from reducing yield and output (Turley, 2002). Vibrations are such a critical issue that fab equipment is frequently mounted on springs or air suspension systems, especially in earthquake-prone areas such as California and Japan.

Specialized air purification and construction requirements add to the enormous cost of equipment and persistent re-tooling, which makes up the majority of a new fab's price tag (McKinsey & Company, 2020). A single fab equipped to manufacture the most advanced 3nm process nodes can cost from $6–7 billion to as much as $20 billion and become obsolete within five to six years (Lewis, 2019). In 2021, Samsung was considering US locations for a $17 billion fab construction project (Patterson, 2021). To put these costs in perspective, capital expenditures for US semiconductor companies amounted to roughly 30% of sales in 2020, compared to 4% of sales for the manufacturing sector as a whole (SIA, 2021).

Older fabs can sometimes be sold "down-market" to mixed-signal or analog companies that are not at the bleeding edge of the technology curve, but these sales are frequently at pennies on the dollar (EETimes, 2003). In Figure 4-14, we can see two fabs – one at SUNY College of Nanoscale Science and Engineering (left) and another at the London Centre for Nanotechnology (right).

Figure 4-14. Wafer Fab Clean Room and Lithography Lab (Bautista, 2015) (Usher, 2013)

Back-End Manufacturing

Assembly and Test

After a wafer has been tested, hardworking fab technicians are ready to enclose the die into its IC Packaging and begin back-end assembly and testing. Most assembly and test work is done by third parties called **Outsourced Assembly, Test, and Packaging Suppliers (OSAT's)**, which are largely based in East Asia and enjoy significant labor cost advantages (Schafer & Buchalter, 2017).

The following steps detail the assembly and test process. There are many different variations of the packaging process, so it is difficult to give a comprehensive list of steps, but this is a good summary. Note that not all steps are performed in every case.

0. **Wafer Bumping:** This step is not always performed, but in cases where the bare die is connected directly to other components, this initial step places small **solder balls** (or **bumps**) directly onto the wafer.

1. **Wafer Dicing:** The next step is **die cutting**, where individual die are cut from a wafer using a diamond saw and sent to a back-end facility for final packaging and assembly.

2. **Die Bonding:** After arriving at the assembly and test facility, the freshly cut die are attached to either a packaging substrate, directly to a PCB in a process called **die attach** (MRSI, n.d.), or simply packaged as bare die (flip-chip). For our purposes, we will assume the die is attached to a packaging substrate. **Epoxy die attach** is the most common bonding process and uses specialized resins as a connecting adhesive, kind of like a gorilla glue for semiconductors (MRSI, n.d.). **Flip-chip bonding** functions as a die attach method as well as a method for forming system interconnects between the die and the rest of the system (Ahmed, n.d.).

3. External Interconnect Formation – Flip Chip or Wire Bond: Next, the attached die are connected to the rest of the system through little wires from the die that lead out to the periphery of the package, forming **interconnects (I/0)** with the rest of the system. This process is called **wire bonding** and results in fewer I/O connections than more advanced Flip-Chip technology (Ammann, 2003). In **Flip-Chip packaging**, die are flipped over and soldered to a **ball grid array** or directly to the **PCB**, forming interconnects throughout the chip's area and increasing the overall speed of the system (Ammann, 2003). Don't worry if this is a little overwhelming now – we will cover IC Packaging in greater detail in the next chapter.

4. Encapsulation and Sealing: In **encapsulation, Surface Mount Technology (SMT)** is used to mount the die onto the IC Package enclosure (Gilleo & Pham-Van-Diep, 2004). Next a **transfer molding** machine heats encapsulant compounds or **molded underfills** before injecting them into the packaging mold, sealing in the **die-package assembly** (Gilleo & Pham-Van-Diep, 2004). We can see a fully "assembled" die-package assembly in figure 4-15.

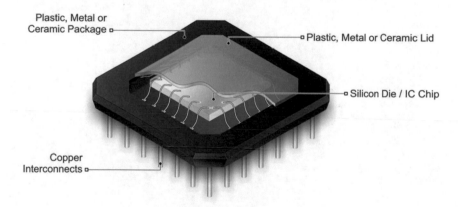

Figure 4-15. Fully Assembled Die-Package Assembly

5. Final Testing: The resulting die-package devices are tested one final time before shipping to the end customer or integrated into an intermediate system or product. It should be noted that in some well-established technologies with very high yield (>90%), this Final Testing may be the only testing of the individual die. When wafer testing is too expensive, it can be more economical to package every single die and test afterward, simply discarding the die that fail at final testing.

The five steps of the back-end manufacturing process are summarized in Figure 4-16. To re-cap, individual die are cut apart from one another during wafer dicing. Each die is then soldered to either a ball grid array (BGA) or directly to a PCB. Once soldered, external interconnects are formed to bond the die to the rest of the system and ensure effective connectivity and quick data transfer. The die-package assembly is then encapsulated and sealed to protect the die from any outside damage and ensure the system's integrity. Finally, the die-package assemblies are tested one last time before shipping to an end customer or device manufacturer for incorporation into a larger product.

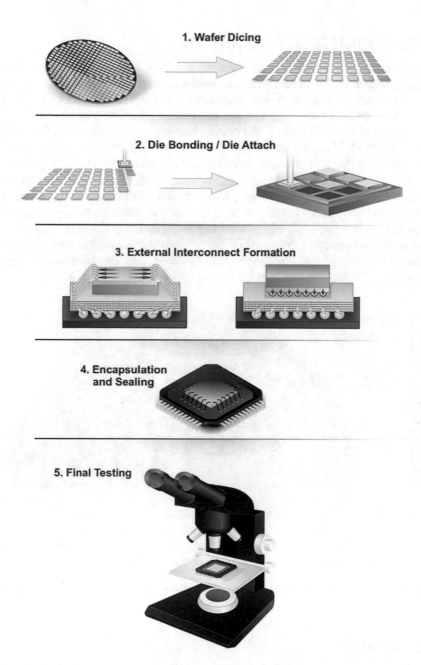

1. Wafer Dicing

2. Die Bonding / Die Attach

3. External Interconnect Formation

4. Encapsulation and Sealing

5. Final Testing

Figure 4-16. Back-End Manufacturing Process – Assembly & Test

Semiconductor Equipment

As we have seen, semiconductor production is an incredibly complex process involving dozens of different types of sophisticated equipment. These devices are as complicated as they are expensive – a single EUV machine can cost upwards of $150 million. We can see the extent of these costs by looking at a breakdown of the $64 Billion semiconductor equipment market in Figure 4-17, which depicts 2019 sales data drawn from the 2021 BCG and SIA report on strengthening the global semiconductor supply chain. Figure 4-17 parses out eleven types of semiconductor equipment, with front-end manufacturing equipment responsible for the vast majority (86%) of overall equipment sales. As chips continue to shrink, the level of difficulty in making them grows, pushing costs for such equipment higher and higher. This is particularly true for core front-end technologies responsible for delivering these increasingly smaller patterns like deposition, lithography, and removal. You may have never heard of these machines before, but you can thank them for your iPhone!

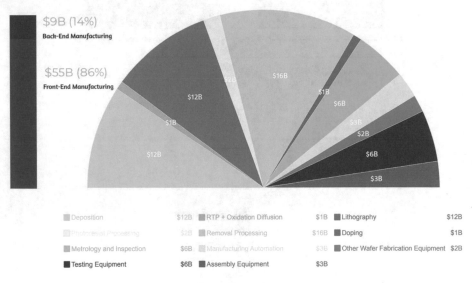

Figure 4-17. Semiconductor Market Equipment Manufacturing Market (Varas et al., 2021)

Summary

In this chapter, we tackled the semiconductor manufacturing process from receipt of a GDS design file to test and assembly. We started with a breakdown of the wafer fabrication and front-end manufacturing. In this stage, engineers build wafers up like layer cakes, running them through expensive equipment using repeating consecutive cycles of four main process types.

1. In **deposition**, key materials and thin films are deposited on the surface of the wafer.

2. In **patterning**, lithographic photomasks are used to break away photoresist and etch patterns onto the surface of the wafer.

3. **Removal** processes are used throughout to dispose of unnecessary materials.

4. **Alteration** processes are used to alter the wafer's physical properties like conductivity.

From there, we reviewed the differences between pre-metal front-end-of-the-line (FEOL) processes used to etch a transistor array onto the wafer surface and post-metal back-end-of-the-line (BEOL) processes used to build local and global interconnects that tie the system together. Once wafer fabrication is complete, finished wafers are tested and probed for defects. We next learned the importance of yield and failure analysis to process improvement and cost cutting. Finally, we broke down the back-end assembly process where OSATs place the finished die into protective IC packaging. We can see the semiconductor manufacturing flow summarized in Figure 4-18.

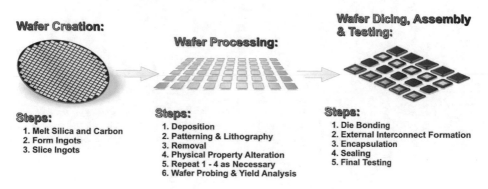

Wafer Creation:

Wafer Processing:

Wafer Dicing, Assembly & Testing:

Steps:
1. Melt Silica and Carbon
2. Form Ingots
3. Slice Ingots

Steps:
1. Deposition
2. Patterning & Lithography
3. Removal
4. Physical Property Alteration
5. Repeat 1 - 4 as Necessary
6. Wafer Probing & Yield Analysis

Steps:
1. Die Bonding
2. External Interconnect Formation
3. Encapsulation
4. Sealing
5. Final Testing

Figure 4-18. Semiconductor Manufacturing Flow – End-to-End

Building functional machines at the atomic scale, much less protecting them from the outside world, requires a plethora of increasingly expensive and ultraprecise equipment and process technology. Tying these technologies together, modern semiconductor fabs are incredible feats of human ingenuity responsible for the proliferation of computing devices across the world.

Your Personal SAT (Semiconductor Awareness Test)

To be sure that your knowledge builds on itself throughout the book, here are five questions relating to the previous chapter.

1. What are the four kinds of processes used for wafer fabrication?

2. Which core process technology is seen as a bottleneck to the rest of the industry? Why?

3. Can you tell the difference between front-end-of-the-line (FEOL) and back-end-of-the-line (BEOL)? How does this differ from front-end and back-end manufacturing?

4. Why is yield such an important metric? What is it used for?

5. What are the five core steps in the assembly and testing process?

Tying the System Together

Millions of dollars and a year of our design team's hard work has been spent, but it was well worth it! The fab has finished and shipped your order – 100,000 freshly minted custom processors are on the way. What now? If you're reading this on a kindle or a laptop, you may have noticed that a screen is in front of you, not a die-package assembly. The truth of the matter is that a well-designed IC is only as good as the system it's a part of. As Moore's Law slows down and companies lean more heavily on functional scaling to meet the demands of their customers, system integration has become increasingly important. From advanced interconnects and next generation IC Packaging to signal integrity and power distribution networks, in this chapter we'll explore the technologies that tie systems together.

What Is a System?

The word **system** can be used at different levels to describe a fully functional and discrete structure, like a laptop, or any number of subsystems or **modules** fully equipped to tackle a specific task within the larger design – think of the screen and LED drivers that make up the display module on the Kindle that we mentioned earlier. Many devices are made from a collection of different ICs and components that may have been designed by entirely separate

© Corey Richard 2023
C. Richard, *Understanding Semiconductors*, Maker Innovations Series,
https://doi.org/10.1007/978-1-4842-8847-4_5

companies using proprietary methods and unique microarchitectures – integrating all of them is a complicated and difficult task. In addition, connection points between each module are often a bottleneck for data flow, which can increase **latency** and slow down the overall system. To connect the various sub-systems and make sure power and data get to the right place, a well-designed network of interconnects, strong packaging technologies, and good signal and power integrity analysis are vital to developing a high-functioning system.

Input/Output (I/O)

An integral part of what ties the system together are **interconnects**, commonly termed **input/output (I/O)**. Within a single chip, **interconnects** are the wiring that connects different components, like transistors, with one another to form logic gates and other functional building blocks. At a higher level, interconnects refer to the connections between the chip and the PCB, other components or chips on the PCB, and other parts of the system as a whole. Large chips can have as much as 30 miles of stacked interconnect wiring occupying the various layers of an IC (these layers are formed during the BEOL stage of the front-end manufacturing process covered in the previous chapter) (Zhao, 2017). In sum, interconnects serve as the gateway through which individual components and functional blocks interact with the rest of the system. The system designer has many different options in connecting the I/O within the system, which all starts with selecting the proper package for each IC.

IC Packaging

As we saw in Chapter 4, a finished chip is placed in an **IC package** during the final stage in the electronic manufacturing cycle. Or in the case of wafer-level packaging, the finished chip is already packaged before being cut and separated from the rest of the wafer. Electronic packaging protects the chip from the outside world and supports the electrical interconnects that connect the device to the rest of the system. While we briefly introduced electronic packaging in Chapter 4, here we'll get to drill down and explore all the different package varieties at a deeper level. Feel free to skip ahead and check out Figure 5-2 on Packaging Structures and Architectures to help visualize the various components and configurations as we parse through our discussion of each packaging type.

The most widely used package types include

> **Wire Bond –** When ICs were first beginning to gain traction, packaging interconnects were limited to **wire bonded** connections from **IC bonds** and **landing pads** inside the packaging to **pins** that soldered onto the external board or substrate that supported the rest of the system (Gupta & Franzon, 2020). This arrangement limits the number of possible interconnects from an individual chip, since they can only be located on the border of the die and packaging.

> **Flip-Chip Packaging –** This procedure solves this area problem by enabling interconnects to be placed within the borders of the die itself (Gupta & Franzon, 2020). It accomplishes this by adding steps to the back end of the manufacturing and assembly process.

The Flip-Chip attachment process has approximately six steps. We touched on this back in Chapter 4, but will do a more detailed breakdown of flip chip technology here.

1. Individual ICs are manufactured through wafer fabrication. Attachment pads on the die are treated to make them more receptive to soldering.

2. Small bits of metal called **solder balls** are placed on each of the IC attachment pads through a process called **wafer bumping** (Tsai et al., 2004).

3. After wafer bumping, individual ICs are cut apart through **wafer dicing** and flipped over.

4. The solder balls on the flipped die are aligned with a pattern of corresponding **bond pads** (called a **ball grid array or BGA**) on a substrate or PCB using high-precision robots.

5. The solder balls are remelted and soldered to the underlying substrate or PCB in a process called **flip-chip bonding** (Tsai et al., 2004).

6. Finally, the spaces in between the solder ball interconnects are filled in with materials called **underfills** that mechanically and thermally support the newly mounted chip (Tsai et al., 2004).

Figure 5-1 helps us better understand each step of the flip-chip bonding process. Steps 1 through 4 are pictured in ascending order from left to right. Step 5 (flip-chip bonding) accounts for the bottom left two figures, while Step 6 (underfill) accounts for the bottom two right. Note that this drawing is not at all to scale – the solder balls are very small, typically just a hundred **microns** across.

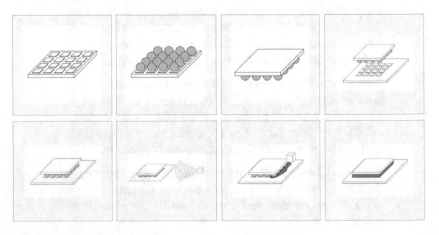

Figure 5-1. Flip-Chip Bonding Process (Twisp, 2008)

Wafer-Level (Chip-Scale) Packaging – In traditional manufacturing processes, a bunch of chips on a silicon wafer are cut apart into individual die, before they are placed in their respective packages. **Wafer-level packaging**, however, begins the packaging process before the wafer is even diced (Lee, 2017). Cutting the die apart later in the process creates a smaller **die-package assembly** that is approximately the size of the chip itself – this is why wafer-level packaging is often referred to as **chip-scale packaging (CSP)**. You can picture this as the difference between putting something in a box vs. wrapping it with wrapping paper. The box will take extra room, while the paper will stick to the edges of whatever you're wrapping. This extra room saved by wafer-level packaging is especially valuable for applications with limited area requirements, like mobile devices. CSP technology only works for small die sizes, which further limits its usage.

Multi-Chip-Modules (MCM) and **System-in-Package (SiPs)** – These two approaches integrate multiple die into a single package and are also useful for limited-space applications. The two are similar except that while MCMs integrate multiple die on a 2D surface, SiPs integrate die both horizontally (2D) and vertically (2.5/3D) (Lau, 2017). The advantages of MCMs and SiPs are that they allow engineers to modulate parts of the design and more easily incorporate licensed IP (Gupta & Franzon, 2020). Instead of having to include a CPU, memory, and a GPU all on one SoC, for example, each could be designed separately, and then packaged together in one larger module. Engineers can mix-and-match each block with other parts, but at the cost of performance and power disadvantages when compared to more tightly integrated SoCs. While suffering some integration disadvantages, modulated packaging architectures allow the use of a cheaper silicon process for the analog functions of the system, and only use the expensive lower-geometry processes for the critical high-speed processing and memory functions. SiPs also allow for passive devices like capacitors and inductors to be integrated into a single package which can improve performance by minimizing the distance between components. The tradeoffs between SoC chip-level **monolithic integration** and package-level **heterogeneous integration** is a pressing question facing many system architects and engineering leaders today – we will explore this topic in greater detail in future chapters.

2.5/3D Packaging – Advances in IC Packaging have improved performance and made electronic systems more efficient. It used to be that all packages and their enclosed chips were attached to a PCB or other substrate through **metal pins**, which then connected that chip to another part of the system through a network of wires (Gupta & Franzon, 2020). Today, system architects have many more options. Breakthroughs in **die stacking** technology have allowed design teams to stack multiple die on top of one another. In this configuration, die are stacked using vertical interconnects called **through silicon vias (TSVs)** to form **2.5/3D packaging** architectures

(Lapedus, 2019). In 2.5D packaging, die are connected to a shared substrate, called an interposer, which in turn is connected to a PCB while in 3D packaging, die are stacked directly on top of one another (Lapedus, 2019). This configuration may not be as tightly integrated as a 3D die stack, but is less costly and is more tightly integrated than a separately packaged wire bond configuration (Gupta & Franzon, 2020). New **copper hybrid bonding** technology uses copper-to-copper interconnects to connect stacked die with greater interconnect density and lower resistance, enabling quicker data transfer and faster processing speeds than traditional TSVs (Lapedus, 2020). These advanced packaging technologies have also enabled the design of integrated modules including die from different silicon processes. For example, a 22nm processor chip and a 180nm high-power audio amplifier can be included together in a single plastic module.

Stacking technology was first applied to memory systems like **Hybrid Memory Cube (HMC)** and **High Bandwidth Memory (HBM)**, where a relevant memory component might be stacked with its relevant processing chip (memory-on-logic) or additional memory die (memory-on-memory), but applications have broadened since then (Lapedus, 2019). Stacking chips vertically enables increased **I/O density**, which reduces the amount of processing time it takes to move a **signal**, or information, from one part of the electronic system to the other while saving valuable silicon real estate (Gupta & Franzon, 2020). This can be especially useful for more compact electronic devices, like smartphones, where space is limited and valuable.

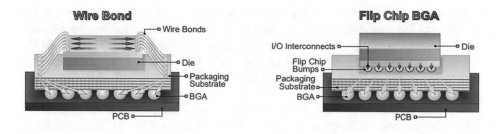

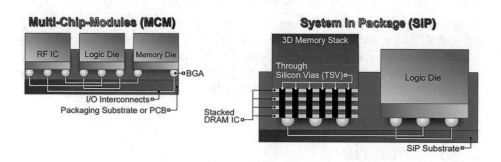

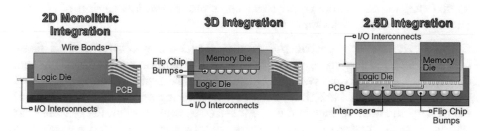

Figure 5-2. Packaging Types and Architectures

Figure 5-2 illuminates each of the various packaging types and architectures we've discussed in considerable detail. Comparing each sub-diagram to its horizontal counterpart(s) reveals key features that differentiate each packaging configuration. In the first row, **wire bonded** die use wires on the border of the die surface to connect to **pads** on the **packaging substrate**. These connections are used to tie the die to the rest of the system, whether directly through **via's** (connecting wires) on the **PCB** or through a **ball grid array (BGA)** soldered to the PCB. Because **wire bonds** require excess wiring, they are slower than their **flip chip** counterparts, which use **bumping** and **through silicon vias (TSV)** to connect the die to the underlying packaging substrate more efficiently. In the second row, **Multi-chip Modules (MCMs)** and **System in Packages (SiPs)** look relatively similar. Their key difference is that MCMs integrate multiple die side by side on a 2D surface within the same overall package. SiPs, on the other hand, use both **2D** and **2.5/3D** stacked die configurations to integrate multiple die within the same overall package. In the bottom row, we scrutinize the nuances of 2D Monolithic Integration, 3D Integration, and 2.5D Integration. **2D Monolithic Integration** attaches die to a substrate side by side within the same package. **3D Integration** attaches die on top of one another within the same package. **2.5D Integration** connects two or more die on an **interposer** that sits between the die and the base substrate, before integration within the same package (both horizontal 2D and vertical 3D integration elements).

While comprising a relatively small portion of our total system cost, making up just $30 billion of the over $440 billion in total 2020 sales reported by the SIA, IC Packaging has an outsized impact on system performance and has seen a resurgence of interest from engineering leaders desperate to squeeze more performance out of existing process nodes (Semiconductor Packaging Market by Type, 2021).

Signal Integrity

As components are packed tighter and tighter in integrated systems, signal integrity has become increasingly important. It is derived from the study of electromagnetics, an area of physics that explores the interaction of electric currents, or fields, with one another.

Digital Signals are electric pulses that travel along **transmission lines** carrying information from place to place throughout an electrical system (MPS, n.d.). In electronic systems, these signals are typically represented by a **voltage** (MPS, n.d.). Let's think back to what we learned in our discussion of electricity and how voltage and current relate to one another. Remember that voltage acts like water pressure in a pipe, driving current along the wiring and circuitry that comprises an electronic system – the current in question here is the signal itself. Currents with higher voltages sufficient to open transistor gates are ON (1) signals, while currents with lower voltages are OFF (0) signals. If we zoom in even further, we can see that a current is made up of charges moving in the same direction. When you hear the term **bit** used in computer engineering, the bit is made up of these charges. Strung together, patterns of bits comprise signals that different components of a computer can interpret as information. At each junction in the transmission process, a **transmitter** sends a signal to a **receiver** along a **transmission line** that connects them (Altera, 2007). To be clear, the transmitter and receiver in this case are physically connected by a wired transmission line, unlike a transmitter and receiver in a wireless system. In complex electronic circuits where wires can be literally a few nanometers from each other, neighboring signals can interfere with one another and the surrounding environment as they pass along transmission lines through the various components of the system. These transmission line effects on signal integrity can result in data loss, accuracy issues, and system failure.

To mitigate these effects, **signal integrity engineers** conduct electromagnetic simulations and analysis to identify and resolve potential issues before they arise. Common forms of **interference** include noise, crosstalk, distortion, and loss.

1. **Noise** occurs when energy that is not part of the desired signal interferes with the signal being transmitted (Breed, 2010).

2. **Crosstalk** occurs when energy from one signal inadvertently transfers to a neighboring transmission line (Breed, 2010).

3. **Distortion** occurs when the signal pattern is damaged or warped. In extreme cases, distortion can be so severe that incorrect data is delivered to the receiver (Breed, 2010).

4. **Loss** can occur for several reasons, including **resistive loss** from transmission line conductivity issues, **dielectric loss** from a loss in signal velocity, and **radiation loss** in unsealed systems (Breed, 2010).

At high **bit rates** and great distances, signals can degrade to a point where an electronic system fails completely.

Bus Interfaces

One of the key performance bottlenecks in electronic devices is the transmission of data between each of the system's constituent parts. Doubling a processor's power doesn't mean anything if it takes too long to get the information it needs to do its job from the rest of the system. To unlock the power of advanced circuits, **bus interfaces**, the physical wires through which data travels between the different components of a system or PCB, have become increasingly important. That 64-bit processor in your computer has to move 64 bits of data together on a single bus interface. **Bus interfaces** can have three primary functions (Thornton, 2016):

1. To transmit data (**data bus**)

2. To find specific data (**address bus**)

3. To control the operations of different parts of the system (**control bus**)

Together, these three buses are called a **system bus** and collectively control the flow of information to and from a CPU or microprocessor (Thornton, 2016). The block diagram presented in Figure 5-3 illustrates the relationship between the system bus, its constituent data, address, and control buses, and key system components like the CPU, memory, and i/o interconnects that tie them all together.

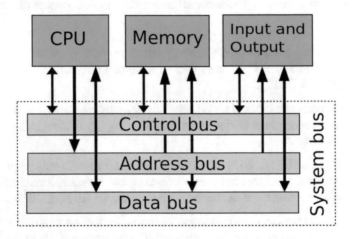

Figure 5-3. System Bus Block Diagram (Nowicki, 2019)

Data buses for PC's can accept information flow to and from the central processor ranging from 8- to 64-bits at a time. Like a hose unable to pump more water than its diameter allows, a bus connected to a 32-bit processor cannot deliver or receive more than 32-bits at a time (per-clock cycle). In this way, the bit number functions as a measurement of bus "diameter" or "width" (Thornton, 2016).

Much of the development in bus interfaces has occurred in the personal computing space. In the early days, bundles of wires called a **bus-bar** would separately connect each component to one another, but this approach was slow and inefficient (Wilson & Johnson, 2005). To increase speed and improve performance, PC companies migrated to an integrated structure that reduced the number of interface junctures from a cluster of haphazardly connected components and modules down to two chips – the Northbridge and the Southbridge **chipset architecture**.

In this configuration, the **Northbridge** interfaces directly with the CPU via the **front-side bus (FSB)** and connects it with components that have the highest performance requirements, like memory and graphics modules (Wilson & Johnson, 2005). The Northbridge then interfaces with the **Southbridge**, which in turn connects to all the lower priority components and interfaces like Ethernet, USB, and other low speed buses (Wilson & Johnson, 2005). These non-Northbridge bus interfaces are collectively known as **Peripheral Buses** (PCMAG, n.d.). The Northbridge and Southbridge are connected to one another at a juncture known as the **I/O Controller Hub (ICH)** and together they are known as a **chipset** (Hameed & Airaad, 2019). We can see this chipset architecture clearly depicted in Figure 5-4.

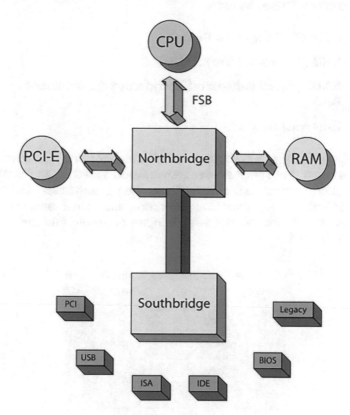

Figure 5-4. Simple Chipset Diagram (Oyster, 2014)

Bus interfaces can be classified by the way they transmit bits between two digital devices (Newhaven Display International, n.d.). **Parallel interfaces** run multiple wires between two components and transmit bits across at the same time (Newhaven Display International, n.d.). This works well over short distances, but signal integrity issues can arise as the distance between two components increases. Common **Parallel Interface Buses** include **DDR (Double Data Rate)** which is used for memory, and **PCI (Peripheral Component Interface) buses**. **Serial interfaces**, on the other hand, transmit and receive data between two components across a single wire one bit at a time, but at much higher speeds (Newhaven Display International, n.d.). This reduces the chances of signal integrity issues since a bit cannot be received until the one before it has been processed. Serial data transmission is less likely to experience crosstalk issues since individual data lines are not bundled next to each other. However, serial data is susceptible to another type of interference called **Intersymbol Interference (ISI)**, where a data bit can be affected by the bit transmitted just before (Kay, 2003). Common **Serial Interface Buses** include

> **PCIe (PCI Express Bus)**
>
> **USB (Universal Serial Bus)**
>
> **SATA (Serial Advanced Technology Attachment Bus)**
>
> **Ethernet Bus**

Beyond signal integrity advantages, serial interfaces are less costly due to lower wire count, but suffer slower transmission speeds (Kay, 2003). Parallel communication, by contrast, enables faster data transmission, but is costlier and has limited efficacy over long distance and when operating at high frequencies (Kay, 2003). We can see examples of parallel and serial interfaces depicted in Figure 5-5.

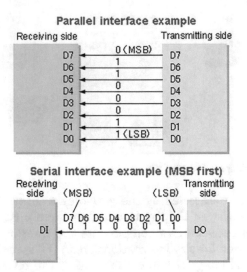

Figure 5-5. Parallel vs. Serial Interfaces (Ashri, 2014)

Unless you specialize in Signal Integrity or interface circuit design, it probably isn't so important that you know all the bus interface flavors, but rather that you understand why they are so important to the overall system. The key takeaway to remember is that bus interfaces form the connective tissue responsible for delivering data, distributing instructions, and tying together the major components of the overall system.

Power Flow in Electronic Systems

To most of us, the power that fuels our electronics is like magic. We plug our phones and laptops in and Boom! they work. Harnessing the power of "power" is the subject of a vast field of engineering and numerous subdisciplines. Taking a page from our review of transistors, it's helpful to think of system power flow like the flow of water through a water utility system. It might be useful to take a look at Figure 5-6 and follow along as we track each step.

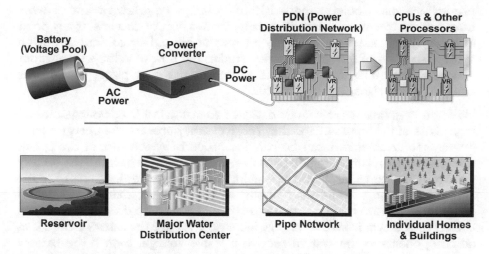

Figure 5-6. Power Flow in Electronic Systems – Water Utility Analogy

Our world is becoming more and more mobile every day, so we'll focus on battery-powered systems for this discussion. In our analogy, the **battery** acts like a reservoir of charges whose **voltage** is comparable to a municipal reservoir of water. A **power converter** converts AC Power to DC electric current, much like a major water distribution center might decrease the water pressure as water gets closer to its destination. As it turns out, AC power is much better for transmitting power over long distances (think utility-grade transmission lines in your city's power grid), while DC power is much better for power transmission over short distances (think of the power home appliances might use). Batteries often store power in DC form as well, but for the sake of illustration, we'll pretend this battery stores AC power that needs to be converted before use.

Next, the charges or electric voltage from the battery are transported through a network of metal planes, called a **Power Distribution Network (PDN)**, to the different processing centers of the system, like a utility pipe network delivering water to the homes and buildings of end users like you and me.

To transport water to individual homes and buildings, utility providers use varying levels of water pressure to push H_2O through the system. This is a delicate balancing act – if the water pressure gets too high, the pipes in the system may burst, but if it drops too low, then water won't get through the pipes to its end destination. In electronics, we have a similar problem with voltage. If the voltage gets too high, the circuit may become damaged, or may overheat and fail, but if the voltage drops too low, then the circuit will not have enough energy to function. To prevent this from happening, **power engineers** must build a network of **voltage regulators** and **power converters** to ensure that voltage is never too high or too low at any point in the system. Like Signal Integrity analysis of bit and signal flow through a system, the field of **Power Integrity** studies the flow of voltage throughout a system to ensure that voltage is getting to the right place, in the right amount, at the right time (Mittal, 2020).

Voltage regulators are circuits designed to maintain a fixed voltage output, regardless of the input voltage they receive – they process the energy from a power source so that it can be handled properly by the rest of the circuit (MPS, n.d.). This is important in battery-powered systems because the battery voltage is not constant. If you're walking down the street listening to music and get a phone call and your phone screen lights up, that takes a lot of instantaneous power and can cause the battery voltage to drop significantly as the current drawn from the battery increases. Voltage regulators ensure that all components in the system receive a stable voltage, even if the battery voltage is moving around. There are a wide variety of voltage regulators, including **DC/DC converters**, **PMUs** (power management units), **Buck converters** (a specific type of DC/DC converters), **Boost** and **Flyback** converters.

Summary

In this chapter, we first discussed I/O interconnects and their importance to connecting the various components of an overall system. With as many as 30 miles of wiring in a single chip, interconnects are a key factor in limiting or boosting device performance. From simple wire bond packaging to high I/O density flip-chip and wafer-level packaging, we dove deep into the various packaging architectures and the processes that make them possible. Next, we discussed the differences between multi-chip-modules and system-in-packages, introducing key concepts like heterogeneous and monolithic integration. We learned about advanced die stacking technology used in high bandwidth memory (HBM), HMC, and other 2.5/3D packaging architectures. From there, we explored the role of signal integrity in maintaining the pace and quality of information flow throughout an electronic system. Building on our understanding of interconnects and signal integrity, we then tackled the three buses – control, address, and data – that facilitate information flow between a CPU, Memories, and external sources of data. Finally, we explored the flow of power through an electronic system like water through a utility system – tracking voltage through power converters and a power distribution network to its end destination.

A company may source and design the perfect assortment of ICs and components to create a market-leading product, but having the right parts is not enough on its own. Building high caliber devices requires tight system integration with plenty of interconnects, the right IC packaging architecture, and strong signal and power integrity performance.

Your Personal SAT (Semiconductor Awareness Test)

To be sure that your knowledge builds on itself throughout the book, here are five questions relating to the previous chapter.

1. What are interconnects and what makes them so important?

2. What is the difference between wire bonding and flip-chip bonding? How do these impact the number of interconnects and transmission speed of a system?

3. Why do signal integrity engineers exist? What kinds of interfaces and transmission methods might they encounter?

4. In a chipset, why are the CPU, the northbridge, and southbridge arranged the way that they are? What do each of these bridges handle and how are they different?

5. Describe the four main stages of power flow in an electronic system. Which components or modules handle each stage? Can you relate each of them to similar components in a water utility system?

Common Circuits and System Components

From basics to ASICs, we've covered a lot of ground in Chapters 1–5. We started with foundational electronic physics and transistor structure, then focused on how semiconductors are designed, manufactured, and integrated into larger systems. Though our discussion has helped us build a holistic model of electronic systems, thus far it has largely treated semiconductors as a monolith devoid of differentiating features. In this chapter, we will break apart this monolith, exploring the numerous types of common circuits and system components that comprise the semiconductor family. Before we explore each of these major subcategories, we'll first explore the differences between digital and analog technology.

© Corey Richard 2023
C. Richard, *Understanding Semiconductors*, Maker Innovations Series,
https://doi.org/10.1007/978-1-4842-8847-4_6

Digital vs. Analog

There are two main types of components that get their names from the type of signals that they use – **digital** and **analog**. **Digital signals** act like a light switch – they are either on (1) or off (0) (MPS, n.d.). These patterns of 1's and 0's are used to convey information and constitute the **binary computer language** that most people are familiar with when they think of electronics (MPS, n.d.). Digital signals are usually also **synchronous** – they run on a **reference clock** to coordinate the processing of different functional blocks and ensure proper timing (MPS, n.d.). Though their predictability and synchronous timing make them great for storing and processing information, digital circuits are unable to transport information over any sort of distance without physical wiring to move their signals from place to place.

While digital electronics operate with synchronous timing and discrete values, analog devices process information continuously as a range of values (MPS, n.d.). Their ability to capture and transmit **electromagnetic energy** makes them well suited for applications like wireless communication. To the experts in the audience, yes, wireless communication can send digital signals, but this is typically done by **modulating** an analog signal **frequency** or **amplitude** and then recovering those bits using a receiver. We can picture analog signals like the sine and cosine graphs from basic geometry. Much of the energy from real-world signals are analog in nature – sound and light, for example, exist as analog "wave" signals. We can see the differences between binary digital signals and analog wave signals clearly pictured in Figure 6-1.

Figure 6-1. Analog vs. Digital Signals

Analog signals are distinguished from one another by their **frequency**. **Frequency** describes the number of times an analog signal wave completes an up and down cycle, or repeats itself, over a fixed period. For a given signal, frequency is inversely proportional to **wavelength** and directly proportional to **power** – the greater the frequency, the shorter its wavelength, but the greater its energy level (NASA Hubble Site, n.d.). To remember this dynamic, I find it helpful to picture an exhausted parent taking their restless child to the park after a long day of work. The child running around the park may be smaller but has much more energy and higher frequency of movement than their larger parent, who lumbers from swing set to monkey bars. Electrical **frequency** is measured in units called **Hertz (Hz),** which describes the number of times an electromagnetic signal completes an up-down cycle per second (Encyclopædia Britannica, n.d.). The unit Hertz is named after Heinrich Hertz, a German physicist who performed early research into properties of electromagnetic radiation. By receiving and processing different frequencies, analog electronics can perform all kinds of useful things from detecting external stimuli (sensors) to wireless data transmission and communication (RF technology).

We can see the relationship between wavelength, frequency, and energy visualized in Figure 6-2. High-frequency signals have higher energy and a shorter wavelength, while low-frequency signals have less energy and a longer wavelength.

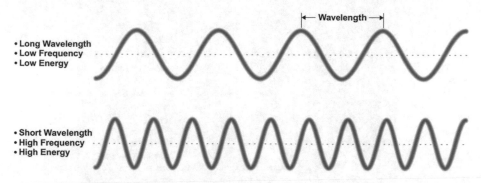

Figure 6-2. Wavelength vs. Frequency vs. Energy

The differences between Analog and Digital signals make them more useful for distinct parts of electronic systems. Storage and processing parts of the system (the "computing" parts) are typically made up of **digital components,** which are better at storing and processing data (MPS, n.d.). Devices that receive information from the outside world, like the sensors in your earphones or in your camera, however, are more likely to be made up of **analog components** (MPS, n.d.). In many electronic systems, analog and digital components work together to "translate" real-world analog signals into digital signals a computer can understand, then re-translate the digital response from the computer back into analog signals we humans can understand. To accomplish this, **mixed-signal devices** called **data converters** are used to convert between each type of signal. Data converters can be **Analog-to-Digital (ADC)** or **Digital-to-Analog (DAC)** (MPS, n.d.). We summarize the differences between Analog and Digital technology in Table 6-1 and will discuss Analog and Wireless Technologies in greater detail in the following chapter.

Table 6-1. Analog vs. Digital Signals

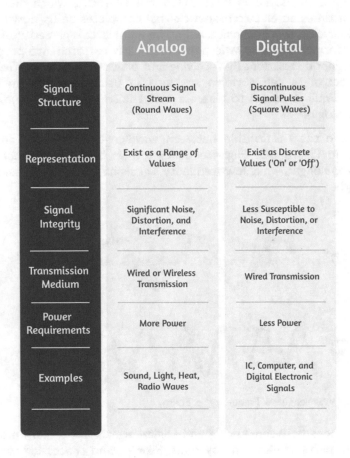

	Analog	Digital
Signal Structure	Continuous Signal Stream (Round Waves)	Discontinuous Signal Pulses (Square Waves)
Representation	Exist as a Range of Values	Exist as Discrete Values ('On' or 'Off')
Signal Integrity	Significant Noise, Distortion, and Interference	Less Susceptible to Noise, Distortion, or Interference
Transmission Medium	Wired or Wireless Transmission	Wired Transmission
Power Requirements	More Power	Less Power
Examples	Sound, Light, Heat, Radio Waves	IC, Computer, and Digital Electronic Signals

Common System Components – The SIA Framework

So we now know that there are two types of components – digital and analog – but what do all of these components do? When building a system, designers and architects have a multitude of individual parts to choose from, each with its unique advantages and disadvantages. Driven by demand in the six end-use markets (communications, computing, consumer, automotive, government and industrial electronics), the component market is diverse and highly competitive. The variety of individual products and devices can be daunting, so it's helpful to use the Semiconductor Industry Association's framework, breaking the market into five constituent segments (SIA, 2021).

1. Micro Components (Digital): Micro components include all non-custom digital devices that can be plugged into another system and used for computation or signal processing. You can think of them as generic subcomponents and specifically include microprocessors, microcontrollers, and digital signal processors (DSPs) (SIA, 2021).

2. Logic (Digital): Logic encompasses all non-micro component digital logic. This segment primarily refers to specialized circuitry and includes application-specific ICs (ASICs), field programmable gate arrays (FPGAs), and more versatile, but application-specific digital logic devices (SIA, 2021).

3. Memory (Digital): Memory is used to store information and is usually classified based on whether it can store data with or without power. Volatile memory (RAM) requires power to store memory, but enables quicker access, while non-volatile memory (ROM) can retain memory without access to power. Dynamic random access memory (DRAM) is the most common type of volatile memory, while NAND flash is the most common type of non-volatile memory (NAND is not actually an acronym, but rather stands for "NOT AND", a type of boolean operator and logic gate) (SIA, 2021).

4. Optoelectronics, Sensors and Actuators, and Discrete Components – OSD (Analog and Digital): Optoelectronics include laser devices, display technology, and other photonics-based electronics. Sensors include all kinds of specialized devices used to measure everything from temperature to air pressure. Actuators include devices that initiate movement or take other actions in response to a stimulus detected by a sensor (SIA, 2021). Discrete components are individually packaged, specialized transistors or other basic components, like resistors, capacitors, and inductors.

5. Analog Components: Analog ICs process analog signals and are classified as either standard linear integrated circuits (SLICs) or application-specific standard products (ASSP). SLICs are generic, plug-and-play analog devices that can be integrated into a larger system. ASSPs are components designed for a specific application, but can still be integrated into multiple systems within that application category. As we discussed in the last section, analog electronics process real-world signals like radio waves, light, sound, temperature, and other sensory signals.

From the 2020 semiconductor product segment sales figures in Figure 6-3, we can see that the market is led by memory, micro components, and logic, followed by OSD and analog electronics (SIA, 2021). We will cover each of these in the following sections.

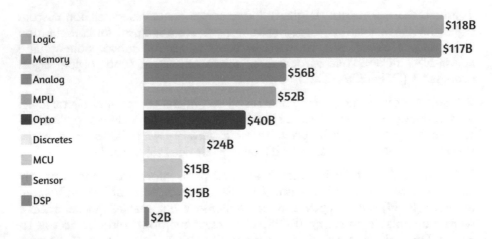

Figure 6-3. 2020 Distribution of Semiconductor Sales by Component Type (SIA and WSTS)

Micro Components

Microprocessors and Microcontrollers

In its simplest form, a **processor** is a chip that receives input, processes said input, and produces an output that can be used for some intended purpose. The term **microprocessor (MPU)** is generally used to describe more complex digital circuits, like CPUs, that connect to a larger system. They perform a general computing function and require an external bus to connect to memory and other peripheral components (Knerl, 2019).

While microprocessors handle general computing tasks, **microcontrollers** perform specific functions and are integrated with memory and I/O connections all on one chip (Knerl, 2019). Generally, microcontrollers are smaller, less powerful processors that can serve as plug-and-play computing power for simple operations (Knerl, 2019). They are used widely in low power IoT devices and embedded systems. PCs and Servers account for the largest share of microprocessor sales, while automotive, industrial, and computing account for most sales in the microcontroller segment (SIA, 2021).

It is important to distinguish microprocessors and microcontrollers in the Micro Component segment from processors in the Logic segment. **Logic devices** are custom designed for a specific application, while **Micro Components** provide more generic processing that can be combined with other components in all kinds of systems (Schafer & Buchalter, 2017).

Digital Signal Processors (DSP)

Digital signal processors (DSPs) are used to process multimedia and real-world signals like audio, video, temperature, pressure, position, etc. (Analog Devices, n.d.). Digital electronics have trouble accurately representing the real world in 1's and 0's, so they need DSPs to make sense of them in a way they can understand. They are usually fed converted analog signal data from an **Analog-to-Digital Data Converter (ADC)** for quick processing, before sending their output to other processors or back out into the world through a **Digital-to-Analog Converter (DAC)**, depending on the application (Analog Devices, n.d.). There's a DSP in your mobile phone, for example, that enables modes like Bass Boost to change the nature of the sound coming out the headphones. DSPs are adept at high-speed, real-time data processing and are highly programmable, which makes them easy to implement in a wide variety of devices and systems (Analog Devices, n.d.).

Micro Component Market Summary

Figure 6-4 uses data drawn from SIA and WSTS's 2020 End Use Survey to break down the Micro Component market. Microprocessors (MPU), Microcontrollers (MCU), and Digital Signal Processors accounted for a combined $69 billion in sales, or about 16% of the $440 billion of total industry sales in 2020 (SIA Databook, 2021). Comprising 57% of the segments' end-use applications, Micro Components are much more heavily weighted toward computing applications than other components in the SIA Framework (SIA End Use Survey, 2021).

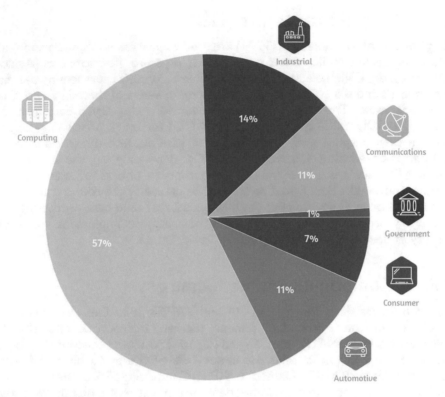

Figure 6-4. 2020 Microprocessors, Microcontrollers, and Digital Signal Processor Market by End Use (SIA and WSTS)

Logic

Special Purpose Logic

Special Purpose Logic encompasses all ICs designed and sold as standard products. This includes a range of specific ICs, including wireless controllers like Ethernet and WLAN, Modem SoCs, image and audio processors, PC Core Logic, and GPUs (SIA, 2021).

Special Purpose Logic Devices are **Application-Specific Standard Parts (ASSPs)** that are designed and integrated into a system the same way **Application-Specific Integrated Circuits (ASICs)** are (Maxfield, 2014). The term "standard parts" here just means that the same part can be used in many different products. For example, the same "standard" 12-bit video DAC (Digital to Analog Converter) can be used on a Ring doorbell, an LCD TV, or a handheld game console. A "custom" part is specifically designed for a single device. High-volume consumer products like iPhones utilize many different custom chips – when you're selling hundreds of millions of iPhones, it's worth it to squeeze every last bit of performance using specialized silicon. The main difference between the two is that ASICs are designed and optimized for a specific use in a single system (i.e. Samsung designs an ASIC CPU for its smartphone or AMD designs an ASIC GPU to power Microsoft's Xbox video game systems) as opposed to a more generalized application (Intel designs a server-based CPU aimed at all Data Center customers) (Maxfield, 2014). Standardized product types such as Input/Output (I/O) circuits like USB or PCIe are also classified as ASSPs (Maxfield, 2014).

Central Processing Unit

Central Processing Units (CPUs), as the name implies, are the main processing center for most computing systems (Encyclopædia Britannica, n.d.). They are a type of microprocessor and are likely the first thing that comes to mind when you think of a computer's inner workings, but don't let the term CPU limit your thinking to the computer on your desk, or the laptop in your bag – from smart speakers to automotive control systems, any device that processes information can have a CPU. There might even be a CPU in your coffee maker.

You can think of a CPU as the digital "brains" of a computer, processing and executing instructions as needed. The core processing of a CPU is handled by something called the **Arithmetic Logic Unit (ALU)**, which performs numerical and logic-based operations necessary to run all the software it was intended to deliver (Fox, n.d.). CPUs are complicated circuits and can house billions of transistors on a single die.

CPUs are typically connected with other modules through a **bus** or **chipset** that feeds information into the CPU for processing and directs output data to memory for storage or to other system components (Thornton, 2016). To connect with other memory chips holding instructions awaiting processing, CPUs use **registers** as the physical entry and exit point for data flow to and from the rest of the system. Instructions and data must enter and exit through these registers, which act like an "information security team" keeping unauthorized people from getting into a club or private party. Each CPU has a fixed number of registers through which data can flow, with typical register capacities measuring 8-, 16-, 32-, or 64-bits "wide" (Thornton, 2016). These numbers indicate the number of bits a CPU can access from its memory at a given time. If a CPU is a water tank, its register bit count indicates the diameter of the hose used to fill it up or empty it out.

An individual microprocessor in a CPU or GPU may be referred to as a **core**, which can be combined with other "core microprocessors" to tackle complex tasks and run more taxing applications (Firesmith, 2017). When computer manufacturers advertise their powerful, **multi-core architecture** – this is what they are referring to.

Together, the CPU and other components are "integrated" onto a single IC (SoC) or a larger system. One laptop may include a separate CPU, memory, GPU, power source, and multimedia processors, while another may integrate all of these onto a single SoC or Multi-Chip-Module (MCM).

Intel is a leader in developing CPUs that power devices like personal laptops, though many other companies like AMD develop CPUs as well.

Graphics Processing Units

Graphics processing units (GPUs) are best known for driving the graphics and 3D visual processing in electronic devices (PCMAG, n.d.). They use **parallel processing** as opposed to **serial processing** used by CPUs. **Serial processing** enables a processor to run through a series of tasks very quickly, but can only complete instructions in order, one bit at a time (Caulfield, 2009). **Parallel processing**, on the other hand, enables a processor to break down more complex problems into smaller constituent parts (Caulfield, 2009). CPUs are excellent at performing a few complex operations using a modest number of cores but are inefficient at breaking up problems into smaller chunks (Caulfield, 2009). GPUs, on the other hand, can perform thousands of specialized operations using hundreds of cores, though they are not as efficient at handling more diverse operations (Caulfield, 2009). The display on your computer is such a regular structure that GPUs have been massively optimized to perform just that image display task. In sum, CPUs are better at performing a high variety of tasks like running all the programs and functions of a PC, while GPUs lend themselves to applications that require high-volume, repetitive calculations like graphics processing (Caulfield, 2009). We can see the differences between CPUs and GPUs illustrated in Figure 6-5.

CPU

GPU

Steps:
- Serial Processing
- Instructions One Bit at a Time
- Few Complex Operations
- High Task Variety
- General Processing

Steps:
- Parallel Processing
- Instructions Multiple Bits at a Time
- Many Simple Operations
- High-Volume Repetitive Tasks
- Machine Learning and Visual Processing

Figure 6-5. CPU vs. GPU

Some of the more recent and exciting applications of GPUs are in **artificial intelligence** and **machine learning** (Dsouza, 2020). **Deep learning** and other AI techniques require the execution of multitudes of relatively simple arithmetic calculations. Machine learning involves lots of computation of two-dimensional arrays of numbers, called **matrices**. When you think about it, a computer display is just a big matrix of individual **pixels**, so it was natural to look to GPUs as the ideal matrix processors. And because GPUs can break down complex problems into smaller, constituent problems, they are well equipped to handle the millions and billions of small trial-and-error calculations necessary to deliver arduous AI solutions (Dsouza, 2020). That same number-crunching power that makes GPUs good at machine learning also makes them good at mining cryptocurrencies. GPUs can complete the hash operations of cryptocurrency mining much faster than a CPU. In fact, the same way companies created custom GPUs for graphics years ago, companies are now creating processors custom-built just for cryptocurrency mining.

While most of the semiconductor industry has been consolidating, innovations in AI-centric GPUs have led to a significant growth area where new companies have been able to compete. Specific applications ideal for GPU processing include autonomous driving, machine vision and facial recognition, **high performance computing (HPC)**, complex simulation and modeling, data science and analytics, bioinformatics, and Computational Finance, to name a few (NVIDIA, 2020).

ASICs vs. FPGAs

ASICs and FPGAs represent two different approaches to chip design and development, each with their own pluses and minuses.

ASIC stands for **Application-Specific Integrated Circuit**. As the name implies, ASICs are designed for a specific purpose (Maxfield, 2014). By designing a chip from the ground up, ASICs have several performance advantages including high speed, lower power consumption, smaller area, and lower variable manufacturing costs at high volumes (Maxfield, 2014). The main drawback for ASICs is the significant upfront development costs that go into their design (Cadence PCB Solutions, 2019). Building a chip is a capital and labor-intensive process that requires teams of highly qualified and well-paid engineers. Even if a chip is **taped-out** (finished) and sent to the fab for manufacturing, there is always the risk that yields are low, or that the ASIC does not function as intended. No amount of verification, validation, and failure analysis can eliminate the risk of serious flaws, and this risk must be considered when deciding whether developing an ASIC makes sense.

Another drawback of ASICs is that they are typically so customized for a given application that they can't be used in another area. For example, audio devices use digital-to-analog converters (DACs) to convert digital voice or music data which is driven as an analog signal to a speaker. The DAC driving the speaker in your phone is customized for the frequency and performance levels needed for audio. That same DAC can't be used to convert the digital video signals to drive the LCD screen. Each application needs a different chip, which adds to cost and complexity.

FPGA stands for **Field Programmable Gate Array**. As the name implies, these chips are "programmable," which means they can be customized to serve a specific function after they have already been manufactured (Cadence PCB Solutions, 2019).

Most FPGAs can, in fact, be erased, then "re-programmed" to serve a new purpose, which makes them ideal for prototyping new designs (Cadence PCB Solutions, 2019). An engineer can program an FPGA with a new design, test how it functions in the real world, and iterate from there to perfect their design before moving it to manufacturing. This programming step can be performed in minutes, compared to months or years to design and manufacture an ASIC. Devices called **emulators** are essentially a box with a bunch of FPGAs working together that allow ASIC designers to iterate their designs before moving to manufacturing (Xilinx, n.d.). Emulators are becoming more and more important as chip manufacturing costs increase. Fine-geometry processes can cost millions of dollars for the first tape-out of a new custom chip, so it's critical that the design is correct. Emulation is a way to further verify how a given design performs in the real world and be sure it will function correctly when it comes back from the fab. We can see the various applications FPGAs are used for in Figure 6-6.

While ASICs can take as much as a year to design and cannot be reprogrammed after manufacturing, FPGAs offer "off the shelf" solutions that enable companies to quickly bring a chip to market, albeit at a much higher per-unit price point (Cadence PCB Solutions, 2019).

For the last decade, the FPGA market has been dominated by two main players Xilinx and Altera. Altera was acquired by Intel in 2015, which now controls about 32–35% of the market. Xilinx controls between 50-55% and was recently acquired by AMD for $35 billion (Mehra, 2021).

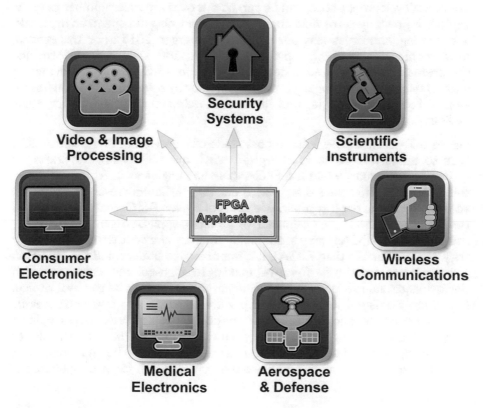

Figure 6-6. Potential Applications of FPGAs

ASIC or FPGA – Which to Choose?

A key decision for many companies in need of an IC is whether to build a custom ASIC or use an off-the-shelf FPGAs. At the crux of the dilemma is a trade-off between performance and price. ASICs can take months or years to develop and cost well into the millions, even billions of dollars, in upfront R&D with no guarantee that the finished product will perform as intended (Trimberger, 2015). Because of their custom design, however, ASICs have considerable speed and power efficiency advantages over FPGAs that still must perform programmed tasks while carrying extra circuitry "dead weight" that isn't needed for its programmed application.

If you are working with short time-to-market constraints or lower-than-expected manufacturing volumes, FPGAs are usually the better choice, assuming there is some wiggle room for poorer performance (Trimberger, 2015). As expected volumes increase, however, the per-unit cost of ASICs becomes increasingly attractive (Trimberger, 2015). At higher volumes, high up-front development costs can be spread out over a greater number of units, capitalizing on long-term yield improvements, reducing net spend on materials, and costing companies less per device (Trimberger, 2015). For this reason, most companies with high product volumes and stringent performance requirements have invested in developing custom ASICs, either by partnering with a fabless design company like Qualcomm or by developing them in house. Apple, Facebook, Google, and Tesla all develop custom ASICs for their devices for example.

Figure 6-7 visualizes the volume-cost trade-offs between FPGAs and ASICs. Due to the high fixed costs of a given ASIC, the ASIC value line starts off higher on the y-axis, while the FPGA value line begins at 0. At low volumes, this fixed cost difference is a game ender for ASICs. However, as projected volumes increase, the lower variable costs of a given ASIC eventually make up the difference. ASICs are optimized for a specific application and do not carry the deadweight FPGAs carry in additional circuitry and cost structure. Though they are less flexible than FPGAs, it is important to understand the inflection point of this trade-off. If you're building a high-volume chip with high performance and low power requirements, an ASIC might be the best choice. If you are building a low-volume chip without stringent power constraints, FPGAs may be the quicker and cheaper option. Of course we've oversimplified things a lot with this graphic. For a given technology or industry, the slopes and starting points of these lines may change significantly. The important thing is to do a thorough analysis and make the right decision for your application.

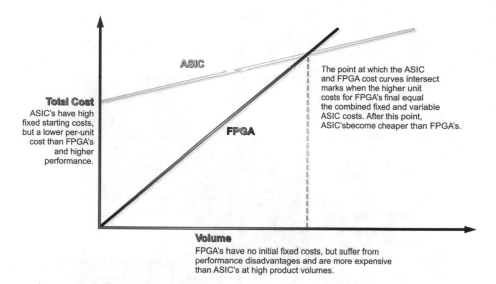

Figure 6-7. FPGA vs. ASIC Cost Analysis

One option that combines the strategies is to use FPGAs to initially prove out a new product idea and demo a solution to generate customer interest. Once that hurdle is cleared, it can be easier to secure funding or corporate buy-in for the much larger expense for ASIC development. The various advantages and disadvantages of FPGAs and ASICs are summarized in Figure 6-8.

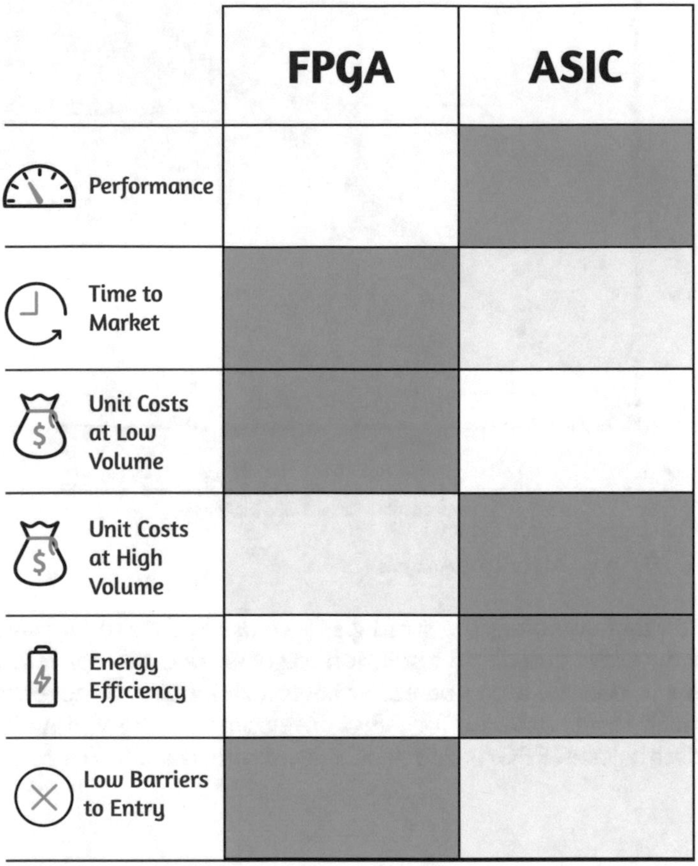

	FPGA	ASIC
Performance		
Time to Market		
Unit Costs at Low Volume		
Unit Costs at High Volume		
Energy Efficiency		
Low Barriers to Entry		

Figure 6-8. FPGAs vs. ASICs – Advantages and Disadvantages

System on Chip

System on Chips (SoCs) are a complex and highly integrated type of ASIC that can house billions of components on a single silicon chip. As the name implies, SoCs contain an entire functional device all on one IC substrate – a single unit may have a CPU, memory, GPU, power management unit, wireless circuitry, and other components or functional modules. To be considered an SoC, an IC must have at a minimum, microprocessors and/or microcontrollers, DSPs, on-chip memory, and peripheral functions like **hardware accelerators** (Maxfield, 2014).

For larger devices with greater power accessibility like PCs, design teams may have plenty of space and flexibility to design the system with distinct modules, perhaps deciding to integrate the system at the package level with MCM. For smaller applications like cell phones, however, multiple chips may require too much space and power. Tighter integration mitigates these problems, enabling engineers to fit entire computing systems in the palm of your hand. SoCs are used pervasively in mobile devices like cell phones, tablets, smartwatches, and other battery-powered devices where space and power are limited. Though SoCs are used most in embedded and mobile devices, they have been increasingly used for laptops and other devices that can still leverage their performance advantages.

Differentiating between ASICs, ASSPs, and SoCs can be a bit confusing, we can better visualize how they relate to one another in Figure 6-9. The main difference between the two is that ASSPs are designed to serve multiple companies and end systems, while ASICs are designed for a single use by a single company or product. ASSPs or ASICs that contain a processor are considered SoCs, while those that don't are not.

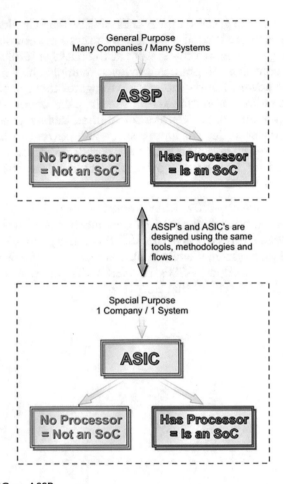

Figure 6-9. ASIC vs. ASSP

Logic Market Summary

Figure 6-10 uses data drawn from SIA and WSTS's 2020 End Use Survey to break down the Logic market. CPUs, GPUs, ASICs, FPGAs, SoCs, and other Logic devices accounted for a combined $118 billion in sales, or about 27% of the $440 billion of total industry sales in 2020 (SIA Databook, 2021). Comprising 44% of the segments' end use applications, Logic is more heavily weighted toward Communications than other components in the SIA Framework (SIA End Use Survey, 2021).

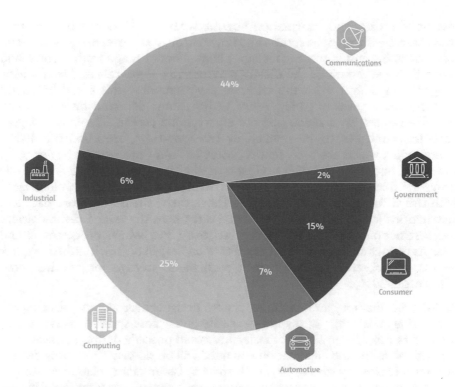

Figure 6-10. 2020 Logic Market by End Use (SIA and WSTS)

Memory

Since the birth of the electronics industry in the 1960s and 1970s, the market needs for data storage has skyrocketed, driving demand for more advanced memory chips to new heights year after year.

Memory Stack

Memory's primary function is to store data and information for use in the processing centers of larger systems (Nair, 2015). Storage capacity is no longer the dominant performance constraint for many of today's advanced memory devices. Over the past decades, the bridge between memory and the core system processors has instead become a key bottleneck for device performance, driving the development of new memory chips and **microarchitectures** (Nair, 2015). Getting the data in and out of the memory is now the critical parameter. Extra memory capacity is useless if your processor can't retrieve and deliver information faster than it can process the data you've stored.

Instruction, data, and information flow between the CPU and the memory stack starts with an input source and flows through the **memory hierarchy** for processing and storage. This input stimuli could range from a command typed into a keyboard or the click of a mouse to a signal released by a sensor triggered by stimuli from the external environment – this could be sound captured by a speaker ("Hey, Alexa"), movement detected by your home security camera, or a swipe on your smartphone screen. The input triggers core **instructions** to be readied by the long-term, **non-volatile ROM memories**, which are then sent to **volatile RAM memories** higher up in the stack (closer to the CPU) (Tyson, n.d.). These instructions are quickly transferred to Level 1 and Level 2 **cache memories**, which directly interfaces with the CPU registers (Tyson, n.d.). These cache memories store data and instructions for quick access. Through a **data bus**, the level 1 cache delivers the instructions and necessary data to the CPU, which processes it and returns output instructions that can either be held in up-stack cache for quick re-use or delivered to down-stack permanent storage for another time (Thornton, 2016).

In designing memory architectures, system designers are always balancing the competing constraints of memory capacity and access speed. Massive, dense memories can deliver all the capacity you could possibly desire, but searching for and retrieving the information you need will be slower. This is why designers use a **memory hierarchy**, with smaller, faster cache memories used to store frequent, time-sensitive operations that can be accessed quickly, and larger but slower memories used to store broader datasets that are needed less often.

Memory can be classified into two broad categories, **temporary storage volatile memory** and **permanent storage non-volatile memory** (Shet, 2020). The first important distinction between the two is that volatile memories require power to store data, while non-volatile memories do not (Shet, 2020). Once power is removed to volatile memory, all the data is lost. Permanent storage non-volatile memory is used for operations that never change – like the **booting instructions** your computer uses to turn on. Volatile memory, on the other hand, is used for operations that underlie any programs or applications you might be running. When you turn on your computer, it's using non-volatile memory, and when you open the web browser, it's using volatile memory. The second important distinction denotes each memory's read/write ability – **RAM (Random Access Memories)** allow a processor to both read or "take" input data and write or "deliver" output data to memory, while **ROM (Read Only Memory)** can only be programmed once and cannot be easily re-purposed (Shet, 2020). You can think of RAM like a white board that you can read from or write on until you need to write something else, while ROM is more like a diary that is not particularly useful once you run out of pages.

In general, ROM memories are used for permanent data storage, while RAM memories are used for running programs and storing temporary data close to the CPU for quick access (Shet, 2020). We summarize the difference between ROM and RAM in Table 6-2.

Table 6-2. ROM vs. RAM

ROM	RAM
Non-Volatile	Volatile
No Power	Needs Power
More Storage	Less Storage
Long-Term Memory	Short-Term Memory
Start-Up Functions	Normal Operations
Slow Data Transfer	Fast Data Transfer

Taking our knowledge of the various types of memory, we can build a memory hierarchy from those memory components closest to the end processor (top) to those farthest from the end processor (bottom) (see Figure 6-11). Starting at the top, CPU registers serve as the bit interface where data is physically transferred from memory to processor for any given clock cycle. Cache is the closest pure memory component (registers are technically part of the CPU) and functions as active working memory, drawing from different RAM sources to keep whatever data the processor has requested readily available. Below the cache, RAM, DRAM, and SDRAM act as general working memory. If cache helps process information for what needs to be in a conversation, RAM, DRAM, and SDRAM represent the active knowledge one has of the subject being talked about. Following quick access RAM memories are long-term non-volatile ROM memories and external data collection interfaces which comprise the final part of the hierarchy.

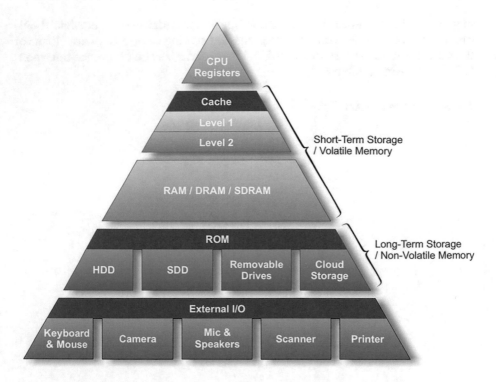

Figure 6-11. Memory Hierarchy

It may be useful to think of ROM like a library and RAM like a student who's checked out a book (see Figure 6-12). In this analogy, the rows of books are the ROM or Hard Disk, the backpack is RAM, the book is the cache memory (type of RAM), and the student is the CPU. The student does not want to have to go to the library every time they go to a new class, so they keep the books that they will soon need in their backpack for easy access. To retrieve the right information to work on, data and instructions are taken off the ROM bookshelf and stored in the more quickly accessible RAM backpack. From there, the student CPU can directly access the cache book when needed.

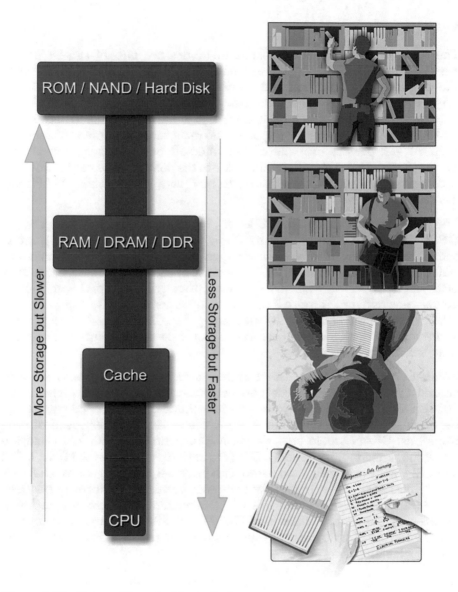

Figure 6-12. Memory Hierarchy Library Analogy

There are numerous kinds of volatile and non-volatile memories available. We cover them in the following sections.

Volatile Memory

The most common types of volatile memories are DRAM and SRAM. As **random-access memories**, they function as the CPU's short-term memory, allowing it to quickly access and process information (Shet, 2020). **DRAM (Dynamic Random-Access Memory)** can hold more data than an **SRAM (Static Random-Access Memory)** but is slower overall (Shet, 2020). SRAM may have faster access speeds but requires more power to function properly – a perfect example of the trade-off between performance and power (Shet, 2020). This differential is due to the number of storage transistors each has – SRAM has six transistors to hold data locally, while DRAM only has one.

The RAM memory closest to a CPU or processor is called **RAM Cache**, or **CPU Memory**, often referred to simply as **cache**. Cache has the greatest speed requirement of any memory type and typically stores instructions waiting to be executed (Shet, 2020). Because of its speed advantage, SRAM is often used as cache, while DRAM, which has greater capacity and lower power requirements, is more frequently used as temporary working memory (Nair, 2015). In the library-backpack analogy, if the student waiting to process information is the CPU, then the cache would be an individual book on the desk, waiting to be read.

In addition to cache-level data transfer rates, computing speeds are also limited by the transfer speeds between memory DRAM and cache (Shet, 2020). During each **clock cycle**, a fixed amount of data can be transferred between DRAM and cache. On its own, the limited transfer speed of even traditional DRAM would be a significant processing bottleneck. To mitigate this issue, a technology called **DDR (Double Data Rate RAM)** or **DDR SDRAM** was developed. Compared with prior DRAM generations, DDR has greatly increased the speed of data transfer, boosting connectivity between DRAM and cache. Big picture, it's less important to know the technical nuances of the various flavors of DRAM and SRAM, as much as it is to understand RAM as a category and how it relates to other parts of the memory hierarchy.

Non-Volatile Memory

There are two types of non-volatile memories – **primary memory** and **secondary memory**. All RAM memories are considered primary, while some **read-only memories (ROMs)** are classified as secondary. Primary memories are the main working memories of a computer – they can be accessed more quickly by the processor, but have limited capacity and are usually more expensive. Secondary memories, also known as **Backup** or **Auxiliary memories**, can only be accessed through interconnects and are much slower. You can think of primary memories like the space at a storefront with all the inventory you need to do business day to day and secondary memories like cheap warehouse space where you store everything else. You may bring new inventory to the store from the warehouse when needed, but don't have the budget or the floor space to keep it all at once.

Primary Non-Volatile Memory

There are five major types of non-volatile memory:

- **Standard ROM** cannot be adjusted or rewritten and must be programmed when it is created (Shet, 2020). The data is literally hard-wired when the chip is **manufactured.**

- **PROM (Programmable Read-Only Memory)** can be programmed after manufacturing but cannot be changed once programmed. PROM is essentially ROM that is programmable a single time through a process called **burning** (Shet, 2020).

- **EPROM (Erasable Programmable Read-Only Memory)** addresses most of the issues with ROM and PROM and can be erased and re-written many times (Shet, 2020). To erase EPROM, however, requires a special tool that uses the energy of UV light to destroy stored data without destroying the underlying electronics. Unfortunately, this method does not allow for selective erasure and the whole EPROM must be re-written before re-use (Shet, 2020).

- **EEPROM (Electrically Erasable Programmable Read-Only Memory** (Try saying that five times fast!) tackles some of the issues with EPROMs. Namely, the whole chip does not have to be erased and no UV-light tool is required to erase the EPROM (Shet, 2020). The main drawback of EEPROM is that they must be changed one byte at a time, making them relatively slow to erase and re-program. This slow erasing speed led to the final type of ROM, NAND Flash.

- **NAND Flash Memory** is a type of EEPROM that overcomes the limits of other types of ROM. It can erase information, write data in chunks (as opposed to one byte at a time) and works considerably faster than EPROM (Shet, 2020). Flash NAND is the primary type of ROM used to store data in electronic devices today (Shet, 2020).

Secondary Memory (HDD vs. SSD)

Secondary memories are external non-volatile RAM memories used for permanent storage and core device functions like boot drive. The most common types of secondary memory are **Hard Disk Drives (HDD)** and **Solid State Drives (SSD)**. Hard Drives are built from a **magnetic disk** with a read/write arm that can store data indefinitely (Brant, 2020). An SSD performs a similar function but uses interconnected NAND Flash memory chips instead of a disk (Brant, 2020). NAND Flash memories are faster and more reliable than HDDs but are more expensive and have lower capacity (Brant, 2020). Moore's Law, however, is making NAND Flash cheaper and denser every year. That cheap, dense Flash memory has made all our portable electronics possible – imagine if your cell phone needed a spinning hard drive platter to function!

If cost and storage capacity are your main drivers, then HDDs are probably the better choice. If versatility and reliability are more important, it might be better to go with an SSD. As memory densities keep improving, SSDs continue to gain share in mobile applications. We summarize the trade-offs between HDDs and SSDs in Table 6-3.

Table 6-3. HDD vs. SSD

	HDD	**SSD**
Performance	Slower	Faster
Reliability	Less Reliable (Moving Parts)	More Reliable (No Moving Parts)
Heat	More Heat (Moving Parts)	Less Heat (No Moving Parts)
Cost	Cheap	Expensive
Power	More Power	Less Power
Size	Larger	Smaller

Stacked Die Memory (HBM vs. HMC)

In many systems, it is the interconnect between chips that limits performance. Rather than mount chips onto a PCB and wire from chip-to-chip, new die stacking technologies connect chips directly to each other without the performance disadvantage of wiring from chip to chip. Die stacking technology breakthroughs and 2.5/3D Packaging Architectures have enabled new, tightly integrated memory architectures with significant performance advantages. **High-bandwidth memory (HBM)** and **Hybrid Memory Cube (HMC)** are industry standards used to build 3D memory devices (Moyer, 2017). Structurally, HMC uses a **3D memory-on-logic architecture**, whereby DRAM memory chips are vertically stacked on top of a logic device and connected to one another with a **Through Silicon Via (TSV)** (Moyer, 2017). HBM takes a slightly different approach. It splits the core logic and stacks the memory die on top of one the split parts, while leaving the other half on its own. The new memory-logic die stack is now connected to the recently separated logic via an **interposer** in a **2.5D Packaging** configuration (Moyer, 2017). Separating some functions for the base of the die stack enables integration of silicon from a more diverse set of suppliers. As you may recall from our sub-section on IC Packaging, the main difference between **2.5D** and **3D packaging** is that individual die are connected to one another with a piece of **substrate** that sits on top of the **PCB** (a significant connectivity improvement over wire bonding to the board itself). We can visualize the structural differences between HBM and HMC in Figure 6-13.

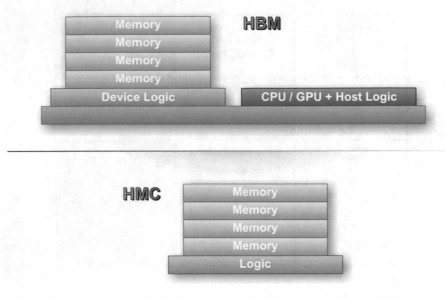

Figure 6-13. High Bandwidth Memory (HBM) vs. Hybrid Memory Cube (HMC)

Memory Market Summary

Figure 6-14 uses data drawn from SIA and WSTS's 2020 End Use Survey to break down the Memory market. DRAM, SRAM, Flash NAND, Stacked Memory, and other Memories accounted for a combined $117 billion in sales, or about 27% of the $440 billion of total industry sales in 2020 (SIA Databook, 2021). Memories are distributed across the different end-use applications at roughly the same proportions as the overall SIA Framework. This distribution is not surprising considering that nearly all end-use applications require memory for core functionality (SIA End Use Survey, 2021).

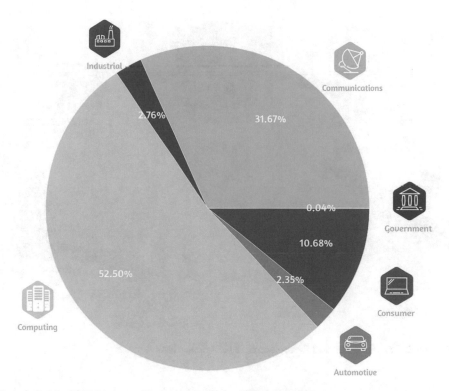

Figure 6-14. 2020 Memory Market by End Use (SIA and WSTS)

Optoelectronics, Sensors and Actuators, Discrete Components (OSD)

Optoelectronics

Optoelectronics are semiconductor devices that produce and receive light waves and are used for a variety of applications, including light detection and image sensors, LEDs, information processing, fiber-optic telecommunications, as well as display and laser technologies, to name a few. **Photonic integrated circuits (PICs)** are commonly used as **optical transceivers** for data center optical networks, which enable **data centers** to transmit information more effectively and efficiently across greater distances than copper cabling (Photonics Leadership Group, 2021). We can see the various applications of photonic and optoelectronic ICs in Figure 6-15.

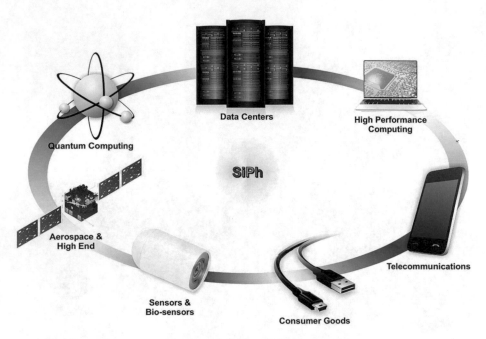

Figure 6-15. Photonic and Optoelectronic IC Applications

Sensors and Actuators

At their most basic level, **sensors** detect real-world inputs (heat, pressure, light, sound, or other physical phenomena) and convert them into electrical signals. They can be classified as either **active**, which require an external power source to function, or **passive**, which require no power to generate output (GIS Geography, 2021). While sensors these days are mostly active devices with many onboard chips, you do still see passive sensors still being used for select applications, like old-fashioned mercury thermometers. Sensors are often used in **control systems**, like altimeters used to adjust airplane flight patterns or proximity sensors that trigger a car's automatic braking system. All kinds of semiconductors are used in sensors for a multitude of applications, including optical sensors, pressure sensors, gas sensors, speed sensors, weight sensors, among others (Teja, 2021).

Actuators are like reverse sensors – they revert electrical signals back into real world outputs. Actuators are primarily used in industrial and manufacturing applications like robotics but are beginning to see applications in consumer and automotive markets as well.

The modern revolution in industrial automation and autonomous driving are both made possible by the rapid proliferation of silicon-based sensors and actuators. We can see many of the common sensors and actuators found in a mobile device in Figure 6-16.

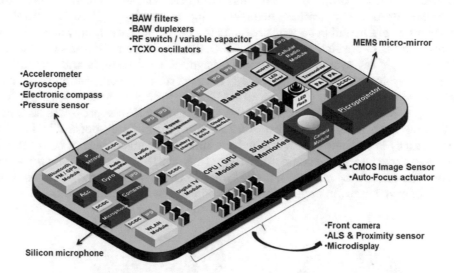

Figure 6-16. Mobile Device Sensors and Actuators (IntelFreePress, 2013)

MEMS

MEMS (Micro-Electro-Mechanical Systems) are tiny mechanical devices that operate gears or levers at a microscopic scale and are manufactured using semiconductor fabrication techniques (SCME, 2017). We can see some pictures of MEMS devices up close taken by Sandia National Laboratories in Figure 6-17. Sandia is a federally funded government research and development lab supporting the U.S. Department of Energy's National Nuclear Security Administration (NNSA) and drives technological innovation across a number of key scientific areas.

Figure 6-17. MEMS Up Close (Sandia National Laboratories, n.d.)

MEMS are technically not semiconductor devices, since they don't use electricity to process and store information, but are often grouped together because they compete with semiconductor-based sensors and are manufactured using similar manufacturing technology. Their mechanical properties are useful in sensor products for detecting threshold values across a diverse set of physical attributes (SCME, 2017). These products vary widely, including air bag systems, gyroscopes, magnetic field sensors and navigation systems, microphones and speakers, temperature sensors, biomedical and chemical sensors, etc. (MEMS Journal, 2021). MEMS devices in airbags, for example, may be designed to trigger bag deployment if an appropriate amount of force is applied. Unless you work in the MEMS field specifically, it isn't necessarily important to understand the underlying mechanics of how MEMS work, as much as understand what they are, what they are used for, and what key differences they have with more "traditional" semiconductor devices. We can observe common applications of MEMS and Sensors in Figure 6-18.

Figure 6-18. MEMS and Sensor Applications

Discrete Components

Discrete components are high volume, individually packaged components used as enabling devices for more complex systems. They generally help route signals and power to different processing centers in a given device. Common discrete components can vary from simple resistors, capacitors, and inductors, to more complex power transistors, switching transistors, diodes, and rectifiers.

Discrete Components vs. Power Management ICs (PMIC)

Power delivery used to be handled exclusively by discrete components that performed functions like voltage regulation, power conversion, battery management, and so on. Power management involves high voltages and signals moving around at high frequencies which can create massive interference issues. Integrating this function onto an IC alongside critical sensors is a difficult problem. But technology is always advancing, and the quest for greater integration and efficiency has led to growth in PMICs and PMUs.

PMUs (Power Management Unit) are a type of **microcontroller** specific to digital devices. PMICs and PMUs help convert power to a usable form, regulate battery usage and charging, and convert control voltage and flow of electricity to other components in the system like the CPU, memory, and more. Tighter integration does not come without costs, however – clustered components experience higher **parasitics** (unwanted interference from other components) and other **power integrity issues** (Texas Instruments, 2018). When a "noisy" power management chip is placed next to a sensitive circuit like a microphone, for example, it can cause performance issues and reduce audio quality. Upfront design costs are higher for PMICs, but their overall performance advantages and efficiency improvements often make PMUs a competitive long-term option.

PMICs are integrated circuits used for a family of chips and modules that are responsible for **regulating power** and **voltage** in a system or device (Intersil, n.d.). Typically, unique components in a system require different voltages to operate effectively – 1.0V for processors and memory, 1.8V for **interface drivers**, and 2.5V for **power devices** is common. A PMIC ensures that each of these system components receives the correct voltage level according to its unique requirements.

Optoelectronics, Sensors and Actuators, and Discrete Components Market Summary

Figure 6-19 uses data drawn from SIA and WSTS's 2020 End Use Survey to break down the OSD market. Discrete Components, Optoelectronics, Sensors, Actuators, and MEMS accounted for a combined $79 billion in sales, or about 18% of the $440 billion of total industry sales in 2020 (SIA Databook, 2021). Comprising a combined 77% of the overall segment, the communications, industrial, and automotive industries make up a much higher percentage of the end use market than the overall SIA Framework (SIA End Use Survey, 2021).

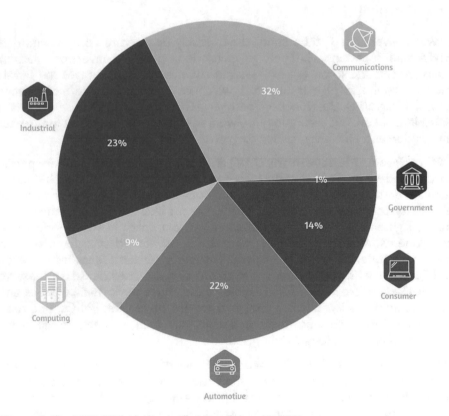

Figure 6-19. 2020 OSD Market by End Use (SIA and WSTS)

Analog Components

While digital chips have come to dominate for processing and storing information, as we will see in the *Wireless Technology* Chapter, our physical world is still "analog," requiring specialized **analog chips** to help make sense of it. These devices include sensors, wireless technology, and power supplies.

General Purpose Analog ICs vs. ASSPs

There exist two types of Analog circuits: general purpose analog ICs and application-specific standard products (ASSPs). **General Purpose Analog ICs** are used as broad plug-and-play analog components that may be optimized to perform a specific function, but can be used across many different systems, much like the Micro Component segment on the digital side. They include comparators, voltage regulators, data converters, amplifiers, and interface ICs (WSTS, 2017). In complex systems, these General Purpose Analog ICs frequently sit between an analog sensor and a processor, amplifying and converting the analog sensor signal into a digital signal for use by the processor.

Analog **Application-Specific Standard Products (ASSPs)** are Analog ICs designed for a specific application, similar to the Logic segment of the SIA Framework. Many ASSPs have digital components in them and are effectively mixed-signal devices. **Mixed-signal chips** include both digital and analog components. Typical examples are radio transceivers, audio amplifiers, as well as many varieties of RF (Radio Frequency) ICs, which will be covered in the following chapter.

Analog Component Market Summary

Figure 6-20 uses data drawn from SIA and WSTS's 2020 End Use Survey to break down the Analog Component market. General Purpose Analog ICs, ASSPs, and other Analog Components accounted for a combined $56 billion in sales, or about 13% of the $440 billion of total industry sales in 2020 (SIA Databook, 2021). Analog Components are most utilized in the Automotive, Industrial, and Communications segments, which each comprise about 25% of their end use applications. Like the Discrete Component, Optoelectronics, Sensor and Actuator Segment, Analog Components are least used for Computing Applications (SIA End Use Survey, 2021).

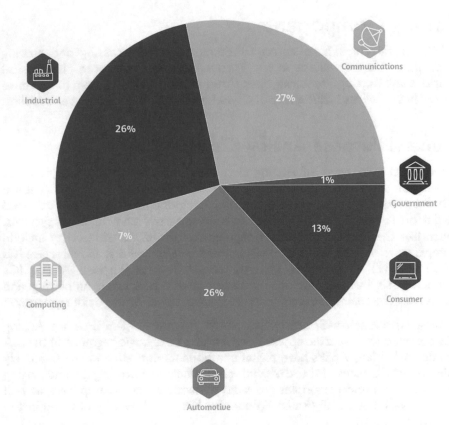

Figure 6-20. 2020 Analog Component Market by End Use (SIA and WSTS)

Signal Processing Systems – Putting Components Together

To understand how many of these components tie together, it is useful to think of electronic systems as signal processing devices. To illustrate, let us examine how a music producer's laptop records and mixes music using the five different components from the SIA framework. To start, a microphone records an analog audio signal, and **analog-to-digital converters (ADCs)** in the laptop absorb the real-world sound of an instrument they want to use in a new track. The ADC then feeds that signal to a **digital signal processor** (micro component), which accepts the incoming digital stream and can apply some simple **signal processing algorithms**. The producer may want to increase the bass content, or adjust the volume. From there, the newly converted **digital signal** is sent to the **central processor**, in this case the CPU, that runs the mixing software the producer uses for editing. The central "system" processor (logic) may use **volatile memory**, like **DRAM**, to store the collection of sound signals temporarily while it performs other tasks as directed by the mixing program. Once the producer is done, she can tell the central processor to store the finished track for later using the system's **non-volatile memory**, like **NAND flash**. When the music producer is ready to play the finished song, the digital signal is sent to another digital signal processor, followed by a **digital-to-analog converter (DAC)** which converts it into an **analog signal**. The analog signal is finally sent to an **analog processor**, or perhaps merely an **amplifier**, which amplifies it out into the real world through the laptop's speakers as music. Throughout the system, various **discrete components** perform functions like **system timing** and **power management** that enable the device to run properly.

Another way of thinking of a computer is like your central nervous system (see Figure 6-21). In this analogy, the **CPU** or other **microprocessor** performs high-level brain functions, like logical reasoning and problem solving. **Cache** and other **RAM** act as short-term memory that your brain can use to perform pressing tasks like remembering a name of someone you just met, while **ROM memories** (**Hard Disks** or **Solid State Drives**) function as long-term memory. The **northbridge** and **southbridge** that make up a chipset act like the brain stem that connects your brain to your spinal cord and the rest of your nervous system. The chipset then communicates with the rest of the system through the **system bus**, which acts like the rest of the spinal column. Finally, **I/O devices**, **sensors**, and other peripheral components act like the outer sensory neurons that allow you to sense and respond to the outside environment. If you touch a hot stove, the nerves in your fingers shoot a signal down your arm, up your spinal cord, through your brain stem to your brain, which then sends a signal back through your nervous system to tell your hand to move. In a similar fashion, a gaming computer may sense that its core temperature is getting too hot through an internal sensor. The signal from the sensor will travel to the system bus, through the chipset to the cache and finally to the CPU, which will send a signal to the cooling fans to pick up the pace!

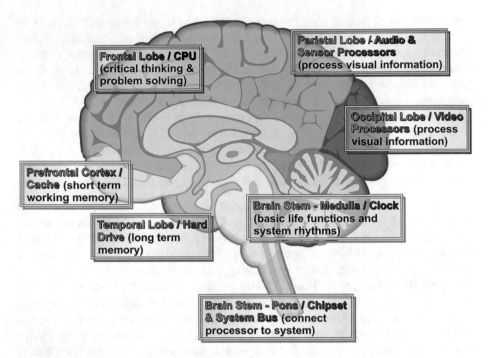

Figure 6-21. PC as a Central Nervous System

Chapter Six Summary

In this chapter, we first broke down the analog and digital electronics – capturing their differences in signal structure, data transmission methods, and power requirements. We also introduced key signal characteristics like frequency and wavelength and classified their uses along the electromagnetic spectrum. From there, we summarized the five system component categories in the SIA Framework before breaking each down in detail:

1. **Micro Components** are plug-and-play digital processors that include microprocessors (MPU), microcontrollers, and digital signal processors (DSP).

2. **Logic** encompasses digital processors designed for a specific purpose and includes special purpose logic and ASSPs, central processing units (CPU), graphics processing units (GPU), ASICs, FPGAs, and SoCs.

3. **Memory** chips are used to store data either short-term (RAM) or long-term (ROM) and are structured in a hierarchy to enable quick data availability for the CPU or other processors in the system.

4. **Optoelectronics, Sensors and Actuators, and Discrete Components (OSD)** includes, well, optoelectronics, sensors and actuators, and discrete components.

5. **Analog Components** are useful for many applications like wireless technology and power supply and are often mixed with digital circuitry to create mixed-signal chips capable of signal conversion from analog to digital (ADC) or digital to analog (DAC).

Though memory, micro components, and logic are responsible for the majority of industry revenues, all five are integral to the semiconductor ecosystem.

Your Personal SAT (Semiconductor Awareness Test)

To be sure that your knowledge builds on itself throughout the book, here are five questions relating to the previous chapter.

1. Compare and contrast analog and digital signals.

2. In the SIA Framework, what is the difference between Micro Components and Logic?

3. Which memory type sits closest to the CPU in the memory hierarchy? Why?

4. What makes MEMS similar and different from integrated circuits? If you were to categorize MEMS devices, which SIA component family would you choose?

5. Why are analog components well suited for wireless communication? Why not digital components?

CHAPTER

7

RF and Wireless Technologies

We began Chapter 6 by discussing the differences between Analog and Digital signals and the various subcomponents designed to process them. In Chapter 7, we pay particular attention to the analog world as we break down the exciting work of RF and Wireless electronics. From car radios to cell phones, the advent of wireless technologies has enabled instantaneous access to information and entertainment across the globe and on the go, transforming the way we live our daily lives. Before we track this evolution and the hardware technologies that make it possible, we'll need to survey the electromagnetic spectrum.

RF and Wireless

To better understand wireless systems, it is helpful to consider two forms of energy. The first form is **electrical energy**, which we discussed in Chapter 1. Electrical energy runs along a **conductor** and is the result of a **voltage** difference that causes **current** to run through the internal wiring and circuits in an electronic device. The second form is the **wireless** "airborne" energy that travels from place to place in waves like a ripple through water. As scholars with boundless creativity, we will refer to this as **wave energy**.

© Corey Richard 2023
C. Richard, *Understanding Semiconductors*, Maker Innovations Series,
https://doi.org/10.1007/978-1-4842-8847-4_7

By manipulating these two types of energy – electrical energy and wave energy – humanity manages to create, store, and communicate nearly three quintillion bytes of information every day (Bartley, 2021). Electrical engineers perform this magic by controlling the intensity of electrical energy over time, creating electrical "patterns" or **signals**. Computers use these patterns to communicate with one another – sending, receiving, storing, and processing the information that we use in our everyday lives.

RF Signals and the Electromagnetic Spectrum

So what exactly are radio frequency signals? **RF Signals** are analog "wave" signals used to transmit information from one place to another without a physical cable or wired connection (NASA, 2018). The semiconductor revolution that started in the 1960s was limited by those physical connections, but wireless technology enables us to take the technology with us wherever we go. These analog wireless signals can exist across a broad range of intensity and frequencies, called the **electromagnetic spectrum** (NASA, 2018).

What sets RF signals apart from other analog "wave" signals like Sound and Video? **Frequency.** Frequency is what electronics use to distinguish between one signal and another (NASA, 2018). If you've ever wondered how you're able to listen to the radio and talk on the phone at the same time without them interfering with one another, here is your answer: Radio, television channels, telephone, and Internet service providers all use different ranges of frequencies, called **frequency bands**, to deliver different types of information (Commscope, 2018).

The **Federal Communications Commission** (FCC) strictly regulates who can use which frequency ranges (bands) for which types of communication in order to avoid people interfering with each other's signals (FCC, 2018). Even so, sometimes our devices will interfere with each other – try using your Bluetooth earbuds too close to your microwave oven and it might ruin your podcast!

Each band is reserved for a particular communication protocol to ensure that all users are abiding by the same standards (AM, FM, CDMA, 802.11, etc). Service providers only have a finite amount of **frequency range** they can work with (**bandwidth**) to deliver an ever-expanding suite of services like Internet and television to their customers (FCC, 2018). Because of this, providers are incentivized to fit as much information for as many people as possible into a fixed amount of frequency range. They aim to squeeze as much revenue out of their allotted bandwidth as possible, investing billions in wireless technologies like **CDMA** (more on this in a bit). In simple terms, when phone companies and TV providers brag about "bandwidth" and network speed in their commercials, what they're really saying is "we use our frequency range to deliver the quickest service to the most customers."

As you can see from Figure 7-1, various parts of the electromagnetic spectrum are used for different applications. **Radio Frequency (RF)** describes a part of "spectrum real estate," which we use for radio, TV broadcasting, and others. Within the RF frequency range, a subsection includes **microwaves** whose frequency range is used for Wi-Fi, radar, and cell phone coverage. All electromagnetic waves are **radiation**. Most frequencies are harmless, but at high frequencies, they can be very harmful, as can be seen in the **ionizing** part of the spectrum in the right side of the diagram.

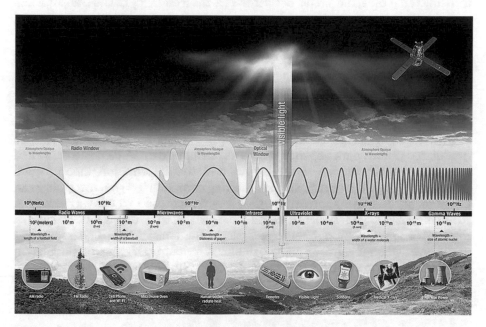

Figure 7-1. Electromagnetic Spectrum by Frequency and Application (NASA, 2010)

RFIC – Transmitters and Receivers

All RF systems have two main components – a **Transmitter** and a **Receiver**. The basic functions of a receiver and a transmitter are straightforward. Information is sent, or *transmitted*, by the transmitter, and accepted, or *received* (hold on to your hats for this one folks) by the receiver. It is possible for a single component to function as both a receiver and a transmitter - this is called a transceiver. More on that later.

Most transmitters and receivers require at least six base components to operate: a source of power, an oscillator, a modulator, an amplifier(s), an antenna(s), and filters (Weisman, 2003). Not all components within a transmitter or receiver require power to function. Those that do are called

active components and those that don't are called **passive components**. We review each of the six basic transmitter and receiver subcomponents in the following section.

1. Power Source – RF waves are a form of energy; this energy must come from somewhere like the battery in your phone.

2. Oscillator – This is the source of the "RF" waves. An oscillator produces RF analog "wave" signals that will act as a "carrier" for the information being transmitted (Lowe, n.d.). This oscillator sets the frequency of the transmission.

3. Modulator – This is where some real magic happens. For an RF "carrier" signal produced by an oscillator to be useful, it needs to be "imprinted" with the digital information that it will be carrying to the receiving system. The modulator does this by making small adjustments to the **frequency** or **amplitude** of the **carrier signal** that are then received and converted back into digital signals by a **demodulator** in a receiver at the other end. A rough depiction of what a modulator does is included in Figure 7-2. This is an amplitude modulation system, because the height (or amplitude) of the modulated output data depends on the digital input data. A *demodulator* would separate the RF carrier signal (wave) and the information input (digital "computer" language signal), so the receiving computer's digital machinery can properly process the information. One key device used to convert between RF Analog and Digital signals is called a modem. A **modem** is a device with a modulator and a demodulator – yes, early communication engineers weren't very clever when it came to naming things. A modem can execute modulation and demodulation algorithms at the same time, allowing it to convert between analog-to-digital and digital-to-analog signals quickly (Borth, 2018).

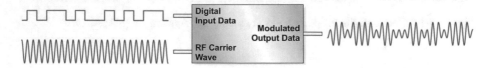

Figure 7-2. Modulator Block Diagram

4. Amplifier – This increases, or *amplifies*, a signal. The more powerful the signal, the farther it will travel and the greater distance it will maintain its accuracy. As RF energy spreads or travels further, it suffers **loss** as it passes through the various media it encounters (where it is partially absorbed), is reflected by objects in its path, or experiences interference from other electromagnetic energy and signals. When a signal gets bigger after passing through a component, the signal is said to have experienced **gain** (the opposite of **loss**). By the time a signal has reached its intended destination, it is likely that it will have lost a considerable amount of its original strength. With such a faint signal, amplifiers can be used to boost the signal back to a usable strength that a computer can process. On the other end, as a signal is on its way out of the transmitter, amplifiers are used to boost the signal so that it can travel greater distances while maintaining its **signal integrity** and deliver an intact message to the receiving device. Amplifiers are used throughout RF systems to boost signal strength for all kinds of technical reasons, but thinking of them as boosters for faint incoming and fresh outgoing signals is a much less abstract way of visualizing what they do (Weisman, 2003).

5. Antenna – Antennas are the components that receive and transmit signals to other systems. Many antennas can act as both, alternating its function between transmitter and receiver (Weisman, 2003).

6. Filters – There are catalogs of RF sub-components well beyond what you probably need to know, but before we move on there is one last device that deserves our attention – **filters**. Conceptually, filters are relatively simple. Their purpose is to let signals with intended frequencies get into the system and keep signals with unintended frequencies out, like a security guard at a private community who checks your license plate as you enter or leave. In the RF world, these unintended signals can come from **interference** or **noise**, which can arise from random environmental disturbances (this is called **EMI**, or **electromagnetic interference**) and from other "artificial" RF noise produced by broadcasts of RF signals operating at similar frequencies. A filter is why when you turn your radio to 94.7FM, you don't also hear the song playing on 94.9FM. The signal at all those other frequencies is "filtered out." There are four main types of filters used in RF systems (Shireen, 2019):

1. **Low Pass:** Filter only lets signals in below a certain frequency.

2. **High Pass:** Filter only lets signals in above a certain frequency.

3. **Band Pass:** Filter only lets signals in between two frequencies.

4. **Band Reject**: Filter only lets signals in outside of a range of frequencies.

To illustrate how all these pieces fit together, Figure 7-3 provides a simple **block diagram** of a transmitter and a receiver. For this example, we've assumed that the data being transmitted is an audio or video signal, but it could be any packet of data. For example, a simple instruction to load your favorite website on your phone. Not every RF system looks exactly like this, but for the sake of conceptual understanding, assume a receiver is processing the RF signal produced by the oscillator in the transceiver that sent the message it has just received. Filters can exist throughout the system, but it is useful to picture them (and they are often placed) in between the amplifier and the antenna.

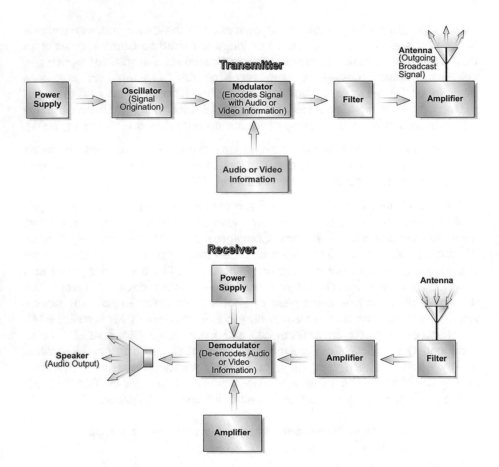

Figure 7-3. Transmitter and Receiver Block Diagrams

If we trace the data path for the transmitter in Figure 7-3, we can see that it originates from the oscillator, which emits a carrier signal. This carrier signal is combined with digital information (audio or visual data in this example) to create a wireless signal that is passed through filters and an amplifier(s) that modify and boost the signal before transmitting it toward the intended receiving device. If we trace the data path for the receiver, we can see that it begins at the antenna, which receives an incoming signal from another device transmitting in its direction. The signal is then passed through filters and amplifiers through to a demodulator, which separates the wireless carrier signal and the digital audio or visual information before passing along the received information for consumption or further processing within the system.

The OSI Reference Model

System designers have a challenging job to do. They must ensure that their system (1) fits together as a properly functioning unit and (2) seamlessly communicates with other devices. For design organizations working on advanced devices, challenge number one can involve coordinating the efforts of thousands of engineers working on dozens of sub-modules. Once this first challenge is overcome and a high performing device is fully functional, integrating with devices made by different companies with separate design methodologies, technologies, and processes would be incredibly complicated if not downright impossible without some sort of shared set of rules or guidelines.

To illustrate further, imagine you are a hardware engineer building a chip intended to help run applications on a mobile device. To be useful, the system must be able to efficiently run the code programmed by your customer's software engineering teams, while at the same time integrate with all kinds of other hardware devices like laptops, Bluetooth devices, and other cell phones. How can you design a system that works with everything else? In a vacuum this would be impossible – every hardware company would build different systems running separate programming languages and have difficulty communicating with one another. With the OSI model, however, you can just "follow the recipe" and build a system that both supports the needs of your software teams while seamlessly connecting with other devices.

The **Open Systems Interconnection (OSI)** model describes the system layers that connect the underlying hardware to the user-facing interface that consumers interact with. The layers themselves are collections of standards and protocols that allow design engineers and system architects to communicate with one another (within layer), with engineers working on other layers (between layers), and other systems within a given network. As you can imagine, with the number and variety of electronic systems that exist today, designing systems and products that can work together and integrate with one another is a complicated and challenging thing to do. A universally accepted model like OSI enables the standardization necessary to produce high performing networks and integrated systems.

The model breaks down networking functions into an **OSI system stack** comprising seven layers, each of which can be designed independently of each other. Layers 1–3 are responsible for the physical transportation of information around the network while Layers 4–7 deal with user applications. Layer 7, or the **application layer**, contains the **user interface** that a consumer interacts with like a web page or app home screen on your phone. As you descend through each subsequent layer, you get closer and closer to the circuitry powering the application. The lowest layer in the model is the **physical layer (PHY Layer)**, where the data itself (a string of 1's and 0's) is transmitted to the underlying hardware. In practice, the PHY Layer comprises an electronic circuit or circuits that connects a device to a larger network. This circuitry is usually composed of mixed signal and analog ICs, RF components like transceivers and receivers, and DSP modules that can interpret and modify incoming and outgoing signals. You can see a more detailed description of each layer in the appendix.

To be clear, the OSI model was primarily designed for inter-system communication between different devices within a larger network. There are many more collections of frameworks and standards used to communicate between design teams working *within* a given system rather than between them. Different **operating systems**, like iOS or Android for example, may have separate protocols and standards that enable **embedded software engineers** working at the **Hardware Abstraction Layer** or **Platform Layers** to communicate with software engineers working at the **middleware layer** at the same company. What's important is that the external-facing endpoints of a system can integrate well with other devices. The variety and intricacies of different reference models is well beyond the scope of this book, but it's useful to picture any computing system as a collection of clearly defined layers stacked on top of one another, from hardware to user. We can create a universal **Macro-System Stack** by adding a "Hardware Layer" beneath the Physical Layer of the OSI model (see Figure 7-4). The "Hardware Layer" in our stack is what this book is all about, but we can't forget the layers above it that make the hardware useful!

The **Macro-System Stack** is a more practical way of thinking about how each of the different levels of a computing system fit together. The **Application Layer** is what you interact with – whether an app on your phone, a program on your computer, or the interface for a website you are visiting. The **Middleware Layer** comprises the **backend application framework**. This is where a traditional software developer would code the "inner workings" of a given application – tying together the various databases, functions, and security protocols that power a software program. **Middleware** is built on a **Platform Layer**, comprised of an operating system supported by **Kernel** and **Device Drivers**, which manage the operations of the various hardware components like memory and CPU time (GeeksforGeeks, 2020). The **Hardware Abstraction** and **Physical Layers** bridge between the software and hardware that power it. Between and across the Hardware Platform, Hardware Abstraction, and Physical Layers lie embedded software and firmware. **Embedded software** and **firmware** are types of software that sit "closer" to the hardware than typical, middleware layer or application layer code. Firmware, for example, might be used to carry out low-level tasks such as analog-to-digital or digital-to-analog conversion. The terms can be used interchangeably, though embedded software usually refers to code that impacts higher-level features or functions of a device that is often "farther" from the core circuitry than the firmware might be. All of this is built on the **Hardware Layer**, which comprises the physical circuity and core silicon which we learn about in this book.

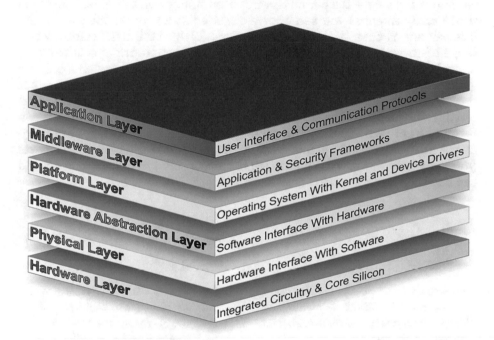

Figure 7-4. Macro-System Stack

RF and Wireless – The Big Picture

You should by now have a general understanding of the inner workings of RF devices, but how does this network of devices work together to bring you your favorite shows, talk to your friend in another city, or connect you to the Internet?

To understand this "big picture" of wireless networking systems, we will track the path of a typical long-distance phone call (see Figure 7-7).

To start, a phone making a call will transmit a signal (from its transmitter's antenna), which will likely be picked up by a cell phone tower or base station. A **base station** is a relay point that extends a service network to a specific area (Commscope, 2018). Because RF signals lose strength and accuracy the farther they travel (due to **interference** and **noise**), service providers have spent billions building robust networks of base stations across the globe to make sure you don't lose your signal (Commscope, 2018).

You can think of a **base station** as a giant receiver and transmitter with a router that receives an incoming phone call or broadcast and directs and amplifies the signal to another base station or "information exchange center" on its way to its intended destination (Wright, 2021). Base stations come in all shapes and sizes – cell phone towers, small stations on top of buildings, and those tacky antennas you see poorly disguised as a tree on the side of the freeway are all base stations (Commscope, 2018). Each base station has a range of coverage called a **coverage cell**, and the patchwork of cells make up a service provider's coverage area. As a rule of thumb, the smaller a cell, the greater the signal strength (less distance = less interference and noise), but the smaller the coverage area (Weisman, 2003). The reason you may have terrible service when you go hiking in a remote area is because you are too far away from a base station your phone can connect to. Service providers are constantly weighing the benefits of a stronger network against the costs (more base stations). We summarize the major cell types in Figure 7-5 and can see their coverage areas illustrated in Figure 7-6.

 **Macro Cell**

Large cell towers providing a wide area of coverage. Towers can stretch from 50-200 feet tall with ranges that can stretch from a few miles to over 20.

 **Micro Cell**

Pole mounted devices about the size of a pizza box providing block, facility, or small neighborhood-level coverage. Typical range is just over a mile.

 **Pico Cell**

Small structure or pole mounted devices providing building or street-level coverage area. Typical range is around 200 yards.

 **In-Building Systems**

Very small devices about the size of a license plate providing floor or room-level coverage. Also called femtocell or home base stations.

Figure 7-5. Different Types of Base Stations

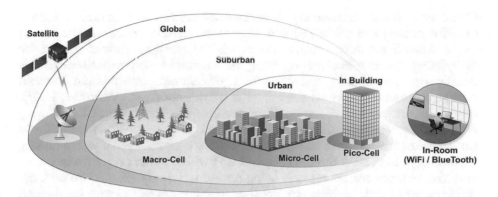

Figure 7-6. Different Types of Coverage Cells

Once it has received the signal from your phone, the base station then sends your call to a central exchange, where it can be routed to any number of places. If a call is across the country, for example, your call will likely be routed to a satellite, which will then route the call to another exchange center close to the location to which the call has been directed. That exchange point will then route the call to another base station or a landline, which can finally connect the call to the intended receiver.

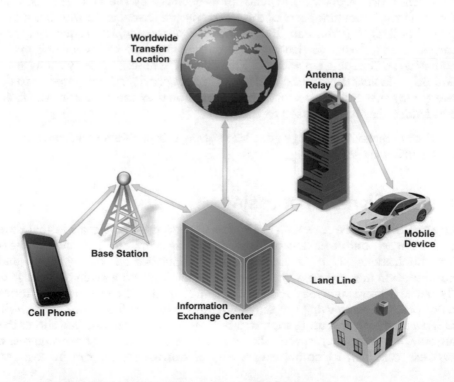

Figure 7-7. Signal Path of a Long-Distance Phone Call

Of course, directly connecting via satellite or landline is a possibility (hence satellite phones and cable TV) and oftentimes, hard connections are routed to get from one hub to another. Hardwired information transfer is great for processing time and information integrity, but can be very expensive, so it is usually used over shorter distances, for significant data transmission between exchanges, and for uses where speed is extra important (Weisman, 2003). High-frequency Financial Trading firms, for example, have spent billions laying fiber-optic cables from Chicago to New York to shave milliseconds off the time it takes financial data to reach their trading centers. Even if you're making a call using a landline, if the call recipient isn't within a short distance of where you live, chances are your call is being routed wirelessly via satellite or long-distance fiber-optic cabling to another routing center closer to its end destination.

Broadcasting and Frequency Regulation

With so many devices and users of limited bandwidth available, a dizzying amount of RF signals are flying around at any given moment.

If a base station receives more than one call at a time, how does it know which signal is which and where each signal is supposed to go? To mitigate this problem, strict regulation of spectrum frequencies by the FCC ensures that we don't the important parts of the electromagnetic spectrum with too much "signal pollution" (Weisman, 2003). The FCC dictates which frequency bands can be used for what so that your call doesn't interfere with your neighbors' addiction to "Keeping Up with the Kardashians." These frequency bands are a limited and valuable resource, and it is in service providers' best interest to do everything they can to maximize the information they can send using the fixed bandwidth they have allotted to them.

A lot of complex technology goes into solving this problem which we'll cover in the following sections.

Digital Signal Processing

Digital Signal Processors (DSP) are used to process signals in real time and convert between analog and digital signaling. In RF and wireless communications, DSP technology uses sophisticated mathematics and computation methodology to fit more information into a given digital signal. By packing more information into the same signal, we can send a lot more from place to place using the same, limited amount of frequency bandwidth. DSPs accomplish this using sophisticated algorithms to encode and shrink the amount of "frequency space" that a given piece of information requires, a process called signal compression. **Signal compression** can be lossless, which takes advantage of special algorithms to encode the exact information with less storage or lossy, which uses complex theories on what humans can see and hear to only store information that we can perceive.

The second technologies important to understand are the different kinds of multiple access standards. In essence, **multiple access standard technology** allows service providers to route multiple calls through the same base station, or across a given amount of bandwidth. The two most common multiple access technologies used today are TDMA and CDMA.

TDMA and CDMA

TDMA (Time Division Multiple Access) separates or **multiplexes** (in engineering speak) calls into a time domain within the same **frequency channel** first by converting a caller's voice into digital bits, and then breaking these digital bits into defined "chunks" of time. These "chunks" of call time from different conversations are then sent, one after the other, using the same small amount of bandwidth (this is what we mean by **channel**). This all works because voice is actually a very low bandwidth signal. Voice is frequently sampled at 4kHz, and if the TMDA channel has 4MHz of bandwidth, we can cram 1000 voice signals into that one channel.

You might expect that breaking a conversation into so smaller parts and sending them separately would lead to an unintelligible mess. The magic of TDMA is that the system can put the "conversation chunks" back together so quickly that there is no detectable lapse in the conversation, even though there is a break in between when each chunk is received (ITU, 2011). And remember, all these components are running at very, very fast clock speeds. A 1GHz chip (1 billion operations per second), can perform a million operations on your phone call data in just one millisecond. Trust me, you'll never notice.

You can think of TDMA like two jugglers tossing different colored balls to one another (each color being a different conversation) along the same path then dropping the balls into separate "call buckets." The jugglers in this analogy can toss the balls so quickly though, that it looks like they are just playing a simple game of catch, with no break in the conversation for the listener on the other end of the call.

CDMA (Code Division Multiple Access), on the other hand, uses algorithms to code digitized voice bits or other data and transmit it across a wider channel (greater frequency range), which is then "de-coded" on the receiving end (ITU, 2011). Instead of alternating between which bits are sent from which device along a given channel, CDMA can send data from numerous senders to numerous receivers at the same time and use algorithms and digital signal processing (DSP) technology to ensure the data gets to the right place intact.

Figure 7-8 helps bring our juggler analogy to life. While TDMA multiplexes data into chunks that can be sent using the same frequency channel one after the other, CDMA uses digital signal processing to send data at the same time across a wider frequency channel. Lightning-fast digital signal processing techniques help both methods establish uninterrupted signals and strong, uninterrupted service.

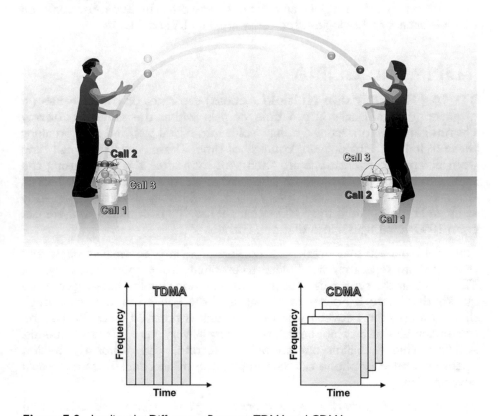

Figure 7-8. Juggling the Differences Between TDMA and CDMA

Where are these technologies used in practice? TDMA is the technology that underlies **GSM (Global System for Mobile Communication)** and is the primary standard for communication networks globally. In the US carriers like AT&T use GSM, while Verizon Wireless uses CDMA.

1G to 5G(eneration) – An Evolution

The world of telecommunications and wireless technologies is always evolving – here's a wide-angle view of how far we've come (Vora, 2015). The original 1G technology could transmit only 4kbps, where today's 5G technology can transmit up to 1,000,000kbps (1Gbps), nearly a quarter million times more!

1G – First Generation: This is when cell phone technology first came into existence, starting in the late 1970s. The first cell phones were big and clunky, with terrible battery life. They used **analog technology** to send RF analog "wave" signals from point A to point B wirelessly.

2G – Second Generation: Here cell phones, using **modulation**, could now transmit digital data wirelessly. **CDMA** and **GSM** technologies were developed that allowed service providers to connect more devices more affordably, though services were limited to voice and text messaging (SMS).

3G – Third Generation: Building on voice and text services, 3G technology expanded wireless capability to deliver email, video streaming, web browsing, and other technologies that made the "Smartphone" possible.

4G – Fourth Generation: High-speed connectivity built on advancements in hardware technologies has allowed for faster data transmission, mobile gaming, video conferencing, high-definition content delivery, and cloud computing capabilities.

LTE (Long-Term Evolution) – You'll often see service providers use this term in conjunction with 4G ("4G LTE") to market their service as better and faster than their competitors. In actuality, LTE is just an industry standard used to make sure the various devices, access points, base stations, satellites, and other components that make up our telecommunications network are able to work with each other to create one big, fully functioning system. Standards like LTE help make sure different technology companies can develop products that are able to work with other parts of the system, which is pretty important if you don't want your service to cut out every time your cell phone is routed to a cell tower operated by a different network provider.

5G – Fifth Generation: Though you probably see 5G all over the place, this generation of networking technology is still being developed and is designed to make 4G much faster and more efficient. To deliver higher "data throughput" connection speeds, 5G technology will require a robust network of thousands of cell towers and tens of thousands of small cell antenna cells deployed across coverage areas.

We can see the evolution from 1G to 5G played out in Figure 7-9. Since the advent of 1G consumer analog systems in the 1970s, telecommunications infrastructure and wireless technology have rapidly evolved to deliver increased connectivity and performance to businesses and consumers across the board. 6G networks are already in development to enable new, data-hungry applications and continued growth in the space.

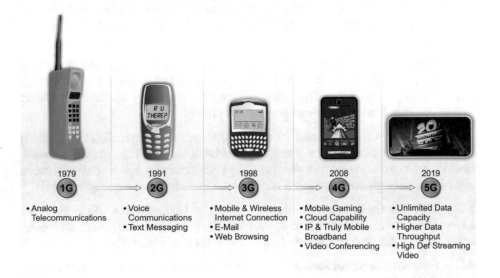

1979	1991	1998	2008	2019
1G	**2G**	**3G**	**4G**	**5G**
• Analog Telecommunications	• Voice Communications • Text Messaging	• Mobile & Wireless Internet Connection • E-Mail • Web Browsing	• Mobile Gaming • Cloud Capability • IP & Truly Mobile Broadband • Video Conferencing	• Unlimited Data Capacity • Higher Data Throughput • High Def Streaming Video

Figure 7-9. The Evolution of 5G

Wireless Communication and Cloud Computing

While the evolution from 1G to 5G has delivered exponential improvements in data transmission and brand-new technologies like mobile gaming, video conferencing, and high-definition video streaming, these faster rates have driven an insatiable demand for **cloud computing**. The "cloud" is an elusive mystery to many of us but is a much simpler concept than one might expect. What we call the cloud is really just countless servers housed in giant rooms called data centers. By storing, or hosting, applications on higher performance computers, companies and consumers can store information, run applications, and boost capacity without having to invest in and manage all their own infrastructure. This is only possible because communication networks are so fast today. You wouldn't think to store 1MB worth of photos in the cloud if you had to use your 56k modem to view it each time. But when data exchange rates are lightning fast, why buy an external hard drive or a top-of-the-line 512GB iPhone when you can get to all your photos, music, and movies in seconds? By the same token, why set up a private company server, when AWS (Amazon Web Services) or Google Cloud can handle it for a lot less trouble at a fraction of the cost? Prior to the boom in wireless innovation over the last couple of decades, the bottleneck to centralized computing operations like data centers was moving the data to and from end users. With this bottleneck alleviated, cloud computing is here to stay. The problem has now shifted from limited bandwidth to building and powering data center infrastructure that can support ballooning demand.

We can see examples of two data centers in Figure 7-10, which pictures a data center built in a shipping container used by Microsoft to process and redistribute Bing Map data (left) and the bird's eye view of Google's Data Center in Council Bluffs, Iowa (Right) (Scoble, 2020) (Davis, 2019). With 200,000 square feet of space, it pales in comparison to the China Telecom Data Center in Hong Kong, which, at over 10 million square feet, is the largest data center in the world (Kumar, 2022)!

Figure 7-10. Data Center Used by Microsoft's Bing Map Team (Left) and Google's Data Center in Council Bluffs, Iowa (Right) (Scoble, 2020) (Davis, 2019)

Chapter Seven Summary

In this chapter, we did a deep dive into the RF portion of the Electromagnetic Spectrum and learned about how different frequency bandwidths are carefully regulated by the FCC. Next, we broke down the two main parts of all RF systems – transmitters and receivers – into their constituent parts. By interweaving the six primary subcomponents – oscillators, modulators, amplifiers, antennas, filters, and power sources – with thousands of unique wireless building blocks, engineers are able to build intricate systems capable of long-distance, high-frequency remote processing and mobile communication. Following our analysis of RF subcomponents, we took a step back for a wider view of the OSI Reference Model and broader macro-system stack. From there, we compared the different types of base stations and followed the path of a signal from an international caller across the globe to a receiver on the other side of the world. Having traced a call from one end of the world to the other, we pondered the question – how do so many signals travel using the same bandwidth and airspace? We found the answers in TDMA, CDMA, and Digital Signal Processing Technologies that help maximize throughput with different signal dicing and timing schemes. We followed these bandwidth-optimizing technologies through the telecommunications evolution from the 1st Generation Analog devices in the 1980s and 1990s through high frequency 5G networks in development today. Finally, we touched on the downstream impacts of wireless technology advancements and the rise of cloud computing.

All RF systems depend on RF Transmitters and Receivers to send and receive information. Leveraging technologies like TDMA, CDMA, and DSP, service providers and device manufacturers are able to squeeze the most they can out of a limited amount of bandwidth. As technology has progressed, each successive generation of wireless devices and telecommunications infrastructure boosts what we can transmit and receive over the airwaves. The foundation on which nearly all RF systems are built, semiconductors have revolutionized the way we communicate with one another, entertain ourselves, and process information.

Your Personal SAT (Semiconductor Awareness Test)

To be sure that your knowledge builds on itself throughout the book, here are five questions relating to the previous chapter.

1. What do we mean when we say "RF"? Which key characteristics set one RF signal apart from another?

2. How does the FCC manage shared frequency bandwidths? What technologies are used to fit more information into a given amount of bandwidth? How does each technology accomplish this task?

3. Name the five key base components to any transmitter or receiver. Which component is number six and what makes it special?

4. Why is the physical layer so important in the OSI model? What are the other six layers and how do they function?

5. What makes each generation of telecommunications technology unique? How have these advancements enabled the growth and success of cloud computing?

CHAPTER

8

System Architecture and Integration

Having completed our tour of RF and Wireless Technologies in the world of analog electronics, we will now shift our focus back to digital as we dive deeper into the computational workhorses of the semiconductor ecosystem – microprocessors. Microprocessors are the "brains" of computing systems – they contain the arithmetic, logic, and control circuitry necessary to execute instructions, process data, and run sophisticated software programs. With the most advanced personal computing microprocessors today containing over 100 billion transistors, system complexity and design challenges have never been greater (Apple Newsroom, 2022). To overcome such challenges, design leaders must pay close attention to both Micro- and Macro-architectural decisions, carefully balancing the trade-offs between flexibility and performance with the cost and complexity of tighter system integration. In this chapter, we will analyze the architectural decisions and trade-offs these leaders face as they build the next generation of electronic devices.

© Corey Richard 2023
C. Richard, *Understanding Semiconductors*, Maker Innovations Series,
https://doi.org/10.1007/978-1-4842-8847-4_8

Macroarchitecture vs. Microarchitecture

The term "architecture" can be used in semiconductor engineering to mean one of two things – System Architecture or Microarchitecture.

System Level, or macro-level silicon architectures that are used to define entire chip families, are technically described by different kinds of **Instruction Set Architectures (ISA)**. ISAs describe the way in which instructions are delivered from the programmer to the computer (Thornton, 2018). Because software serves as a conduit between the programmer and the physical hardware it lies on top of, the type of architecture used to build the hardware can have a measurable impact on the type of programs that a processor can run and how the overall system will perform.

Microarchitecture, on the other hand, describes the way an ISA is actually implemented into the hardware design itself. A CPU, GPU, and PMU may all be designed using a single ISA that governs the design of the whole SoC, but still have unique microarchitectures.

Historically, there are two main types of machroarchitectures.

Common Chip Architectures

Von Neumann Architecture vs. Harvard Architecture

The **Von Neumann Architecture** is a macroarchitecture developed by the physicist and mathematician John Von Neumann in the 1940s and is what most modern computers are based on to this day. The Von Neumann framework relies on three components – the CPU, input/output interfaces, and memory. Inside the CPU, there exist (1) **registers**, where data and instructions are delivered by and given to the memory; (2) a **control unit**, which determines which instructions should be executed; and (3) the **arithmetic** and **logic unit**, where instructions are carried out and information is actually processed (BBC, n.d.).

The **Harvard Architecture** has most of the same system components – CPU, memory, and I/O interfaces. The two are different primarily in how they access (input) and distribute (output) information. In a Von Neumann device, the CPU both receives instructions and data from memory and distributes output using the same I/O interfaces (armDeveloper, n.d.). A device with a Harvard Architecture, on the other hand, parses instructions and data into two separate memory banks, with a unique bus for each type of input (Khillar, 2018). By keeping data and instructions separate from one another, Harvard devices can theoretically access both memory and instruction sets at the same time, reducing the **clock cycles** necessary to perform a single instruction. The difficulty comes in properly timing, or **pipelining**, instructions and data to get to the CPU at the same time (Khillar, 2018). Because the Von Neumann framework has only a single bus, design is less complex and thus less costly (Khillar, 2018). We can see the differences between Von Neumann and Harvard Architecture visualized in Figure 8-1 and summarized Table 8-1.

Harvard Architecture

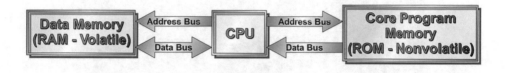

Von Neumann Architecture

Figure 8-1. Harvard vs. Von Neumann Architecture

Table 8-1. Von Neumann vs. Harvard Architecture

	Von Neumann	Harvard
Memory	Same memory address for instructions and data.	Separate memory addresses for instructions and data.
Frequency & Clock Cycles	Two clock cycles to execute one instruction - one for instruction retrieval and one for data retrieval.	One clock cycle per instruction.
Data Transfer & Instruction Delivery	Cannot be done simultaneously.	Can be done simultaneously.
Chip Design	Simpler, faster, cheaper.	Expensive, slower, complex (two buses instead of one).
Processing Type	Serial Processing	Parallel Processing
Real World Applications	Computers, Mobile SoCs, Complex Digital Electronics	Microcontrollers and Specialized DSPs

Von Neumann devices account for the vast majority of complex devices, though Harvard Architecture is used in limited cases for microcontrollers and digital signal processors. To be clear, Von Neumann and Harvard Architectures are more theoretical macroarchitectural categories than specific macroarchitecture options chosen from in practice. The vast majority of IC's use a Von Neumann "type" of machroarchitecture – system designers must weigh the pros and cons to decide which kind Von Neumann macroarchitecture is best for the device they are building.

Instruction Set Architecture (ISA) vs. Microarchitecture

Instruction Set Architectures (ISA) determine the set of instructions that a given processor can support. **Microarchitecture**, on the other hand, determines how the processor receives and executes those instructions at an implementation level. Another way to think about this is that ISAs provide higher-level design requirements that define *which types of instructions* a given system must be able to perform, while microarchitecture provides specific, lower-level design guidelines for *how to build a system that supports these instructions* (Maity, 2022). To be clear, **instructions** here are lines of code written by a programmer that a computer follows, and not the instructions that came with the bookshelf you bought from Ikea. The goal of these instructions is to get the computer to execute a specific task, or **function,** and perform the directed operation.

We can better visualize these differences by drawing back to a more detailed version of the macro system stack from Chapter 7 that we will call the universal architecture stack (see Figure 8-2). In our Universal Architecture Stack, we start at the bottom with transistors and move up with increasing levels of abstraction until we reach the application layer containing the user interface that you or I might interact with. This abstraction can be clearly seen at each layer of the stack. At the second level in our stack, transistors from the bottom layer are fit together to form the logic gate building blocks used to enable key computing functions and the registers that serve as an interface between the CPU and peripheral circuitry. Above that, microarchitecture determines how these logic gate building blocks fit together to form the functional modules that constitute the system. The modules shaped by the microarchitecture of individual design teams must abide by the macro-level instruction set architecture in layer 4 that determines which types of instructions the system must be able to perform. Above the bottom four hardware layers, the platform layer containing the operating system is connected to the hardware via firmware. Finally, the middleware layer containing the core back-end software programming logic and application layer containing the user interface run on the operating system from the layer below it.

Each level is dependent on the collection of the levels below it and must be designed to support the levels above it. Whether you're a student saving a school essay on your laptop or a firmware engineer programming the interface between hardware and operating system, your input ultimately must be carried out by the transistors and functional components that comprise an integrated circuit. The translation process that makes this possible is difficult and requires engineering skill spanning numerous areas and disciplines. Bridging this gap is why abstraction layers are so vital to building high performance systems.

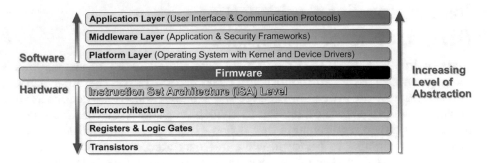

Figure 8-2. Universal Architecture Stack

Beyond the challenges faced *within* systems, another reason these abstraction layers are so important is that they enable hardware designers to maintain compatibility *across* systems, so that software programs can run on different devices that share the same set of basic instructions. Without standardization of basic instructions, software developers would be unable to build applications that run on devices designed by companies supporting separate instruction sets (ISAs). Imagine the headache if every software company had to create a dozen separate versions of their software to run on each kind of laptop their customers might be using!

To further illustrate this difference, we can think about the distinct ISAs developed by separate companies. The popular licensed ISA **ARM Architecture** developed by ARM Holdings may be used by multiple companies at once designing the same type of device but with completely different microarchitectures. Samsung and Qualcomm, for example, might both use ARM Architecture to build a custom processor for the next generation smartphone devices, but each has separate implementations, or microarchitectures, of their licensed ARM ISA, each with unique features, levels of performance, etc.

In addition to determining the *type of instruction* a process will support, ISAs also determine the *format* and *maximum length* of each instruction a system can process (Maity, 2022). These underlie the differences between the two main types of ISAs – CISC and RISC.

Instruction Pipelining and Processor Performance

Before delving into differences of CISC and RISC, it's important that we review the key factors that determine processor performance. These differences are useful to understand in a variety of contexts, but are especially useful in understanding the trade-offs of CISC vs. RISC. From an architectural perspective, there are really three main things we can do to increase the speed of a given processor – we can (1) increase clock frequency; (2) synchronize task performance; and (3) pipeline operations (Engheim, 2021). We'll work through each in the following paragraphs.

Looking to boost our processor's performance, we first look for ways to increase clock frequency. As we covered in previous chapters, **clock frequency** is the number of clock cycles per second and is a common measure of processor performance. A **clock cycle** measures the amount of time between two pulses of a processor **oscillator** (device that releases electrical signals) (Intel, n.d.). We can increase clock frequency and boost processor speed by either making our signal move faster or by reducing the distance it must travel to complete the circuit. But how would this work? To help explain, let's pretend our circuit is the assembly line in a school cafeteria where student lunches are made (see Figure 8-3). For simplicity's sake, we'll assume that it's Taco Tuesday and we start with a single cook on staff who works on each taco plate along a four-step assembly line one lunch at a time.

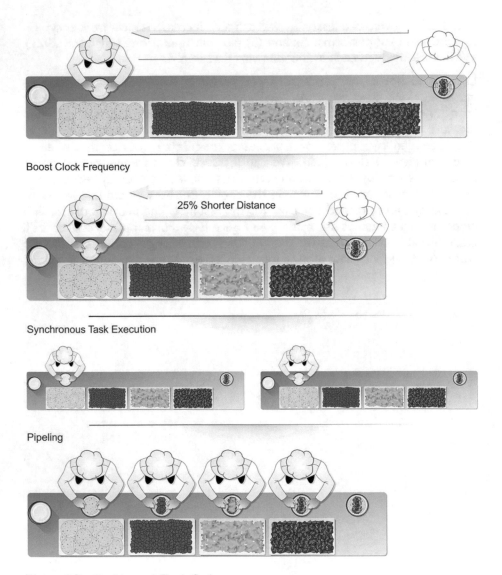

Boost Clock Frequency

25% Shorter Distance

Synchronous Task Execution

Pipeling

Figure 8-3. Cooking and Clock Cycles

If a clock cycle is the time it takes for a signal to move all the way through a processor and complete an operation, then a "cooking cycle" is the time it takes for a plate to move all the way through the food production line as a completed student meal. To speed up the rate of meal production in our school cafeteria, the first thing we can do is shorten the length of the "cooking cycle." In the same way that our clock frequency is reduced and processing speed is increased when we reduce a clock cycle, if we can get our school cook to move faster, then our "cooking frequency" will be reduced and our "meal processing" speed will increase. Unfortunately for us, electrons and school cooks can only move so fast, so there are limited ways to boost performance through processing speed alone. Alternatively, we could try shrinking the size of the processor or shortening the length of the assembly line, which would shorten the distance our signal or lunch must travel, reduce our clock or cooking cycle, and increase our processing speed. We can only shrink this distance so far though, after all, our cook must have a place to put the ingredients and there are physical limits to how much we can shrink our processor. Between reducing our clock and cooking cycle and shortening the distance of our **critical path**, we've been able to boost performance by a significant margin, but there's still more we can do.

The next thing we could do to boost processor performance is incorporate **synchronous task performance**. To do this, we would need to add another processing core(s) to our processor, sometimes called a **co-processor**. Each core can now handle separate tasks in sync with one another, reducing the net amount of time required to complete a given task and boosting overall performance. GPUs are particularly well suited for this kind of parallel processing, demonstrating strong performance for applications requiring high volumes of repeatable calculations like machine learning and visual processing.

In our cooking analogy, we could accomplish synchronous task performance by hiring a second cook. Like a pseudo-independent processor core executing a function in parallel to other cores, our new cook could work on a separate, but identical meal line. The combined effort of these two cooks should be able to complete more lunches in a shorter period. Theoretically, it follows that if we wanted to increase the throughput of school lunches, we could simply keep making new cooking lines until our kitchen was completely full. However, there is only one place we can collect money from students and one counter we can deliver the food to them – at some point we will be making taco plates quicker than students are taking them and they will start to pile up. More cooking lines means more costs as well, which may not be possible on a slim school budget. This is similar to the cost and throughput constraints faced by microprocessors, which have only so much "electronic counter space" (registers) available to accept inputs and deliver outputs (to the cache memory). If only there was another a way to speed up processing time that didn't depend on more cores, while accounting for throughput bottlenecks! Lucky for us, there exists one such method – our third and final option for boosting processor performance, pipelining.

Pipelining is a method of speeding up tasks by breaking up a lengthy workflow into smaller constituent parallel tasks. Unlike synchronous processing that relies on tasks being performed in parallel along *separate paths* (multicore processors), pipelining breaks up a process into smaller constituent parts performed in parallel *along a given path*. Pipelining methodology is by no means restricted to microelectronics and is used across a variety of application areas (like cooking!).

Returning to the cafeteria, what if instead of having our school cook make one full meal at a time, we had four cooks, side by side, getting the meal one fourth of the way done, before passing to the next cook standing beside them? It's taco Tuesday, so the first cook warms the tortillas and arranges them on the plate in the first cook cycle. During the second cook cycle, the second cook throws some chicken on the tortillas, while the first cook warms some new ones. For cook cycle number three, the third cook adds lettuce while cooks one and two repeat their steps. Finally, after cook cycle number four, the fourth cook completes the meal adding some salsa and is ready for the next plate in the following cycle. We may not be able to increase the frequency of a single cycle end-to-end, but we can increase the volume of deliveries in a given period of time.

Turning back to our processor, we can break up our longer, "complex" instructions into four equally sized, "reduced" instructions that each take about a quarter of the time to complete (25% of the clock cycle). After clock cycle one, the first instruction is one quarter of the way there. After clock cycle two, the first instruction is half the way complete, while the second instruction is one quarter done. By clock cycle four, the first instruction is completed in roughly the same time as the lengthier "complex" instruction. However, with a pipeline full of incoming instructions, instead of having one instruction finished every full "complex" clock cycle, one pipelined "reduced" instruction is fully completed every quarter cycle. Herein lies a key advantage of RISC over CISC – its reduced instructions are far better suited for pipelining, providing performance advantages over its CISC counterparts.

Whether we're talking about tacos or electrons, pipelining can significantly improve our **processing throughput**, enabling us to finish more lunches or instructions per cycle than before (Engheim, 2021). This can prove to be a substantial advantage, giving one ISA an edge over another depending on the application.

CISC vs. RISC

The two main types of ISAs are **CISC (Complex Instruction Set Computing)** and **RISC (Reduced Instruction Set Computing)** (Thornton, 2018). Common processors that used CISC architectures include Motorola 68k, PDP-11, and several generations of Intel x86, while notable processors that use RISC ISA's include ARM, RISC-V, MIPS, PowerPC, and Atmel's AVR (McGregor, 2018). There are numerous differences between RISC and CISC, though the most notable is the way in which they process instructions.

Each processor has a **clock cycle** that limits the number of instructions that it can process over a given period of time. Conceptually, you can think of clock cycles like a metronome or a heartbeat – each beat is a window of time for the processor to perform a given task. To understand how this works, it is important to remember what is actually happening when a computer executes an instruction – it is converting software "input" into physical signals (patterns of electrons) and running these signals through the circuit, where they are manipulated and processed before being converted back into some sort of useful software "output." A clock cycle is a single pulse of "instruction signal" coursing through the processor circuitry. The number of clock cycles a processor can run per second (clock speed) determines how fast it can process instructions. The greater the "clock cycle frequency" (clock frequency), the faster the processor. CPUs can run millions of clock cycles per second, notching processing speeds of millions or even billions of **hertz** (cycles per second) (Intel, n.d.).

The key difference between CISC and RISC processors is that RISC processors break down instructions into smaller segments that can run one at a time, while CISC processors run instructions that take more than one clock cycle to execute, hence their names *Reduced* Instruction Set Computing vs. *Complex* Instruction Set Computing (Engheim, 2020). At first glance, our intuition might tell us that CISC processors must be better since they can run more units of instruction per unit clock cycle. However, for many of the processor performance factors outlined in the previous section, RISC is often seen as a more effective option for many applications. Unlike CISC processors which use lengthy, multi-clock cycle instruction sets, RISC processors break up instructions into smaller, standardized instruction sets that are better optimized for instruction pipelining and more easily digested by **compilers**. Pipelining is a complicated scheduling operation that must ensure both the data and the instruction necessary to execute a given task or operation arrive at the CPU at the proper time. RISC processors aim to maintain an instructions-to-clock cycle ratio of 1-1, ensuring a steady and predictable clock cycle, which significantly improves processing speed (Engheim, 2020).

The reason for these differences is rooted in semiconductor history. CISC came about in 1970, followed by the first RISC prototypes about a decade later (IBM, n.d.). This early on in the industry's development, compilers were unreliable and programmers often wrote directly in assembly code. **Compilers** translate high-level programming languages like Java and C# to machine-level language a computer can understand, while **assembly languages** are much closer to the hardware and have many disadvantages to compiled languages, including increased complexity, difficulty of use, and reduced portability (Pedamkar, n.d.). As compilers improved, RISC architecture was more widely adopted by design teams across the industry.

Because they process simplified instructions, RISC processors tend to consume less power, making them ideal for applications where power is particularly limited, such as mobile phones or other battery-powered devices.

This advantage is reduced in higher-performance applications, like servers or personal laptops, which tend to use CISC processors more often.

Though more efficient in many ways, RISC processors do require more **RAM** (to access additional code) and greater programming efficiency (shorter instructions means more lines of code) (Bisht, 2022). This used to be a significant disadvantage when memory chips were a lot more expensive in previous decades when RISC architecture was just gaining traction, but has become much less so as memories have become smaller and less expensive (Teach Computer Science, 2021). The differences between CISC and RISC are summarized in Table 8-2.

Table 8-2. CISC vs. RISC

	CISC	RISC
Clock Cycles	Multiple Clock Cycles Per Instruction	One Clock Cycle per Instruction
Instruction Length	Variable Length	Standard Length
Instruction Volume	Less Instructions	More Instructions
Pipelining	Pipelining Disadvantage	Pipelining Advantage
Memory Usage	Less RAM Usage	More RAM Usage
Design Orientation	Hardware-Centric Design (Less Dependent on Compilers)	Software-Centric Design (More Dependent on Compilers)

Choosing an ISA

Choosing an ISA is a difficult and consequential decision. Many ISAs are licensable, like those offered by **MIPS** and **ARM Holdings**, though some are proprietary or **open source**, like **RISC-V**. Typically, a licensed ISA will come with a pre-designed processing core, while an open-sourced ISA does not (McGregor, 2018). Licensing fees and royalties are key factors in deciding whether to license, build, or borrow.

Often more important than direct costs are the risks that come with each ISA. Depending on which is chosen for a particular design, each will come with advantages and disadvantages. To start, engineering leadership must consider the time and costs of physically developing a core processor in-house. Most ISA licensing companies license processors that serve as the core of any customized end-product. Even if a unique core processor design is completed within a feasible time frame, there are always manufacturing risks that can cause a new processor and architecture to fail.

Perhaps even more important are the downstream software implications. ISAs like **ARM** and **x86** have mature software "ecosystems" with fully developed software development stacks. Building a new processor with a proprietary architecture requires the development of new firmware, operating systems, and development tools (Hill et al., 2016). Even if hardware and software execution is seamless, time-to-market is likely to be an issue. While your company was spending its time developing a core processor and proprietary architecture, the competition was releasing new products.

One question to ask yourself is this: are customers buying the processor, or are they buying what it does. If your customers are buying your new algorithm or integrated processor and sensor system, then licensing an existing ISA may be most attractive. But if the processor itself forms the core of your business or adds some unique value not available in the market, then a custom design may be the right answer. A table comparing the relative risks of different ISA choices is shown in Figure 8-4.

	Proprietary ISA	Licensed ISA	Open Source ISA
Hardware Design Costs	High	Low	High
Software Engineering Costs	High	Low	Mid
Existing Software Ecosystem	Low	High	Mid
Time-to-Market	Long	Short	Long
Manufacturing Risk	High	Low	High
Design Flexibility	High	Low	High
Royalties and Licensing Fees	None	Mid	None

Figure 8-4. ISA Trade-offs – Proprietary vs. Licensed vs. Open Source

Heterogeneous vs. Monolithic Integration – From PCBs to SoCs

Historically, shrinking transistor sizes due to advances in manufacturing and lithographic technologies has enabled semiconductor design companies to continue increasing the performance of their devices without having to pay much attention to device architecture and integration (Gupta & Franzon, 2020). There was enough "wiggle room" so that even if a design included millions of unnecessary transistors, it could still deliver greater performance using less power and space at a lower or equal cost. Even if a company was motivated to make its chip more efficient, the additional design effort required to make fully integrated devices was costly and the rapid pace of Moore's law made time-to-market a critical constraint. In many cases, by the time a fully integrated device was created, the next generation of manufacturing technology would already have well surpassed whatever the design team could have provided in additional efficiency.

The trend of shrinking transistor sizes for increased performance, often referred to as **geometric scaling**, continued unabated until the last decade or so, when the industry ran into three main problems (Gupta & Franzon, 2020).

First, as transistors became smaller and logic devices became denser, **power management** issues became a primary design constraint for advanced systems, displacing **frequency** as the dominant factor (Gupta & Franzon, 2020). Modern CPUs and other advanced devices often cannot use their full "firepower" since the heat required to run at such speeds would literally fry the circuits in question.

Second, **Lithographic Technologies** like **EUV** depend on shrinking light wavelengths that are thin enough to etch increasingly tiny die features (IRDS, 2020). Though these technologies may have sustained geometric scaling to this point, researchers have had trouble finding light wavelengths that can effectively etch smaller features (Brown et al., 2004).

Finally, the thickness of the materials that transistors are made from is now just a few atoms thick with little room for further shrinking (Gallego, 2016). Bluntly put, there won't be enough atoms to make usable feature patterns below a certain threshold.

In addition to these three physical constraints, each successive technology node requires disproportionally more expensive process technology, which increases the cost to build new fabs and drives up manufacturing unit costs. With some modern fabs costing as much as $20 billion, manufacturing chips using the most advanced process nodes is incredibly expensive, which is pushing designers to squeeze more performance out of older nodes (Lewis, 2019).

In sum, as **Moore's law** has slowed down in recent years, the industry has shifted its focus from geometric scaling to **functional scaling**, boosting performance by optimizing designs for specific applications and by shifting system architectures to include more heterogeneous and monolithic integration (Gupta & Franzon, 2020).

In **heterogeneous integration**, numerous chips are integrated with one another either on the same board (PCB) or within the same package, called a **system-in-package** or **SiP** (Lau, 2017). For board-level heterogeneous integration, different chips and components are soldered to the board and wired to one another. For SiP, different chips and functional modules are enclosed in the same package and connected to one another via interconnects or **through silicon vias (TSVs)** that connect chips stacked on top of one another using **2.5/3D die stacking** technology. By keeping functional components separate, system architects and designers are able to better "plug-and-play," while still enjoying the performance advantages of a more tightly integrated system.

In **monolithic** or **homogenous integration**, numerous functional modules are included on a single integrated circuit, yielding a fully functional system called an SoC (System-on-Chip) (IRDS, 2020). The more integrated a system is, the less distance a signal must travel to reach other parts of the chip. However, fully integrated systems like SoCs are complex to design and have numerous drawbacks that must also be considered.

Across the four **PPAC** dimensions – performance, power, area, and cost – heterogeneous (SiP) and homogeneous (SoC) integration have significant trade-offs. Smaller **form factors** (device area) give **SoCs** significant advantages in area and power efficiency, making them popular choices for smaller, battery powered devices like cell phones. They can suffer on performance, however, depending on the application. Each functional portion of a chip may require different materials and process technologies for peak performance, which is difficult or impossible to do on a single wafer (IRDS, 2020). By integrating all components on a single **wafer**, like in an SoC, some parts may function very well, while others perform poorly since they were made with materials and processes that are not optimized to their individual requirements (IRDS, 2020).

Cost differences also play a big role in whether to use monolithic or heterogeneous integration. On the one hand, greater levels of integration require more design work and thus have higher design costs and greater manufacturing complexity (Gupta & Franzon, 2020). This may not lead to lower unit costs for heterogeneous devices in all cases, however. Monolithic devices require less area in aggregate, which enables more chips to be printed on a single wafer and can lower net manufacturing costs (Gupta & Franzon, 2020). At the same time, heterogeneous integration enables a sort of "manufacturing arbitrage," where different **process nodes** may be used for different parts of the system. In a SiP, for example, advanced modules like memory or core logic could be manufactured using the most advanced 3nm process nodes, while less advanced parts, like analog or RF components, could be manufactured using a 130nm process node (IRDS, 2020). By only manufacturing some components using more advanced process nodes, companies can save considerably on portions of the system that use the older, cheaper technology. They can also build a next-generation system by only changing the memory and logic devices to enable more features, while keeping power management or RF components unchanged. Engineering executives must take great care to balance the additional design costs and manufacturing cost differences when deciding which architecture to employ.

We can see these trade-offs played out in Figure 8-5. Monolithically integrated SoCs consume less power and take up less space than heterogeneously integrated systems integrated at the board level. System-on-Boards (SOBs), however, have greater design flexibility, lower design costs, and can be designed more quickly. System-in-Packages straddle between the two, offering greater design flexibility while reaping higher performance, power, and area advantages due to greater integration.

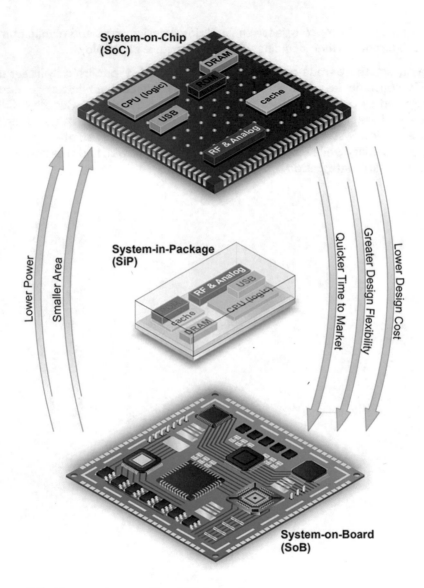

Figure 8-5. Heterogeneous vs. Monolithic Integration

In addition to the core PPAC factors, system architects and design teams must keep in mind time to market – as a rule of thumb, the more integrated a system is, the more design time is needed. If a competitor is pressuring your team with a new product release, perhaps it's best to shy away from designing a new SoC from scratch.

Chapter Eight Summary

In this chapter, we first broke down the difference between macroarchitectures and microarchitectures – system-level Instruction Set Architectures (ISAs) describe how data and instructions are delivered to and received from a core processor while microarchitectures describe how an ISA is implemented in a given circuit. We next compared Von Neumann and Harvard macroarchitectures. While in theory, Harvard Architecture can speed up processing by enabling a CPU to retrieve data and instructions from two separate memory banks at the same time, in practice, increased bus complexity and other factors have limited its performance. Von Neumann architecture limits data and instruction exchange between the CPU and one memory bank, reducing design complexity and lowering costs, and has been the most common architecture used in practice since its inception in 1945.

In the second half of the chapter, we teased apart the differences between CISC and RISC. First arising in the mid-1970s, CISC predates the widespread adoption of RISC by almost a decade and a half (RISC was invented in 1980 but wasn't widely used until the early 1990s). While each has its pros and cons, RISC is widely seen as an improvement due to its pipelining advantages. Moving on from broad macroarchitecture categories, we explored the various ISAs and how to choose between them. Finally, we asked a key consideration facing silicon design teams today – heterogeneous or monolithic integration? Each approach has its advantages and drawbacks. While monolithic ICs like SoCs require less power and take up less area, initial design can take months if not years, which can be prohibitively high. Heterogeneous integration, on the other hand, enables us to capture some PPAC advantages, while retaining design flexibility and quicker time-to-market.

Your Personal SAT (Semiconductor Awareness Test)

To be sure that your knowledge builds on itself throughout the book, here are five questions relating to the previous chapter.

1. What is the key difference between macro- and micro-level architectures? Where do ISAs fit in?

2. Which theoretical advantages does Harvard Architecture have over Von Neumann? Why does this not play out in real life?

3. Name four key differences between CISC and RISC.

4. Which ISA strategy is the most advantageous across the most design- and market-based constraints? What are its shortcomings?

5. Why are cost advantages not so straightforward between monolithic and heterogeneous integration? How do these factors relate to performance?

The Semiconductor Industry – Past, Present, and Future

Having spent eight chapters dissecting everything from transistor structures to System Architecture, we should be well familiarized with semiconductor technology. The question now begs, how does all this technology play into the big picture? Since its beginnings in the 1960s, the semiconductor industry has faced two ongoing major challenges – rising design costs and increasing manufacturing costs. These two challenges have driven the field from fully integrated design companies to multi-faceted fabless design models we see

© Corey Richard 2023
C. Richard, *Understanding Semiconductors*, Maker Innovations Series,
https://doi.org/10.1007/978-1-4842-8847-4_9

today. In the following sections, we outline drivers of design costs and manufacturing overhead followed by a discussion of the transformation of the semiconductor ecosystem over the last fifty years.

Design Costs

Designing advanced ICs is an increasingly complex and costly endeavor. Each chip must undergo architecture and IP qualification, design verification, physical design, software licensing (EDA), prototyping, and validation before it can be sent to a fab for manufacturing (McKinsey & Company, 2020).

In the nascent stages of the semiconductor industry, design costs were largely driven by a lack of universally accepted standards and tools. Most companies developed their software tools in-house, increasing talent training costs and making it difficult to integrate with components designed by other companies. To tackle these challenges, **Electronic Design Automation (EDA) Companies** began developing tools to automate the design process and drove the adoption of universal **hardware description languages (HDL)** like **VHDL** and **Verilog**, which helped "modulate" the design flow so it could be better targeted for additional investment and enabled design firms to build larger systems at aggregated, more manageable levels of abstraction (like C++ instead of **assembly language**) (Nenni & McLellan, 2014). The separation between design houses and EDA tool companies boosted efficiency, reduced design costs, and re-organized companies to better align with their core competencies in software and hardware. An advanced analog semiconductor company could focus all their R&D spending on developing analog design expertise using licensed, off the shelf EDA tools rather than developing custom tools in house. Today's EDA industry is dominated by large firms like Cadence, Synopsys, and Mentor Graphics, with expansive tool portfolios that cover the design flow end-to-end. EDA and design software account for nearly 50% of design expenditures and continue to be significant drivers of burgeoning design costs (Venture Outsource, n.d.). To put into perspective the growing influence of EDA, one only needs to look at the size of EDA companies themselves. EDA giant Synopsys, for example, doesn't make any actual silicon, but has a market cap of over $50B, roughly the size of Ford Motor Company (Yahoo! Finance, 2021).

Through the 1980s, most integrated circuits were medium in size and complexity. To create a fully functioning product, **systems companies** would purchase different chip types and integrate them into their device by soldering them to a **PCB** or other connecting device. As semiconductor technology grew more advanced and systems companies sought higher levels of integration, demand for **Systems on Chips (SoCs)** skyrocketed. SoCs enabled companies to fit all the traditionally separate functional components (memory, processor, etc.) onto a single chip. As the need for closer integration increased, so too did the complexity of each system component, making design even more difficult and expensive. To ease the complexity and stamp down on costs, **Semiconductor IP Companies** began to flourish. IP companies did two things to reduce design complexity – (1) they offered base designs of common modules that could be used as a foundation for an application specific circuit, and (2) they offered **cell libraries** that could be used by circuit designers to generate even more complex designs. In return for upfront licensing fees, per-product royalties, or library access subscriptions, design companies could quickly acquire the undifferentiated parts of a new design and focus their efforts on the parts that made their chip unique. Successful semiconductor IP companies today fall into one of three categories – **microprocessors** like those offered by ARM Holdings, **communication architectures** that enable different parts of an SoC to talk to one another like those offered by Arteris, and **Analog IP**, which has become harder and harder to design at each successive process node. IP companies in these three areas continue to play an important role in keeping design costs under control. If you're an analog company, these IP providers can supply all the digital functions you need (like microprocessor and memory), and if you're a digital company, they can provide the analog functions (like oscillators and power reference circuits).

As **lithography** and **manufacturing equipment suppliers** enable increasingly smaller transistors, semiconductor R&D and design have become progressively more difficult – complicated by phenomena like **quantum tunneling** and **current leakage** (McKinsey & Company, 2020). The cost to design the most advanced 3nm SoCs already costs between $500 million to $1.5 billion, according to research and consulting firm IBS (International Business Strategies) (Lapedus, 2019). Remember, this is just the cost to design an advanced SoC. That doesn't include the cost to manufacture the design at the 3nm node. Designing ICs using less advanced process nodes can reduce costs, but even dated technologies cost a significant amount of money – estimated design expenditures for 7nm and 10nm chips are $300 million and $175 million, respectively (McKinsey & Company, 2020). Silicon design is expected to become increasingly complex in the coming decade, providing unique challenges to chip providers' forward progress (McKinsey & Company, 2020).

Manufacturing Costs

Though design costs have posed significant challenges to profitability, further down the value chain, dramatic increases in manufacturing costs have had even greater repercussions. Each generation of process technology node requires increasingly complex and expensive manufacturing equipment like dicing machines, polish grinders, masks, and steppers, to name a few (Varas et al., 2021). A single dust particle can ruin an entire chip, so the air in a **fab** must be incredibly pure, which requires expensive specialized equipment of its own. All told, an advanced semiconductor fab with a usable life of five years can cost between $7 billion and as much $20 billion today, and that does not include the variable costs of chemicals and materials (Platzer, Sargent, & Sutter, 2020). Front-end manufacturing technology like **lithography equipment** has historically accounted for most of the manufacturing costs, though back-end manufacturing has received greater attention as the industry shifts focus to **advanced packaging architectures** and **heterogeneous integration** to boost performance. We can see soaring R&D and Fab Construction Costs visualized in charts from Figure 9-1. The data for these charts was derived from IBS and McKinsey.

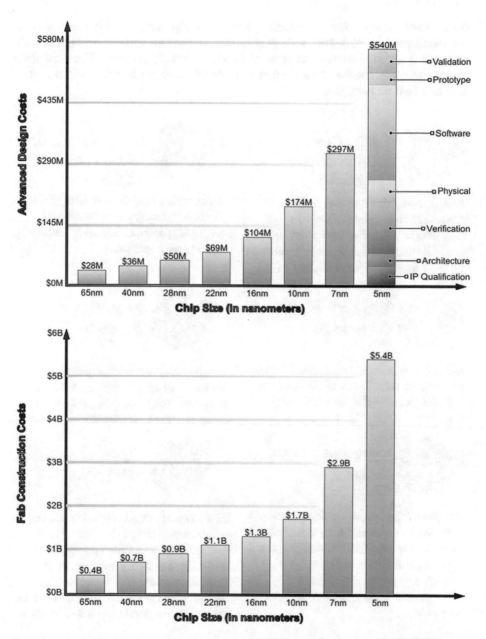

Figure 9-1. Design and Manufacturing Costs (McKinsey & Company, 2020) (IBS, n.d.)

Together, supply-side design and manufacturing costs and demand-side pressures for greater variety of customized designs have transformed the industry from the fully integrated semiconductor companies of the 1960s, 1970s, and 1980s to the mix of fabless design companies, specialized IP and

EDA tool companies, system design companies, integrated device manufacturers (IDMs), and pure-play foundries we see today (See Figure 9-2). This is a great real-world example of David Ricardo's theory of comparative advantage – the market functions optimally when everyone focuses on what they are best at providing.

 Fully Integrated Semiconductor Companies

 **Integrated Device Manufacturers (IDM)**

Design, manufacture, market, and sell semiconductor components and ICs using their own fabs. Fairchild Semiconductor was one of the earliest semiconductor firms to get off the ground and is an example of a Fully Integrated Semiconductor Company.

Design and manufacture some of their ICs, while outsourcing some production to pure-play foundries. Intel and Samsung are examples of IDMs.

 Fabless Design Companies

 Pure-Play Foundries

Design ICs, but outsource all manufacturing to pure-play foundries or IDMs. Qualcomm and AMD are examples of Fabless Design companies.

Contract manufacturers that fabricate custom circuit designs, but do not design ICs themselves. TSMC and Global Foundries are examples of Pure-Play Foundries.

 Semiconductor IP Companies

 System Design Companies

Design and license system architectures, EDA tools, and reusable design modules. ARM Holdings is an example of a Semiconductor IP Company that creates and licenses ISAs, while Synopsys is an example of a Semiconductor IP Company that provides EDA tools.

Companies that create and sell their own end-products, but have brought some of their semiconductor design activities in-house. Apple and Tesla are examples of System Design Companies that have built out their own semiconductor design divisions to build custom processors for their products.

Figure 9-2. Semiconductor Business Models

Evolution of the Semiconductor Industry

1960s–1980s: Fully Integrated Semiconductor Companies

From the commercial introduction of the IC by Fairchild Semiconductor in the 1960s through the 1980s, the semiconductor industry was largely composed of **Fully Integrated Semiconductor Companies**. These early firms would forecast demand for a product, then design, manufacture, and package it before marketing it to potential customers. Each company invested significant resources into its own **fab(s)** to manufacture the chips it sold. High fixed costs left firms vulnerable to volatile demand swings – if sales for their products dipped even slightly, fab utilization could drop significantly, spreading revenue across a greater cost basis and cutting into profit margins (Nenni & McLellan, 2014).

1980s–2000: IDM + Fabless Design + Pure-Play Foundry

The fragmentation of different parts of the value chain began to take hold in the 1980s and 1990s. The costs of building and owning a fab were increasingly expensive, requiring greater amounts of up-front capital investment for each successive technology node. Once built, companies were driven to maximize their output and contribution margin, even if they weren't covering their fixed costs. As a result, even **Integrated Device Manufacturers (IDMs)**, like Intel, which design, manufacture, and sell their own integrated circuits have started to lease out parts of their **fab capacity** (Nenni & McLellan, 2014). Former IDMs like Texas Instruments and AMD have become fabless in the last couple of years. Processor companies would sell their older fab facilities "down-market" to analog companies that could utilize those older technologies for many more years.

In the mid-1980s, companies like Xilinx (founded 1984) and Qualcomm (1985) began with a business model designed to take advantage of this excess capacity (Nenni & McLellan, 2014). By only designing the chips and signing contracts with an IDM to utilize additional manufacturing capacity, they were able to forego high upfront capital investments into their own fab and essentially convert these fixed costs into variable expenditures built into the price charged for each wafer. Not only did this **fabless** model reduce the required capital for new entrants, it also better matched variable supply economics to variable demand.

In 1987, shortly after Xilinx and Qualcomm were founded, the first **pure-play foundry**, TSMC, opened its doors (Nenni & McLellan, 2014). TSMC had an entirely new business model – it focused completely on manufacturing other company's designs. By specializing in fabrication technologies, **foundries** are thus able to focus on a smaller set of core competencies, take advantage of more stable demand and consistent volumes (since they draw orders from multiple customers instead of just their own designs), and strategically position themselves in markets with lower labor costs like Taiwan and other parts of Southeast Asia. Geographically, this balance has continued, with US dominance in **fabless design** and Southeast Asian dominance in **manufacturing**- and **assembly**-related activities. Xilinx and other fabless design companies quickly shifted away from IDMs to lower-cost domestic and overseas foundries, a model that has dominated the market ever since. Even the few remaining IDMs that have their own fabs, like Samsung and Intel, still depend on pure-play foundries for more advanced technology nodes, typically using their own manufacturing capacity to produce devices requiring less demanding, older process nodes.

At the same time the fabless design model took hold in the late 1980s and 1990s, an important shift was happening further up the value chain on the design side as well. As **EDA tools** made building **front-end design** easier to do, systems companies that had historically depended on out of the box products or custom silicon from fabless design companies and IDMs began building their own chips better suited to their specific needs. Tools had entrusted them with front-end and back-end capability that in theory could enable them to bypass chip design companies and work directly with foundries, but they still lacked the complex, back-end expertise necessary to carry out physical design and downstream value chain activities. New players like VLSI Technologies and LSI Logic as well as established players like Qualcomm met this demand with innovative, ASIC-centric business models (Nenni & McLellan, 2014). Pure ASIC companies like LSI handled front-end designs developed by systems companies then coordinated with manufacturing and assembly suppliers to bring their product designs to fruition. Design services companies like Xilinx and Qualcomm drew much of their revenue from a similar model, though they also began to focus on specific markets, developing unique expertise and growing product portfolios of their own (Nenni & McLellan, 2014). Xilinx (now owned by AMD), for example, controls over 50% of the market for FPGAs, programmable chips that can be repurposed for different uses after manufacturing, while Qualcomm is a world leader in custom silicon for wireless connectivity and infrastructure products.

2000–Today: Fabless Design Companies + Foundries + IDM Stragglers + System Company In-House Design

Today, the semiconductor industry is driven by fabless design companies and pure-play foundries in addition to a select few remaining IDMs, supported by an ecosystem of EDA tool developers, equipment manufacturers, and IP providers. Systems companies are playing a growing role as they continue to eat into what used to be traditional fabless semiconductor business. These large integrated technology companies are now doing their own silicon development. Examples of systems companies designing their own chips are numerous and expanding – Apple launched its own silicon engineering division about a decade ago and uses its chips to power the iPhone and Mac product lines; Facebook built its own chip division to develop ICs capable of powering their VR Oculus Headsets; and Tesla developed semiconductor technology capable of powering its Driver Assist and Autonomous Driving platforms. From IDMs to System Design Houses, Figure 9-3 illustrates the changes in semiconductor industry over the past several decades, with the key competencies of each business model highlighted in green.

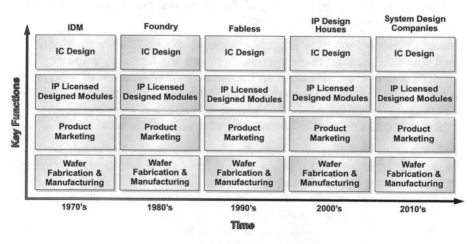

Figure 9-3. Historical Evolution of Semiconductor Business Models

The motivation for these companies to develop their own silicon may primarily be motivated by cost, but there's also a motivation to protect their intellectual property. If Apple is working with a silicon provider on a chip for their newest, most cutting edge iPhone, for example, they may have to reveal too many details of their system in order for the silicon company to provide the ideal solution. Pulling that all in-house keeps those key discussions from leaving the corporate campus.

The pace of change in the semiconductor industry has been so fast that an engineer entering their retirement years in the 2020s has lived through all four of these eras. She may have started her career at a Fully Integrated Semiconductor Company like Fairchild, designing the chip, literally walking it across the building to the fab, then seeing it tested and shipped out the loading dock in the back of that same building. In fact, she may have done some of the testing herself. Now, she may be working at Apple, designing a single block in a massive chip that is manufactured, tested, and shipped offshore. She may never actually see the final silicon. Quite a change for someone that has never changed industries.

Fabs vs. Fabless Design – The Case Against IDMs

There exist today three primary types of semiconductor business models – Fabless Design Companies, Pure-Play Foundries, and Integrated Device Manufacturers. As manufacturing and fab construction costs continue to grow, IDMs are having to rethink the way they do business. Owning a fab can provide numerous advantages, including greater process control, faster time-to-market, and tighter design integration. These benefits, however, have been increasingly outweighed by the costs.

One of pure-play foundries' biggest advantages over IDMs are their ability to **pool demand** across multiple customers and **fully utilize capacity**. This smooths out revenue over time and prevents underutilization of fixed assets. As the cost of manufacturing equipment and foundry construction continues to rise, underutilization becomes increasingly expensive – scaling directly with fabrication costs and causing disadvantages in unit-economics.

Intel may argue that owning a fab gives their company **greater control** over the manufacturing process and allows them **time-to-market** advantages over fabless companies, whose products may have to wait in line behind other foundry customers. While this may be true for smaller companies with low-volume or low-margin orders which can be deprioritized in foundry production schedules, any technical delays at an IDM's fab can represent a significant obstacle to meeting delivery targets. Intel's next generation 7nm chips were recently delayed until 2022, and the company now may have to contract with foundries to produce some of its products (Fox, 2020). Operating an IDM in the 2020s is truly a feast-or-famine endeavor. If you hit all your schedule targets and release a manufacturing process that's superior to your competitor's, you have a huge advantage. If you miss those targets, you've sunk billions into failed process development, and may be forced to manufacture your products in the same foundries that your competitor is using. And your internal development may never catch up once you fall behind.

Proprietary **manufacturing IP** and **data capture** is another common reason IDMs may use to justify the costs of fab ownership. Though this may have proved an advantage historically, foundries have unique technological advantages that are hard to match as an IDM. Because they manufacture a wider variety of components and ICs, foundries can iterate process technology at a quicker rate, building important competencies they can then democratize and provide to fabless design houses and other key customers. Remember what we were saying a while ago about comparative advantage?

Tighter integration between design and manufacturing is a substantial advantage that can result in significant cost-reductions and performance improvements. Though fab-owning IDMs may have a material edge here, software tools, design suites, and remote-work networking technologies have made integration between foundries and their customers much more efficient. Fabless Design Companies like Qualcomm and Broadcom can now seamlessly design new chips with fabrication costs and production optimization squarely in mind. Even small startups can access leading integration and manufacturing technologies by utilizing what's called a **shuttle run** where a foundry combines the designs of multiple customers onto a single mask set and manufactures just a few wafers. You may only get a few hundred copies of your chip, but that's plenty to build demo boards, go on the road and showcase your technology. And instead of a $5M fab expenditure, you may only pay $500,000 since that cost is shared among many customers. Yes, that's still a lot of money, but it's a number that many Venture Capital Funds would be willing to risk on a new technology. Then your company has the proof of concept in actual silicon so you can go and raise a larger round of financing.

We can see a summary of fab ownership pros and cons in Figure 9-4.

	PROS	**CONS**
Manufacturing	Control Over Manufacturing Process + Data Acquisition	Excess Capacity and Underutilization
Time-to-Market	Priority Wafer Runs = Shorter Time-to-Market	No Demand Pooling
Org Complexity	Broad Set of Core Competencies (Design + Manufacturing)	Reduced Focus on Each Competency (Design or Manufacturing)
Overhead & Costs	No Margin Paid to Foundries	More Fixed Costs
Tech & Integration	Tighter Design-Manufacturing Integration	Restricted Access to Most Advanced Technology Nodes at Pure-Play Foundries

Figure 9-4. Owning a Fab – Pros and Cons

To better illustrate the disadvantages of fab ownership, we can compare annual revenues and capital expenditures like property, plant, and equipment (PPE) with market value indicators of IDMs vis-à-vis fabless design firms. We can see this comparison in Figure 9-5, which draws from data presented in the Forbes article titled *Intel, Nvidia, Et Al., And American Semiconductor Hegemony* by George Calhoun (Calhoun, 2020). These figures can tell us which business model creates more value from their assets (i.e., return on investment). As we can see, IDMs like Intel and Samsung lead the industry in sales (Calhoun, 2020). However, when we compare their revenue to their capital requirements (as measured by PPE), we find that revenue to PPE Asset ratios heavily favor fabless design companies (Calhoun, 2020). For all the reasons we discussed earlier, design companies are able to produce more income per dollar of capital than IDMs, which may explain why a fabless design company like

NVIDIA has a market value $60 billion greater than Intel, despite having only a fraction of its sales (Calhoun, 2020).

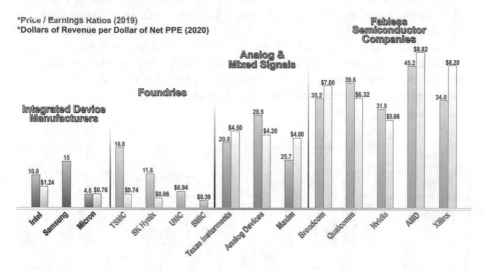

Figure 9-5. Revenue Per Dollar of PPE and P/E Ratios – IDMs vs. Foundries vs. AMS Companies vs. Fabless Design Companies (Calhoun, 2020)

In light of these disadvantages, the few remaining IDMs – namely Intel and Samsung – have shifted or are shifting to a **Fab-Lite model**, whereby they produce some of their own chips, while outsourcing significant portions of their demand to foundries (Patil, 2021). An X-Factor to keep in mind here is the recent global semiconductor shortage and competition between the United States and China. The few remaining US IDMs like Intel and GlobalFoundries are poised to benefit substantially from the $50 billion dollars in government incentives recently passed by Congress to strengthen the industry and shore up domestic supply chains. It is yet to be seen, however, if this renewed support will counteract the fundamental market disadvantages IDMs suffer from today.

Many decades ago, AMD's founder and then CEO Jerry Sanders famously quipped, "Real men have fabs." Some years later, in 2009, AMD spun off its fab into what is now GlobalFoundries (Pimentel, 2009). The lesson – ditch the fab and give your foundry a call.

Industry Outlook

Shaped by a multitude of overlapping variables and market forces, the semiconductor industry is constantly changing. For the next several pages, we will highlight five key trends that shape the industry's history, present health, and future growth prospects.

1. Cyclical Revenues and High Volatility

Semiconductor sales are largely driven by the electronics industry and are highly cyclical and volatile, characterized by boom-and-bust cycles that can last many years (see Figure 9-6). The market most recently contracted in 2019 by over 10% primarily due to decreases in memory prices, but bounced back with close to 7% growth in 2020 (SIA Factbook, 2021). Memory semiconductors, like commodities, are highly price-sensitive and are considerably more volatile than non-memory semiconductors (SIA Databook, 2021).

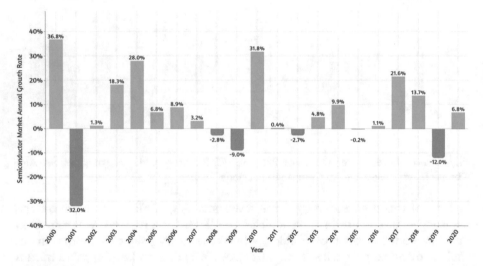

Figure 9-6. Semiconductor Market Sales Annual Growth 2000–2020 (SIA WSTS, 2021)

To manage **Silicon Cycles** and year-to-year volatility, semiconductor companies must be able to control costs, while not sacrificing key investments in R&D. Manufacturing represents the greatest expenditures by US-based semiconductor companies, comprising on average nearly a third of total costs, followed by R&D, Depreciation and Amortization, and SG&A (SIA Databook, 2021). Costs can differ significantly between Fabless Design Companies and IDMs, who have higher capital equipment expenses due to fab ownership. It can be a real challenge to weather an industry downturn if you have massive, fixed costs from a manufacturing facility on your balance sheet. You're stuck paying for all that equipment, even if the fab is only running at 50% capacity. Due to growing manufacturing and capital equipment costs, production expenditures have grown significantly as a percentage of total costs over the last two decades.

2. High R&D and Capital Investment

The rapid pace of technological advancement has driven semiconductor companies to invest markedly high amounts of capital into core R&D. Since 1999, US companies have invested between 15 and 20% of annual revenue into R&D, the highest of any other US high tech sector, apart from pharmaceuticals and biotechnology (see Figures 9-7 and 9-8). In addition, US firms plow 8–20% of sales into new property, plant, and equipment annually, the highest of any industry apart from Alternative Energy (SIA Databook, 2021). Investments in capital and R&D have remained relatively insulated from sales fluctuations as firms protect their long-term competitive edge. According to data from US Semiconductor Companies' 10K and 10Q Filings to the USSEC and SIA Estimates, from 2000 to 2020, Semiconductor R&D and Capital Expenditures have grown by 5.6% year over year, with US companies spending a whopping $74.2 billion in 2020 alone (SIA Factbook, 2021)

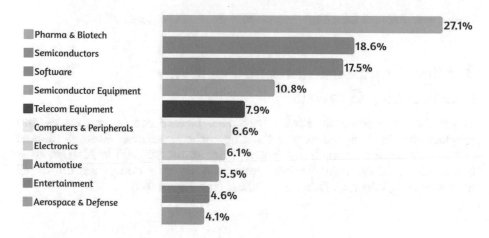

Figure 9-7. R&D Expenditures as a Percent of Sales (SIA Factbook, 2021)

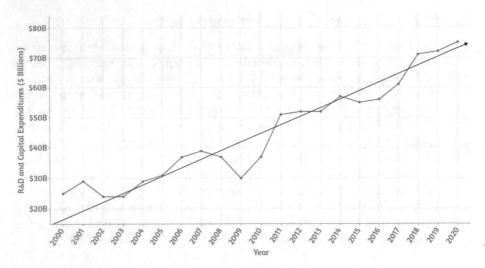

Figure 9-8. R&D and Capital Expenditures 2000–2020 (SIA Factbook, 2021)

3. High Compensation and Positive Productivity Growth

Over the last several decades, a range of factors has led to wages and productivity in the industry outpacing other sectors. Average annual compensation, for example, has grown from about $80,000 in 2001 to over $160,000 in 2019, nearly three times the average compensation of all manufacturing jobs (SIA Databook, 2020) (see Figure 9-9).

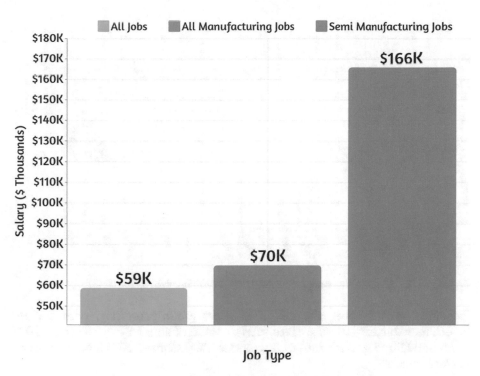

Figure 9-9. Average Salary – Semiconductor Manufacturing Jobs vs. All Manufacturing Jobs vs. All Jobs (SIA Databook, 2020)

In addition, revenue per employee, a strong indicator of productivity, has doubled over the past twenty years, reaching close to $571,000 in 2020 (SIA Databook, 2020). Unlike most industries where average selling prices increase at or above the rate of inflation, per unit costs have decreased at a rate fast enough for companies to maintain profitability without excessive price increases. In lieu of price drops in vital input materials or manufacturing costs, consistent profitability would only be possible by increasing production efficiency.

4. Long-Term Profitability

Well known for wild swings in revenues, as we can see in Figure 9-10, extensive investment in people and technology has nonetheless delivered strong aggregate returns for the industry as a whole. Earnings have concentrated among the biggest competitors with the scale to weather downturns and who have capitalized on disruptive technologies like PCs and smartphones, collecting pre-tax profits averaging about 20% of sales since 1999 with gross margins reaching between 37 and 57% (SIA Databook, 2020).

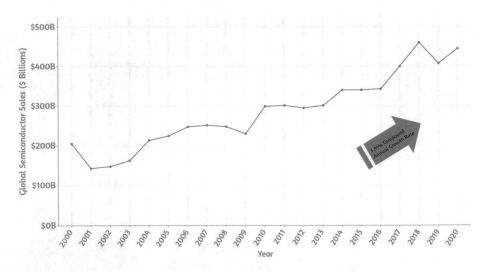

Figure 9-10. Global Semiconductor Sales 2000–2020 (SIA WSTS, 2021)

Expected growth over the next five years looks promising, with current forecasts estimating an aggregate market value of about $775 billion by 2026 at an annualized growth rate of just under 8% (Lucintel, 2021). Major growth drivers include:

1. **Increased demand** for consumer electronics due to rising household disposable incomes, increasing urbanization, and rapid population growth (Fortune Business Insights, 2021)

2. **Fast-expanding emerging economies** with growing demand for ICs (Fortune Business Insights, 2021)

3. **Technological Drivers** including Internet of Things (IoT), Smartphones and 5G Communications, and Artificial Intelligence and Machine Learning (AI/ML) (Columbus, 2020)

For proof that sunny days for the semiconductor industry lie ahead, look no further than the COVID-19 pandemic. At the beginning of lockdowns, analyst forecast a sales contraction of between 5 and 15%, but sales in 2020 actually *increased* from $413 billion in 2019 to approximately $440 billion in 2020, a growth rate of 5.1% (Bauer et al., 2020) (SIA Factbook, 2021). As consumers were stuck at home and not spending money on gas, vacations, or new office wardrobes, they had money to spend on new work-from-home computers and gaming systems. Reduced demand in automotive, industrial, and parts of the consumer market were in turn offset by areas like server demand, PCs, and long-term growth areas like AI and 5G, helping the industry beat expectations and maintain a healthy growth trajectory (eeNews, 2021). NVIDIA, one of the leaders in processors for graphics, AI, and crypto, has set new records for quarterly revenue for every quarter of 2021, peaking at quarterly revenue of $6.5B reported in August of 2021 (Tyson, 2021).

Though new technologies and the explosion of personal computers, servers, and cell phones over the last couple of decades have been a boon for the industry as a whole, high consolidation has adversely affected many companies.

5. High Consolidation

As SoC designs become increasingly complex and transistors are pushed to their physical limits, design and manufacturing costs have never been higher. The industry's profitability has depended on consistent cost-cutting R&D breakthroughs. As a whole, this has been successful, with costs shrinking from $.98 per chip in 2001 to about $.63 in 2019 (SIA Databook, 2020). In addition to pressure to tamp down on per-die unit costs, there has been enormous pressure on companies to get more out of each device – a boon for consumers who gained access to greater computing power at lower costs. These dual pressures for lower cost and greater performance have driven ferocious competition between rivals and resulted in the consolidated behemoths we see today.

This pattern is not unique to semiconductors – capital intensive industries often favor size, since ballooning fixed costs can be spread or amortized across higher annual revenues. It is no surprise that the cost of goods sold (COGS) as a percentage of revenue is significantly higher for smaller firms, who lack the overhead and economies of scale to compete with bigger players. This trend largely tracks with the push toward greater consolidation, with average annual deal volumes stretching to $68.8 billion per year since 2015 (IC Insights, 2021). In 2020 alone, three mega acquisitions were among the industry's top five semiconductor acquisitions – NVIDIA's $40 billion dollar acquisition of ARM Holdings, AMD's takeover of Xilinx for $35 billion, and Analog Devices' swallowing of Maxim for $21 billion (IC Insights, 2021).

With burgeoning design expenditures and fab costs approaching $20 billion, only companies with enough heft and capital can spread fixed costs over a sufficient level of annual revenue and unit volumes. A winner-takes-all dynamic has formed as a result, with the top five companies – Samsung, Intel, TSMC, Qualcomm, and Apple – having a combined annual profit of $35.5 billion as compared with $28.7 billion earned by the rest of the industry (McKinsey & Company, 2020) (see Figure 9-11). Such a dynamic has pushed companies to get big or go broke, leading to a period of rapid consolidation over the last several years. According to a McKinsey report from 2018, while there were 29 companies offering advanced fab services in 2001, there are now only five, including just two main foundries, a handful of EDA companies, and a single lithographic equipment supplier (ASML) (9).

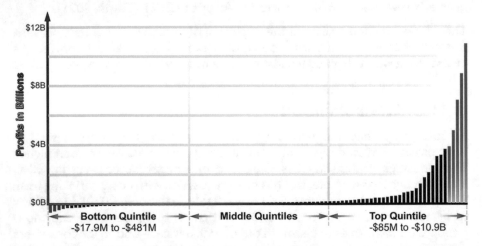

Figure 9-11. Average Yearly Profit of Semiconductor Companies by Quintile (S&P, 2019) (McKinsey & Company, 2020)

The consolidation trend has gained speed in recent years – well over half of the most valuable 51 Semiconductor acquisitions have occurred since 2015 (Design and Reuse, 2021). Continued consolidation appears likely, though it is unclear for how long, considering how few major US semiconductor companies remain independent.

This momentum is captured clearly in Figure 9-12, which depicts Semiconductor M&A Activity over the previous decade. In such a capital-intensive industry and with the top 10 semiconductor companies owning 55% of the market, smaller companies struggling to survive have had to grow to stay competitive (Hertz, 2021).

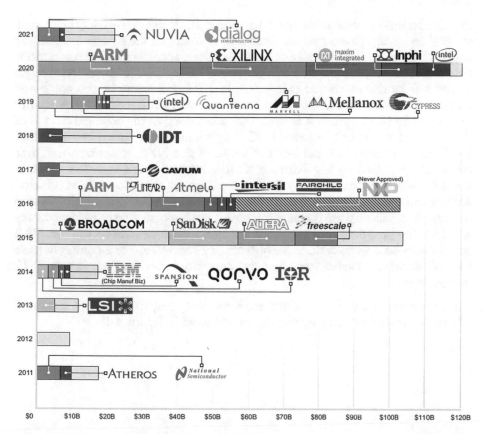

Figure 9-12. Value of Semiconductor M&A Agreements 2011-2021 (See Appendix B for Full List of Sources)

There are a couple of things that are important to note to contextualize this diagram: (1) These are deal announcements, all deals did not necessarily follow through. This could be for a variety of reasons, including rejection by shareholders, management resistance, and a lack of regulatory approval, as was the case of Qualcomm's failed bid to purchase NXP for nearly $40B in 2016. (2) The base cumulative valuation data for the years 2011–2020 were drawn from IC Insights 2021 McClean Report (IC Insights, 2021). The base cumulative valuation data for 2021 was estimated at $22B, but only included the first eight months of reported M&A announcements (Design & Reuse, 2021). (3) We borrowed the baseline assumptions from the IC Insights 2021 McClean report, assuming most notably that coverage includes "purchase agreements for semiconductor companies, business units, product lines, chip intellectual property (IP), and wafer fabs, but excludes acquisitions of software and system-level businesses by IC companies... transactions between semiconductor capital equipment suppliers, material producers, chip packaging and testing companies, and design-automation software firms."

In full disclosure, while we tried to mimic IC Insight's restrictions for all spotlighted deals, there may be deals that should not have been included or overestimation of the net value of individual deals according to the restrictions they used, for which a portion of a given deal or the deal itself may have fallen under one of the restricted categories. In 2016, for example, the combined value of all acquisitions alone comprises more than the $103B in M&A activity estimated by IC Insights – it is likely that a proportion of each deal or one of the deals itself was not included in IC Insight's net estimates. There was also a difference in their estimate of the value of the NXP acquisition that was eventually rejected by regulators – IC Insights estimated this deal value at $38.5B, while we quoted the $47B valuation at the time the acquisition announcement was made. These errors are not important to the overall message that this diagram is meant to convey, but important to note for accuracy and that the proportion of any individual deal's value relative to the net M&A activity may be disproportionately high for any given year. For a comprehensive list of sources, please see a fully annotated version of Figure 9-12 in Appendix B.

We've covered a lot of ground in the last five sections; you can see a summary of the five major industry dynamics we reviewed in Figure 9-13.

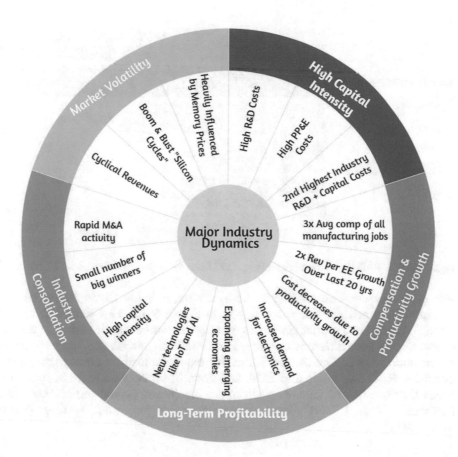

Figure 9-13. Major Semiconductor Industry Dynamics

US vs. International Semiconductor Market

Since 1999, the United States has maintained approximately 50% of semiconductor market share and currently controls about 47% with sales totaling $208 billion in 2020 (SIA Factbook, 2021). The US continues to house most Design Companies and IDMs, and while some design companies are growing in Europe and Asia, these companies are still predominantly US-based design efforts. Manufacturing and Assembly Firms are located predominantly in Taiwan and Asia Pacific, although manufacturing may be moving more to India and South Asia. Long-term market dominance may be related to the high rates of R&D investment by US companies, which spend more on R&D as a percentage of sales than any other country (see Figure 9-14).

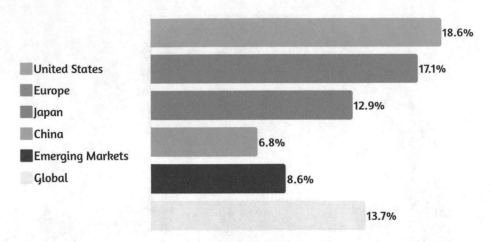

- United States
- Europe
- Japan
- China
- Emerging Markets
- Global

Figure 9-14. R&D Expenditures as a Percent of Sales by Region (SIA Factbook, 2021)

We can see a detailed analysis of Semiconductor Value Chain Activities and Consumption broken down by Region in Figure 9-15. This data was drawn from BSG and SIA's report on Strengthening the Global Semiconductor Supply Chain shows how different countries and regions specialize in separate parts of the supply chain. The United States, for example, leads in areas that require intensive R&D like Logic and EDA and core IP, while Asia focuses more on areas that are labor-intensive and require significant capital expenditure like Materials, Wafer Fabrication, Assembly, Packaging, and Testing (Varas et al., 2021).

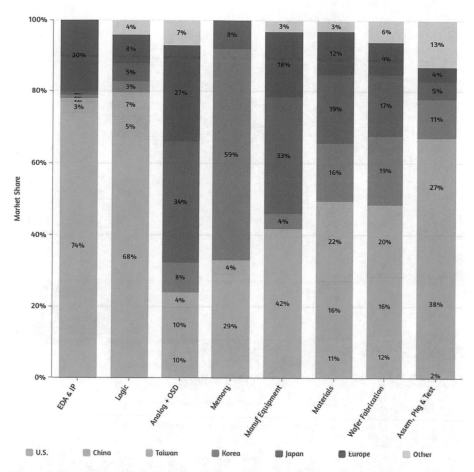

Figure 9-15. Semiconductor Value Chain Activities - Market Share by Region (Varas et al., 2021)

We can further illustrate the broad and interdependent nature of the semiconductor supply chain by tracking the value-add activities required to make a smartphone organized by region (see Figure 9-16). In order to design and manufacture the processor powering the cell phone in your pocket, the efforts of multitudes of companies across the globe specializing in everything from materials procurement to lithographic equipment design must be coordinated and integrated to create a single finished product (Varas et al., 2021). Figure 9-16 is organized by each step of the Semiconductor Value Chain (think back to Figure 1-11 in Chapter 1) and is color coded to match the world map for each step our new IC takes.

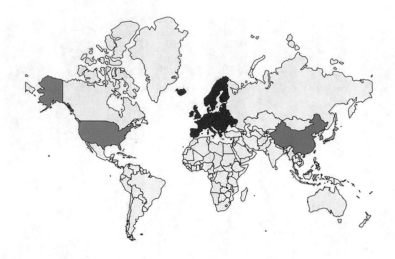

(1) Customer Need & Market Demand

Samsung places an order to Qualcomm for 5 million modem chips to power its newest lineup of next-gen smartphones.

(2) Chip Design

ARM Holdings, an EU Semi IP Company, licenses its ARM ISA to Samsung.

Cadence, a US EDA Co, provides front-end design tools

Qualcomm, a US Fabless Design Co, uses ARM and EDA tools to design the new IC.

(3) Wafer Fabrication and Front-End Manufacturing

ASML, an EU Semi Equip Co, develops advanced lithography machines used in foundries.

Silicon Dioxide is mined and refined in the US.

Silicon is melted and processed into ingots by wafer manufacturers in Japan.

Silicon ingots are sliced and polished into finished wafers by semi companies in S. Korea.

TSMC, a foundry in Taiwan, completes wafer fabrication & front-end manuf.

(4) IC Packaging & Assembly

Die are cut apart and placed in IC packaging at an OSAT in Malaysia.

(5) System Integration

Finished die are sent to a system-level integration company in China.

(6) Product Delivery

New cell phones are delivered to customers.

Figure 9- 16.   Global Journey of a Smartphone

Our silicon supply chain journey starts when Samsung, an IDM based out of South Korea, places an order to Qualcomm, a fabless design firm based out of San Diego, for 5 million modem chips to help power its latest lineup of smartphones. Qualcomm uses an ISA licensed from ARM Holdings, a Semiconductor IP company based in the United Kingdom, and EDA tools from Cadence Design Systems, an EDA tools company headquartered in Silicon Valley, to design the new modem chip. Once Qualcomm finishes the front-end design process, it sends the GDS file to TSMC, a Pure-Play Foundry based in Taiwan, for manufacturing. TSMC cannot finish the manufacturing process on its own, however, without key inputs from various other countries. Its foundries use EUV Lithography machines from ASML, a Semiconductor Equipment company based in the Netherlands, to etch circuit patterns for its most advanced technology nodes. In addition to the equipment on its manufacturing line, TSMC uses wafers made from silicon dioxide sourced from the United States, processed into ingots in Japan, and sliced into wafers in South Korea. Once the wafer fabrication process at TSMC is complete, individual die are cut apart and placed in IC packaging at an OSAT (Outsourced Assembly and Test) company in Malaysia. Finally, the finished die are sent to a System-Level Integration company in China, where they are placed into smartphones and delivered to customers around the world!

Our simple example required inputs from seven separate regions to complete the journey from customer order to product delivery. Real semiconductor supply chains are much more dense, with complex electronic devices requiring thousands of components, tools, equipment, and effort provided by hundreds of suppliers and sub-suppliers.

The United States controls about 60% of logic and analog markets, though it trails in the memory and discrete component markets with about 20–25% market share in each. Contrary to popular belief, the United States still manufactures a considerable portion of the world's semiconductors; it was the third largest export from the United States in 2020, trailing only aircraft and oil (SIA Factbook, 2021). Though still a manufacturing leader, its modern manufacturing capacity relative to overseas competitors will likely shrink as manufacturing capacity has grown at a rate less than five times that of firms overseas, although recent supply chain concerns may slow this decline.

From a demand perspective, Asia Pacific is by far the largest consumer of semiconductors, comprising over 60% of worldwide demand with sales estimated at $271 billion in 2020 (SIA Factbook, 2021). Sales and Demand of Semiconductors is broken down by region in Figure 9-17.

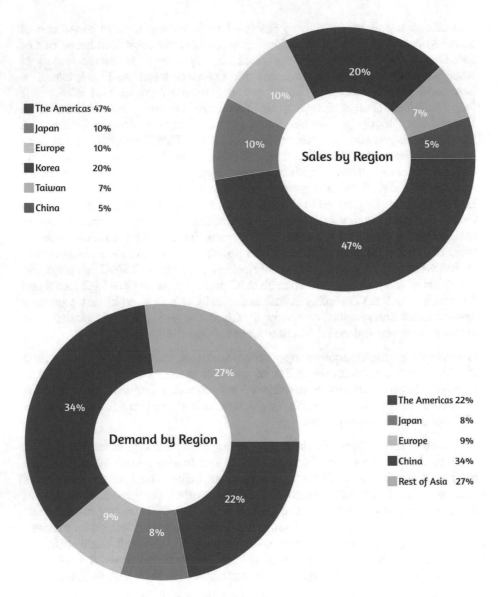

The Americas 47%
Japan   10%
Europe   10%
Korea   20%
Taiwan   7%
China   5%

Figure 9-17. Semiconductor Sales by Region (Top) and Semiconductor Demand by Region (SIA Factbook, 2021)

Though China has been the largest consumer of ICs since 2005, chips that are designed and produced within the country account for only 15% of total purchases (Nenni & McLellan, 2014). To avoid any possible consequences of future trade tensions or over-reliance on the United States, the Chinese government has devoted considerable attention and resources to grow the country's domestic semiconductor industry (Nenni & McLellan, 2014). In

2014, Beijing pumped $20 billion into government-backed private equity funds, like Tsinghua Unigroup, focused on semiconductor technology development (Nenni & McLellan, 2014). More recently, in 2019, the Chinese government created a similar $29 billion fund with the aim of reducing China's dependence on foreign suppliers and developing IC design and manufacturing technology (Kubota, 2019).

COVID-19 and the Global Semiconductor Supply Chain

The COVID-19 pandemic set in motion a global chip shortage that exposed many of the vulnerabilities of the semiconductor supply chain. The shortage has had significant economic consequences, including production cutbacks in the automotive, consumer electronics, medical device, and networking equipment industries, with lead times of many semiconductors stretching as high as one year (Vakil & Linton, 2021). A number of factors are responsible for the current situation. At the beginning of the pandemic, automakers mistakenly forecast a severe long-term drop in vehicle sales and cut back on orders of key chips. Foundries were only too happy to fill that capacity with chips for large at-home monitors, student Chromebooks, and Peloton bikes. By the time automotive demand rebounded, manufacturing lines had already been retooled to produce other consumer products, leaving car companies high and dry with no chips to power their vehicles (Vakil & Linton, 2021). To compound the issue, fires at two Japanese factories that produce advanced sensing ICs and fiberglass used to make PCB's further cut into supply (Vakil & Linton, 2021). Though each of these factors – a global pandemic, inaccurate forecasting and capacity allocation, and fires at two key Japanese factories – may seem like one-time, unavoidable hiccups, the reason they were able to cause so much disruption is structural in nature.

The core weaknesses of the current semiconductor supply chain are (1) **regional stratification** of key activities and (2) resulting **mutual interdependence**. The reasons for regional concentration of important value chain nodes are straightforward – high design complexity and expensive manufacturing require a combination of scale and technical expertise that constrains what each player in the global supply chain can domestically produce. These dynamics incentivize each country to specialize according to their unique competitive advantages and has resulted in the segmented market structure that we see today.

US leadership in R&D and design, for example, can largely be attributed to its existing talent pool and access to a steady stream of new engineers from US Technical Universities. About two-thirds of electrical engineering and computer science graduates at leading US schools are international, but with

80% of students remaining in the US post-graduation, the country is likely to retain a significant edge in engineering talent for the forseeable future. (Varas et al., 2021). The United States also benefits from a vast pool of venture funding, which has the capacity and will to make ambitious bets in the semiconductor industry.

On the manufacturing side, East Asia holds competitive advantages, including skilled and affordable manufacturing talent, robust infrastructure, and higher levels of government incentives. Though talent and infrastructure are both important to manufacturing, the importance of government incentives cannot be overstated. According to a report published by the SIA and BCG, incentives may account "for up to 30-40% of the 10-year total cost of ownership of a new state-of the-art fab, which is estimated to amount to $10-15 billion for an advanced analog fab and $30-40 billion for advanced logic or memory" (Varas et al., 2021). The same report estimated that the total cost of ownership in the United States is between 20 and 50% greater than in Asia and that between 40 and 70% of that difference is due to the lower incentives offered by the US government as compared with Asian competitors (Varas et al., 2021).

We can see these dynamics at play in Figure 9-18, which draws data from BCG and SIA's report on Strengthening the Global Semiconductor Supply Chain. The figure shows how the total cost of ownership (TCO) for a fab in the United States is significantly greater than cost of ownership in Asia. While one might assume that lower construction and labor costs might be the main reason that Asia has an advantage in the manufacturing portion of the semiconductor value chain, the data confirms that it is in fact government incentives that make up the difference, explaining between 40 and 70% of the 25–50% TCO advantage (Varas et al., 2021).

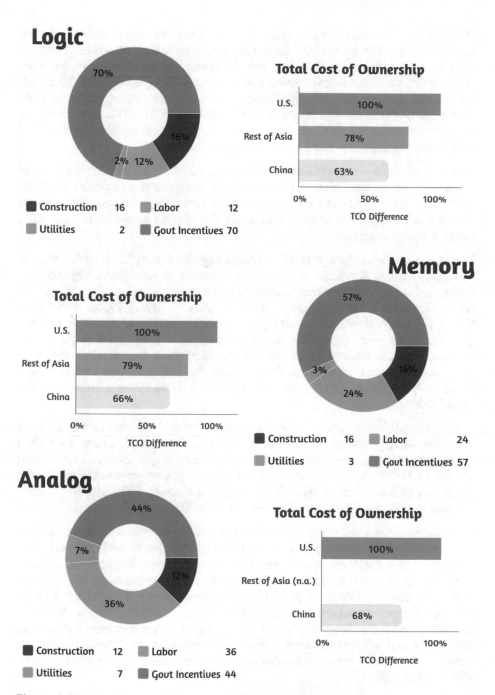

Figure 9-18. Total Cost of Ownership (TCO) Differences by Region and Reason (SIA and BCG) (Varas et al., 2021)

While free trade and specialization have enabled the global semiconductor ecosystem system to thrive, delivering powerful chips at lower costs to consumers worldwide for the last five decades, they have come at the price of a fragile, unstable supply chain. Today, there exist greater than 50 points across the semiconductor supply chain where a single region controls more than 65% of global market share (SIA Whitepaper, 2021). This concentration exacerbates three key risk factors – random variability, geographically clustered manufacturing capacity, and geopolitical conflicts.

The first of these – **natural variability** – cannot be avoided. Any number of accidents can happen, like the two fires at the Japanese factories in 2020. While these occurrences cannot be predicted or completely avoided, a more distributed supply chain would reduce the risk that a single occurrence could cause a major disruption.

The second issue, **geographic clustering**, is a special case of natural variability risk as it relates to physical placement of manufacturing facilities. Advanced semiconductor manufacturing capacity below 10nm, for example, is currently divided between only two countries – Taiwan (92%) and South Korea (8%) (SIA Whitepaper, 2021). Such concentration of activities poses a unique danger – in areas with significant seismic activity, such as Japan and Taiwan, vast swaths of the global fab capacity could be knocked out by a natural disaster like an earthquake, choking the entire system and causing a global chip shortage. While a fire may damage a single factory, an earthquake could damage many.

The third risk factor, **geopolitical conflict**, primarily relates to the political tensions within Asia and between the United States and China. In such a highly interdependent market, tensions between major players can cut off access to suppliers, customers, and investors – like when the United States sanctioned Chinese telecommunications giants Huawei, ZTE, and three other companies citing national security concerns in 2019.

In order to strengthen the supply chain and make it more resilient, experts do not believe every country needs to become completely self-sufficient. Full regional self-sufficiency would require an enormous amount of upfront investment, as much as $1.2 trillion dollars by some estimates, and balloon prices by 35–65% (Varas et al., 2021). However, targeted investment in US semiconductor manufacturing capacity and a greater balance between efficiency and redundancy would go a long way in protecting from future chip shortages and economic downturns, while reducing our over-reliance on other countries for components vital to national security (SIA Whitepaper, 2021).

Chinese Competition

While the United States uses its advantage in education and engineering talent to lead in activities like chip design and manufacturing equipment, East Asia and China control about 75% of semiconductor manufacturing capacity (Varas et al., 2021). Such a wide disparity in manufacturing capacity puts the US economy and national security at risk. In addition to the essential role ICs play in supporting the modern economy, semiconductors power everything from critical infrastructure like telecommunication networks, to advanced cybersecurity and artificial intelligence applications. Shoring up the semiconductor supply chain has become a recent political priority in the US – of the quarter-trillion-dollar Science and Technology bill recently passed by Congress, $52 billion was earmarked for semiconductor manufacturing (Whalen, 2021). The bill drew bipartisan support as a way to counter China's growing economic and military power.

Though the United States still controls many of the key markets for non-memory semiconductor design, its semiconductor manufacturing base has waned over the past two decades. The rising costs of manufacturing have led most US players to sell, spin off, or abandon their foundries, which have been replaced by overseas competitors like TSMC. Today, there remain only five major companies that manufacture semiconductors in the United States – Intel, Samsung, Micron, Texas Instruments, and Global Foundries, which was spun off from AMD in 2009 (Platzer, Sargent, & Sutter, 2020). A handful of smaller analog companies maintain manufacturing capacity for older, niche processes, but these five are by far the biggest players (four if you consider the fact that Samsung is headquartered in South Korea). Though US manufacturing capacity has remained relatively stable, over half of the 27 new fab construction projects targetting advanced technology nodes are projected to be built in China over the coming years (Platzer, Sargent, & Sutter, 2020). We can see this dynamic in Figure 9-19 depicting the forecasted trajectories of US and Chinese chip manufacturing market share according to BCG and SIA's report on Government Incentives and US Competitiveness in Semiconductor Manufacturing (Varas et al., 2020).

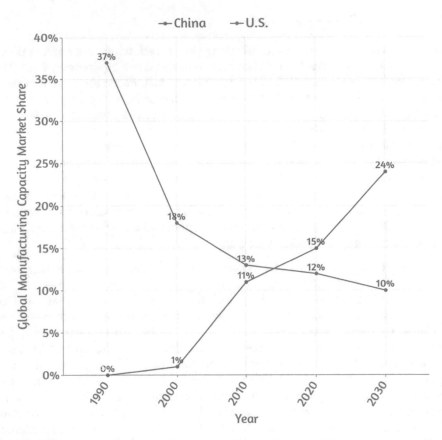

Figure 9-19. United States vs. China – Forecasted Share of Chip Manufacturing (Varas et al., 2020)

China has made development of its domestic semiconductor industry a key piece of its five-year (2020–2025) plan and invested heavily in the space – pledging over $150 billion in investment from 2014–2030 according to the SIA (SIA Whitepaper, 2021). Capital infusions can only go so far, however. Advanced semiconductor manufacturing requires significant pools of relevant engineering talent, a seasoned base of companies with technical know-how, and access to advanced manufacturing toolsets. Despite nearly $50 billion in government incentives delivered over the last 20 years, Chinese companies only account for about 7.6% of global semiconductor sales today, with little presence in advanced logic, cutting-edge memory, or higher-end analog chips (SIA Whitepaper, 2021). To be fair, Beijing's determination to reach semiconductor independence and substantial capital investments have driven annual growth rates of 15–20% and positioned China as a leader in the labor-intensive OSAT market, but the country is still likely a decade or more away from advanced technology nodes like those in Taiwan (Allen, 2021).

Though the subject of Chinese competition in the semiconductor space has made headlines in recent years, don't push the panic button just yet – it is still far behind the United States in terms of market share and technical know-how.

Ultimately, a more diversified and robust manufacturing base in both countries could reduce over-reliance by either country on the other and boost global manufacturing capacity, which would lower costs for consumers across the globe.

From smartphones to infotainment systems, the world has an insatiable appetite for chips. As old markets mature, countries compete for market dominance over the constant stream of new technologies that have come to take their place. Internet of Things (IoT), Smartphones and 5G Communications, and Artificial Intelligence (AI) and Machine Learning (ML) technologies will continue to drive demand for high-performance ICs using smaller-scale advanced process nodes across the globe. Though rising design and manufacturing costs constrain growth and squeeze margins, the semiconductor industry faces a far more existential threat – the fundamental limits of transistor sizes and the slowing down of Moore's Law.

Chapter Nine Summary

In this chapter, we first dug into the two major challenges facing the industry today – rising design and manufacturing costs. We used this context to shape our trip down memory lane, reflecting on the shift from fully integrated semiconductor companies in the 1960s to the fabless-IDM-foundry dynamic we have today. We next focused on a few key trends. With R&D and Capital Investments second only to Biotech, the semiconductor industry has weathered volatile sales cycles and seen consistent productivity growth while delivering high profits and significant pay increases to its workers. Though not without its ups and downs, for the last six decades, the industry has been a growing and profitable sector. Finally, we learned that the United States is still a leader in chip design and manufacturing, though China has grown as a competitive threat in recent years.

As capital requirements bloat, companies have been forced to get big or go bust, consolidating into a handful of top firms. This trend clearly does not favor IDMs who are unable to pool demand and must split resources and attention across both manufacturing and design. Though leading IDMs Intel and Samsung are nominal leaders in revenue, they have trailed in profitability metrics like return on assets and Price/Earning (P/E) Ratios over the past several years. Despite holding some advantages from tighter software-hardware integration, they face perpetual disadvantages to Pure-play Foundries who must worry about only one core competency (wafer fabrication and manufacturing). The slow decay of IDM titans does not reflect the industry's prospects at large, however, with strong growth forecasts and a bright future ahead.

Your Personal SAT (Semiconductor Awareness Test)

To be sure that your knowledge builds on itself throughout the book, here are five questions relating to the previous chapter.

1. How have burgeoning design and manufacturing costs shaped the evolution of the semiconductor industry?

2. Make the case for IDMs. What are some competitive advantages they may have that fabless companies do not? Do you think these are sustainable?

3. List three key current industry trends. Which do you think is most important?

4. What are core drivers of consolidation? Can you think of any drawbacks to being too big (think IDMs)?

5. Describe the distribution of global value chain activities and consumption across the United States and Asia. Which surprising factor is responsible for much of Asia's manufacturing cost advantages?

The Future of Semiconductors and Electronic Systems

As transistors continue to shrink, confronting their physical limitations becomes unavoidable. Lithographic "stencils" can only etch patterns so small, and molecules, after all, can only be divided so many times. Yet, the doubling of computing power every 18–24 months, as Moore predicted, does not have to end any time soon. You could have made a lot of money over the years betting against all the prognosticators claiming the "end of Moore's Law." There are currently many promising research areas, both within existing technology architectures and brand-new sources of computing power, that will continue the technological march of the semiconductor industry for years to come.

© Corey Richard 2023
C. Richard, *Understanding Semiconductors*, Maker Innovations Series,
https://doi.org/10.1007/978-1-4842-8847-4_10

Prolonging Moore's Law – Sustaining Technologies

Within traditional silicon engineering, renewed focus has shifted from shrinking component sizes toward improving design efficiency and integration, as well as exploring new materials and design methods to prolong our ability to keep pace with Moore's prediction. This can be seen by the industry's consistent investment in Research and Development, trailing only pharmaceuticals and biotech as a percentage of sales.

2.5 and3D Die stacking is a promising technology already in use for memory and certain processing applications that enables hardware designers to place multiple die on top of one another, connected by a metal wire called a **through silicon via (TSV)**. We saw examples of die stacking in Figures 5-2 and 6-13. By building up instead of out, the **data transfer rate** between die is vastly improved, costs are reduced, power is conserved, and space is preserved, enabling more transistors to fit on a given substrate. Though promising, 2.5/3D systems greatly increase the complexity of existing designs. Stacking unique processing centers on top of one another can enable tighter integration and boost system performance but will require much more intricate data flow schemas and system architectures. The cost to design a 3nm SoC already costs between $500 million to $1.5 billion, according to research and consulting firm IBS (International Business Strategies) (Lapedus, 2019). Stacked logic will undoubtedly increase design costs further, though high-performance applications like AI will likely continue to drive demand for increasingly complex system architectures. To scale such design techniques, new development tools that encompass all aspects of the design flow will be needed. This presents unique challenges to EDA companies who are better equipped to solve pointed problems at individual design steps.

Gate-All-Around (GAA) Transistors and **new channel materials** are a promising next step in the evolution of transistor technology and offer the most concrete path to prolonging geometric scaling. From their roots in the 1960s, **Planar Transistors** were the dominant transistor structure until about a decade ago. At the 20nm process node and below, planar transistors suffer from crippling **leakage** issues, seeping current even when turned off and costing significant overall system power. Starting in 2011, these planar devices have been phased out in favor of FinFETs for most advanced ICs (Lapedus, 2021). Instead of controlling current flow from source to drain across a 2D plane, **FinFETs** shift gate structure to encompass the channel across three dimensions, which reduces leakage issues and enables greater control at lower voltages (Lapedus, 2021). In FinFET transistors, the bottom of the channel is still connected to the underlying silicon substrate, however, which allows some current to leak out even if the transistor is turned off (Ye et al., 2019). As fabs approach the 3nm and 2nm process nodes, leakage issues have become a critical issue once again. With gate control across four dimensions, **Nanowire** and **Nanosheet Gate-All-Around (GAA) Transistors** aim to solve these issues. GAA Transistors completely wrap channel passages with a vertical gate structure, achieving greater control and resolving many of the FinFET leakage problems (Lapedus, 2021). New CMOS technologies are increasingly expensive at smaller nodes and the process technology required to implement GAA transistors is no different. GAA transistors present unique deposition and etch challenges that likely require new channel materials like strained **Silicon Germanium (SiGe)** to mitigate **electron mobility** issues (Angelov et al., 2019). We can see the structural differences between Planar, FinFET, and GAA Transistors illustrated in Figure 10-1.

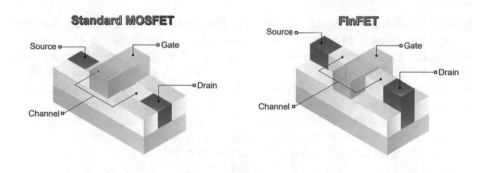

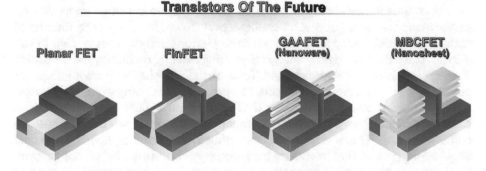

Figure 10-1. Evolution of Transistors – Current vs. Future

As transistors become smaller and more packed together, heat dissipation becomes a major performance constraint, forcing many devices to run below their maximum speed to avoid overheating (Angelov et al., 2019). Traditionally, silicon has been used as the main channel material, but has **power density** (the amount of heat an IC can remove) constraints that limit many of the performance advantages from smaller GAA transistors (Ye et al., 2019). One solution to resolve these power density issues is to use channel materials with greater electron mobility. In **strain engineering**, atoms in elements like **strained silicon germanium (SiGe)** are stretched apart from one another, which allows electrons to pass through more easily while reducing the amount of heat that is released by a circuit (Cross, 2016). Other promising alternative channel materials include **gallium arsenide (GaAs)**, **gallium nitride (GaN)**, and other **III-V elements** (Ye et al., 2019). Together, GAA transistor structures and new channel materials like SiGe can both enable geometric scaling of transistors as well as boost functional performance. Companies have already invested billions into the technology, with Samsung planning to introduce the world's first Nanosheet GAAs at the 3nm process node in 2022 or 2023 (Lapedus, 2021).

Custom Silicon and **Specialized Accelerators** may not boost the nominal computing power of entire circuit generations, but they have proven a successful method for **functional scaling** of application categories and performance improvements of specific products. A great example of this is the functional scaling of GPU processors, whose power has been increasing at an exponential pace. While CPUs are good at doing a bunch of generalized tasks in a sequence, GPUs are particularly good at doing vast numbers of repetitive calculations at the same time, making them particularly well suited for use in artificial intelligence and computer vision, which require quick processing of such calculations. Since 2012, NVIDIA's GPUs' ability to perform key AI calculations have approximately doubled every year, having increased 317 times through May 2020 (Mims, 2020). The phenomena has been dubbed **Huang's Law**, named after NVIDIA's CEO Jensen Huang. Functional improvements in key areas like memory and GPUs can continue improving IC performance, even if geometric scaling slows down. In addition to functional scaling of widely adoptable subsystems, custom silicon design can boost performance through tighter integration using existing technology. Companies like Apple, Google, Facebook, and Tesla are all developing custom chips to power everything from VR headsets to autonomous driving systems. Though cost-prohibitive to smaller players that depend on fabless design companies to design their chips, large product companies are increasingly building custom chips in-house. These companies can afford the cost of building internal engineering groups, and by shifting from commodification to full customization, they are able to sustain competitive advantages in performance that may not be possible when working with third-party providers. In-house design teams also provide quality control advantages and reduce the need to disclose sensitive information.

Structures made from new materials like **Graphene carbon nanotubes**, and other **2D transistors** offer another promising way to extend Moore's Law. As we move toward the point where transistors are only a couple of atoms wide, there becomes a risk that transistor gates (which control current flow) are no longer wide enough to prevent electrons from passing straight through them. This is due to a phenomenon known as **quantum tunneling**, whereby an electron can disappear on one side of a physical barrier and turn up on the other (Fisk, 2020). In anticipation of this problem, scientists have been exploring materials thin enough to enable continual shrinking of ICs without suffering from such **tunneling interference**. There are numerous candidate materials under development, though two have received considerable attention. **Graphene**, the strongest known material with a thickness of only 1 atom, is well suited to resist quantum tunneling (Kingatua, 2020). Future transistors could be made of **carbon nanotubes**, complementary structures made of rolled up graphene sheets that take advantage of graphene's unique properties (Bourzac, 2019). MIT, Stanford, IBM, and other researchers have already built functional chips using graphene and carbon nanotubes (Shulaker et al., 2013). Though promising, carbon nanotubes are difficult to manufacture and will require plenty of additional research before they might be ready for market. We can see graphene sheets and carbon nanotubes illustrated in Figure 10-2.

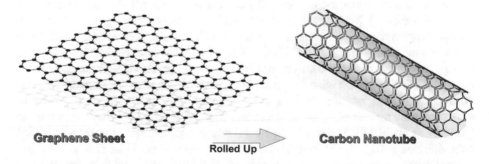

Graphene Sheet   Rolled Up   Carbon Nanotube

Figure 10-2. Graphene Sheets and Carbon Nanotubes

Optical Chips and **Optical Interconnects** aim to harness light instead of electrons as the main signal carrier within and between electronic devices (Minzioni et al., 2019). While a copper wire is limited by one data signal at a time, a single optical wire can transmit multiple data signals using different wavelengths of light (Kitayama et al., 2019). Venture-backed Ayar Labs and teams of researchers at MIT and UC Berkeley working on a DARPA-funded project called the **Photonically Optimized Embedded Microprocessors (POEM) Project** have already begun commercializing photonic chip technology (Matheson, 2018). Ayar has targeted chip-to-chip communication, creating input-output (I/O) **optical interconnects** that are much faster and more power efficient than traditional copper wiring (Matheson, 2018). The significance and breadth of this work has the potential to be huge. You can have the most powerful car engine on earth, but if the pipe from the engine to the gas tank takes too long to deliver fuel, your car will accelerate slowly.

By the same token, processors can only process information as fast as it can be retrieved and delivered to the rest of the system. An SoC may be twice as powerful as its predecessor, but if the circuitry connecting it to other parts of the system is slow, then the extra power is rendered useless. The research on Optical Chips and Interconnects conducted by the POEM Program and at Ayar labs is aimed at alleviating these data-transmission bottlenecks and fully unlocking the power of Moore's Law (Matheson, 2018).

Overcoming Moore's Law – New Technologies

Outside of advances in traditional silicon engineering techniques, there are some truly fascinating technologies in development that could launch us into a post-Moore computing renaissance.

Quantum computing is one technology that gets plenty of press, though experts have many reservations about its practical limitations. In digital computers, a bit must be either a 0 (the transistor is off, no current passes through) or a 1 (the transistor is on, current passes through). In quantum computing on the other hand, a **qubit** can exist as a 0, 1, or a combination of both at any given time (Brant, 2020). The physics of quantum computing are complicated, but in essence, quantum computers harness the **superposition** of qubits in conjunction with a phenomenon called **quantum entanglement**, where two particles are tied to one another over a distance, to execute exponentially more complex calculations than modern computers can handle (Jazaeri et al., 2019). Superposition refers to a property of quantum particles that enables it to exist in two states (in this case 0 and 1) at the same time. Researchers and developers of the technology are striving to achieve **quantum supremacy**, when a quantum computer that functions according to the laws of quantum physics performs better at a given task performed by classical computers that function according to the laws of classical physics like Isaac Newton's law of motion (Gibney, 2019).

Quantum Transistors provide an interesting twist to quantum computing that could theoretically harness current fabrication technologies to create small quantum devices capable of delivering vastly increased computational power. Quantum transistors harness the power of **quantum tunneling** and **quantum entanglement** to process and store information (Benchoff, 2019). In quantum mechanics, tunneling occurs when a particle slips directly through a physical barrier, unlike in classical mechanics where particles cannot pass through such barriers. This becomes more of a problem at the subatomic level and is one of the main challenges to further shrinking of transistor sizes, as we discussed above. At smaller geometries, those barriers become smaller and electrons can easily pass through these tiny barriers. We can see quantum tunneling illustrated in Figure 10-3. Tunneling and entanglement are still not fully understood and maintaining the atomic-scale control necessary to harness such forces is an incredibly difficult engineering challenge in need of considerable investment and inquiry. Quantum Transistors are still in early development, though researchers have been able to develop working prototypes as proof of concept.

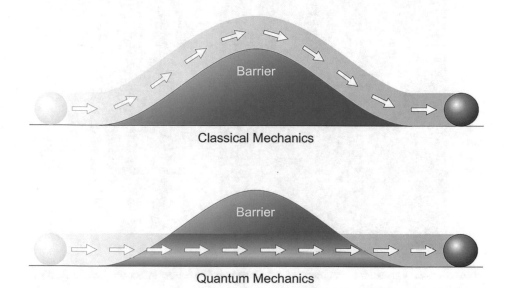

Figure 10-3. Quantum Tunneling

Potential applications of Quantum Technology include data security, medical research, complex simulations, and other problems requiring exponential increases in processing power. Though the tech has great potential, it is prone to frequent errors and requires ultra-precise environmental conditions to function, needing advanced **cryogenic technology** that can cool quantum devices to temperatures approaching physical limits (Emilio, 2020). While such constraints may not sound promising, just remember, the computers of the 1950s that barely fit in a large auditorium now fit in your pocket. Venture-backed companies like Rigetti Computing, as well as big players like Google and IBM, have invested considerable resources into this technology (Shieber & Coldewey, 2020). In 2019, a team of Physicists led by John Martinis working with Google and the University of California, Santa Barbara, claimed to have achieved quantum supremacy, when an experimental quantum computer they built was able to calculate the solution to a problem that would have taken a supercomputer an estimated 10,000 years to complete (Savage, 2020). We can see a picture of a live IQM Quantum Computer in Espoo, Finland (Left) and a better lit rendering of a quantum computer (right) in Figure 10-4 (IQM Quantum Computers, 2020).

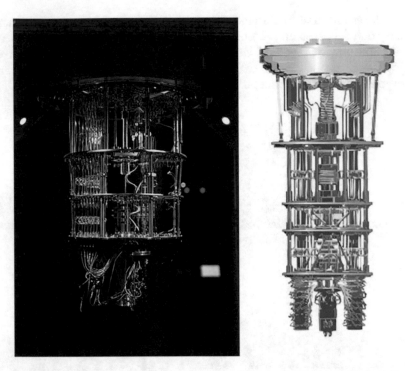

Figure 10-4. Quantum Computers - IQM Quantum Computer in Sepoo, Finland (Left) vs. Rendering of Quantum Computer (Right)

Assuming quantum computers are one day viable, it is highly unlikely they will displace the classical computers we use today – the two are uniquely suited to solving different sets of problems and would be more complements to one another than interchangeable replacements. In Cryptography, for example, Quantum Computers can be used to thwart hackers and make cloud computing more secure. In Medicine and Materials, Quantum Computing power can help make simulations more powerful, accelerating development of new treatments and compounds. In Machine Learning, Quantum Computers can help train ML models more quickly, shortening the time it takes to process massive amounts of data. Finally, as the volume of data grows year over year, Quantum Computers can help with search functions, turning vast seas of individual data points into useful information. Google, the leader in search, has been researching and developing quantum computing technology since 2016 and hopes to have a useful quantum computer by 2029 (Porter, 2021). We can see these various application areas depicted in Figure 10-5.

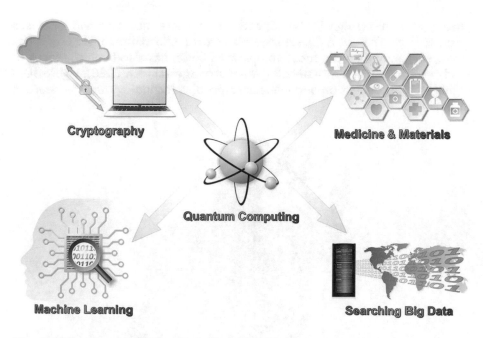

Figure 10-5. Quantum Computing Applications

Neuromorphic Computing Technologies are modeled after living processing structures like neurons and present a fascinating potential avenue for computing progress beyond Moore's Law. Research published in the journal *Nature Electronics* claims that scientists have successfully created a **neurotransistor** which can simultaneously store and process information, greatly improving processing speed, as well as exhibiting characteristics of plasticity; a breakthrough that enables neurotransistors to learn from and change tasks like a human brain (Baek et al., 2020). Additional research at Intel aims to use neuromorphic computing research for AI and other applications using **spiking neural networks (SNN)**, which act like silicon-based neurons in neural networks resembling similar networks within the human brain (Intel Labs, n.d.). The **Human Brain Project (HBP)**, a widely recognized research project focused on building our understanding of neuroscience and computing, has invested significant resources into neuromorphic computing, one of their twelve target focus areas (Human Brain Project, n.d.). The HBP is a collaborative research effort that allows anyone to register and request compute time on one of their neuromorphic machines. It has used both a **SpiNNaker (SNN) System**, similar to Intel's system leveraging numerical models deployed on custom digital circuitry in addition to a **BrainScaleS System** employing analog and mixed-signal components to emulate neurons and synapses (Human Brain Project, n.d.). **DNA**, which stores information millions of times more efficiently than the most complicated SoCs, has also been the focus of study as a potential alternative for **data storage** (Linder, 2020). Figure 10-6 highlights the connection between neuromorphic technology and the neurons in our brain.

Figure 10-6. Neuromorphic Technology

We can think of prolonging and overcoming technologies in terms of **geometric** and **functional scaling**. Prolonging technologies focus on developing existing transistor technologies that can geometrically scale by making components smaller and more efficient. Overcoming technologies, on the other hand, focus on deriving greater performance for a given feature size or rendering feature sizes irrelevant by transforming computing structures to new base components and system architectures. We will need both in the coming decades to fuel the relentless pace of technological development and innovation.

In Figure 10-7, we revisit our functional vs. geometric diagram to compare the potential impacts of technologies that may prolong Moore's Law versus those that seek to overcome it. While Geometric Scaling technologies aim to make transistors smaller, traditional Functional Scaling technologies squeeze more performance out of a given node or feature size. Unlike functional scaling using existing transistor technology, functional scaling here can also be achieved by paradigm shifts in computing performance, irrespective of nm size.

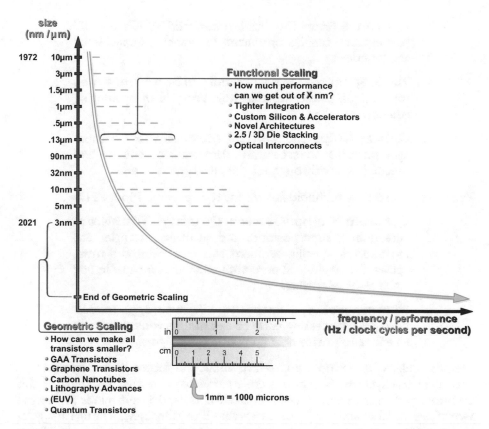

Figure 10-7. Geometric vs. Scaling Technologies

Chapter Ten Summary

In this chapter, we first tackled sustaining technologies that aim to prolong Moore's law:

1. **2.5/3D Die Stacking** allows us to build up instead of out, increasing connectivity (performance), boosting energy efficiency (power), and conserving valuable real estate (area).

2. **Gate-All-Around (GAA) Nanosheet Transistors** are a promising next step in the evolution of CMOS technology and are set to pick up where FinFETs leave off in the upcoming years.

3. **Custom Silicon** like highly integrated ASICs and IC accelerators can be optimized for specific applications and functions.

4. **2D Graphene Transistors** and **Carbon Nanotubes** have unique properties that hold promise of prolonging geometric scaling.

5. **Optical Chips** and **Optical Interconnects** harness light photons to accelerate data transfer speeds and reduce latency throughout the electronic systems.

We next tackled new technologies meant to overcome Moore's Law:

1. **Quantum Computers** and **Quantum Transistors** use qubits, superposition, and quantum entanglement to address specific problem sets that even the most powerful digital supercomputers are incapable or inefficient at solving.

2. **Neuromorphic Computing Technology** models biological processing centers like the nervous system in an effort to create new computing paradigms.

Details aside, what is most impressive about the future of semiconductors and electrical systems is that we are much closer to the beginning of this technology than to where it will ultimately lead us. Brilliant minds across the world are collaborating daily on incredible breakthroughs. Though many of them might seem inconceivable today, tomorrow they could be part of our daily lives.

Your Personal SAT (Semiconductor Awareness Test)

To be sure that your knowledge builds exponentially throughout the book, here are five questions relating to the previous chapter.

1. What advantages does stacking have over traditional "two-dimensional" ICs? Disadvantages?

2. Compare and contrast the structure of planar, FinFET, and GAA transistors. What gives GAA an advantage?

3. Name three promising channel materials. Why are these materials so important?

4. Describe the difference between a bit and a qubit. Which applications might quantum computers be well suited for over traditional digital devices?

5. What questions do geometric scaling and functional scaling ask us? Classify each of the technologies covered in this chapter as more geometrically oriented or functionally oriented in nature.

Correction to: Understanding Semiconductors

Corey Richard

Correction to:

Corey Richard, *Understanding Semiconductors*

https://doi.org/10.1007/978-1-4842-8847-4

This book was published without Series ID, Print ISSN number & Electronic ISSN Number. This has now been updated in the book with the Series ID - 17311, Print ISSN: 2948-2542 & Electronic ISSN: 2948-2550.

The updated version of this book can be found at
https://doi.org/10.1007/978-1-4842-8847-4

© Corey Richard 2023
C. Richard, *Understanding Semiconductors*, Maker Innovations Series,
https://doi.org/10.1007/978-1-4842-8847-4_11

Conclusion

We are living in technologically extraordinary times and the potential for what can be accomplished has never been greater. Those of us that have experienced this remarkable revolution should not forget what an era we have witnessed. It is not unlike the man born in the mid-1800s who grew up riding a horse on muddy tracks and ended his life driving a model T. From the hulking processors of the 1950s that could fill a small house, to the pseudo-supercomputers that fit in our pockets, we too may find our end point in a world far different from where we began.

Whether you participate directly in the electronics industry, work in a related field, or are simply a curious individual seeking hard information about the foundational technology that powers our world, understanding how semiconductors are designed, manufactured, and integrated into systems can be exhilarating, enlightening, entertaining, and worthwhile. For such a complex subject though, it can be frustratingly difficult to form a base of comprehension without a formal education in electrical engineering. My purpose in writing this book was to offer a clear path to that knowledge, weaving together years of painstaking research so that anyone – whether you're narrowly technical or don't know silicon from silly putty – can understand semiconductor technology. I hoped to accomplish this by providing clear, visually engaging explanations of technical concepts going deep enough to develop a broad, holistic understanding of semiconductors, without getting lost in the vast web of theoretical weeds. If I have been successful at that, it is only due to the help of my own teachers and guides. If I have fallen short, it was not for lack of effort. Thank you for reading and may your own path through the world of semiconductors continue to please.

© Corey Richard 2023
C. Richard, *Understanding Semiconductors*, Maker Innovations Series,
https://doi.org/10.1007/978-1-4842-8847-4

Appendix

OSI Reference Model

The **Open Systems Interconnection (OSI)** model is a conceptual framework used in connectivity and telecommunications to describe the inner workings of electronic devices and networking systems.

Layer 7: The **Application Layer** describes what end users of a network actually see. This layer provides protocols like HTTP or FTP that enable software to present data to users as well as send and receive data between users and the underlying system. Examples of an application layer system include a web browser like Google Chrome, email apps, or a proprietary user interface (UI).

Layer 6: The **Presentation Layer** is where an application prepares information for presentation to the end user in the application layer or receives information from the application layer on its way to lower layers for further processing. Encryption and decryption happen at this layer (Imperva, 2020).

Layer 5: The **Session Layer** is the level at which computers and servers open communication channels with one another. This layer initiates and coordinates communication, though actual data transmission happens in layer 4, the Transport Layer (Cloudflare, n.d.).

Layer 4: The **Transport Layer** transports information between different computers and servers in the system. It receives outgoing data from one device, then breaks it into manageable segments before sending to further devices. The segments are then reassembled on the receiving end so they can be used at the Session Layer. You may be familiar with **Transmission Control Protocol (TCP)**, which is built on top of layer 3 **Internet protocol (IP)**.

© Corey Richard 2023
C. Richard, *Understanding Semiconductors*, Maker Innovations Series,
https://doi.org/10.1007/978-1-4842-8847-4

Once an IP address has been found in the network layer, **TCP** is the protocol responsible for delivering data to the end device. You can think of your computer's IP address like a digital house address – it allows network participants on other computers to find you and deliver or request data and information.

Layer 3: The **Network Layer** does three things in a specific sequence. First, data segments from the transport layer are broken up into network packets. Second, those network packets are routed along the optimal path through the physical network using network addresses like **Internet protocol (IP)** to ensure those packets get to the right destination. Finally, those packets are reassembled on the receiving end back into segments that can be used by the transport layer (Raza, 2018).

Layer 2: The **Data Link Layer** establishes a connection between two nodes (physical access points like a computer, cell phone, or server) so that data can be transmitted between them. This layer is composed of two parts. The **Logical Link Control (LLC) Layer** checks for errors and identifies appropriate protocols (set of rules for how data should be transmitted). The **Media Access Control (MAC) Layer** is "below" the LLC and handles interaction with the physical layer. Examples of data link layer protocols include ethernet and Wi-Fi.

Layer 1: The **Physical Layer (PHY)** is responsible for the physical connection between nodes. This is where the data itself (a string of 1's and 0's) is transmitted to the underlying hardware. In practice, the PHY Layer is made up of an electronic circuit(s) that connects an electronic device to a network and is usually composed of mixed-signal and analog circuitry, RF components like transceivers and receivers, and DSP modules that can interpret and modify incoming and outgoing signals. Different kinds of chips can constitute the PHY layer, depending on the device and what it is connected to.

In highly integrated, space-constrained devices like SoCs, PHY and MAC layer functionality is often integrated into the same circuit, commonly referred to as a **network interface controller**. This network could be anything from cell service and Wi-Fi to a broadcast from your favorite TV or radio station.

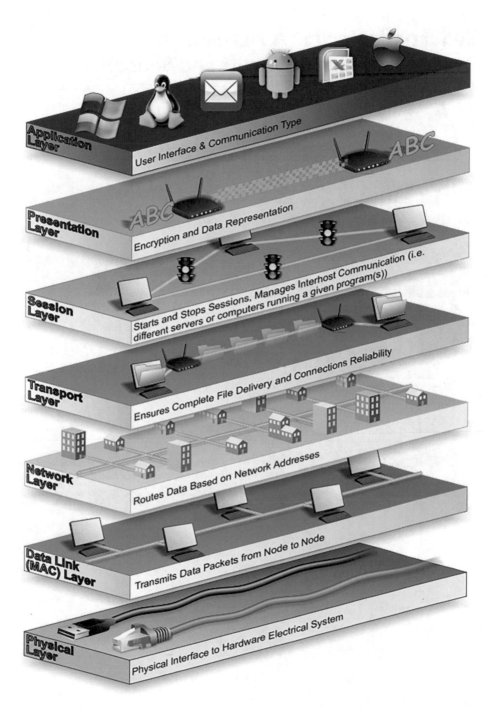

The OSI model comprises seven layers, from the physical layer up through the application layer

Semiconductor M&A Agreement Announcements – Details and Sources

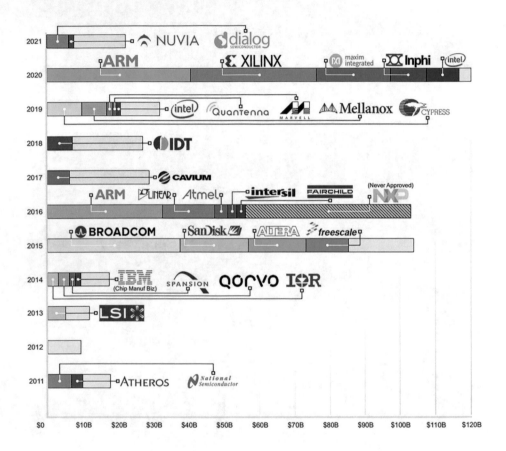

Major Semiconductor M&A Agreement Announcements by Year

2011
- National Semiconductor acquired by Texas Instruments for $6.5B (Rao, 2011)
- Atheros acquired by Qualcomm for $3.1B (Ziegler, 2011)

2012
- Low M&A announcement activity

2013
- LSI Corporation acquired by Avago Technologies for $6.6B (Broadcom, 2013)

2014
- International Rectifier Corporation acquired by Infineon Technologies AG for $3B (Business Wire, 2014)
- RF Micro Devices (RFMD) and TriQuint merged to form Qorvo (Qorvo, 2014). The combined company was valued at $3B at the time of the announcement (Manners, 2015).
- Spansion acquired by Cypress Semiconductor for $1.6B (Silicon Valley Business Journal, 2014)
- IBM Chip Manufacturing Business acquired by GlobalFoundries for $1.5B (Brodkin, 2014)

2015
- Broadcom acquired by Avago Technologies for $37B (Broadcom, 2015)
- SanDisk acquired by Western Digital for $19B (Semiconductor Digest, 2015)
- Altera acquired by Intel for $16.7B (Intel Newsroom, 2015)
- Freescale acquired by NXP for $12B (CNBC, 2015)

2016
- ARM acquired by Softbank for $32B (Kharpal, 2016)
- Linear acquired by Analog Devices for $14.8B (Clark, 2016)
- Atmel acquired by Microchip for $3.6B (Picker, 2016)
- Intersil acquired by Renesas for $3.2B (Design & Reuse, 2016)
- Fairchild acquired by ON Semiconductor for $2.4B (Ringle, 2016)
- NXP acquisition announcement by Qualcomm for $47B (Etherington, 2016)

2017
- Cavium acquired by Marvell Technology for $6B (Palladino, 2017)

2018
- IDT acquired by Renesas for $6.7B (Renesas, 2018)

2019
- Cypress acquired by Infineon for $9.4B (Bender & Dummett, 2019)
- Mellanox acquired by NVIDIA for $6.9B (NVIDIA Newsroom, 2019)
- Marvell Wi-Fi Connectivity Business acquired by NXP for $1.7B (EPS News, 2019)
- Quantenna Communications acquired by ON Semiconductor for $1.1B (Business Wire, 2019)
- Intel's Cellphone Modem Business acquired by Apple for $1B (EPS News, 2019)

(continued)

Major Semiconductor M&A Agreement Announcements by Year

2020
- ARM acquired by NVIDIA for $40B (NVIDIA Newsroom, 2020)
- Xilinx acquired by AMD for $35B (AMD Newsroom, 2020)
- Maxim Integrated acquired by Analog Devices for $21B (Analog Devices Newsroom, 2020)
- Inphi acquired by Marvell Technology for $10B (Marvell Newsroom, 2020)
- Intel NAND Memory Business acquired by SK Hynix for $9B (SK Hynix, 2020)

2021
- Dialog Semiconductor acquired by Renesas for $6B (James, 2021)
- NUVIA acquired by Qualcomm for $1.4B (Qualcomm Newsroom, 2021)

Sources - Text

Ada, L. (2013, June 4). What is an ampere? Retrieved September 2, 2021, from https://learn.adafruit.com/circuit-playground-a-is-for-ampere/what-is-an-ampere

Ahmed, Z. (n.d.). Flip Chip Bonding. Microelectronic Packaging Facility. Retrieved July 27, 2021, from https://advpackaging.co.uk/flip-chip#:~:text=Flip%20chip%20is%20a%20die,down%20onto%20the%20substrate%2Fpackage.

Allen, D. (2021, February 22). China's Computer Chip Industry Plays Catch Up. EastWestBank ReachFurther. Retrieved September 2, 2021, from www.eastwestbank.com/ReachFurther/en/News/Article/Chinas-Computer-Chip-Industry-Plays-Catch-Up

Altera. (2007). Basic Principles of Signal Integrity. Intel. Retrieved July 27, 2021, from www.intel.de/content/dam/www/programmable/us/en/pdfs/literature/wp/wp_sgnlntgry.pdf

Ammann, L. (2003, March 11). The package interconnect selection quandary. EETimes. Retrieved July 27, 2021, from www.eetimes.com/the-package-interconnect-selection-quandary/

Analog Devices. (n.d.). A Beginner's Guide to Digital Signal Processing (DSP). analog.com. Retrieved July 28, 2021, from www.analog.com/en/design-center/landing-pages/001/beginners-guide-to-dsp.html

Angelov, G. V., Nikolov, D. N., & Hristov, M. H. (2019, November 3). Technology and Modeling of Nonclassical Transistor Devices. Journal of Electrical and Computer Engineering. Retrieved September 2, 2021, from www.hindawi.com/journals/jece/2019/4792461/

© Corey Richard 2023
C. Richard, *Understanding Semiconductors*, Maker Innovations Series,
https://doi.org/10.1007/978-1-4842-8847-4

AnySilicon. (2021, April 13). Does size matter? Understanding wafer size. AnySilicon.com. Retrieved July 27, 2021, from https://anysilicon.com/does-size-matter-understanding-wafer-size/

Apple Newsroom. (2022, June 29). Apple unveils M1 Ultra, the world's most powerful chip for a personal computer. Apple Newsroom. Retrieved August 1, 2022, from www.apple.com/newsroom/2022/03/apple-unveils-m1-ultra-the-worlds-most-powerful-chip-for-a-personal-computer/

armDeveloper. (n.d.). Harvard vs von Neumann Architectures. Retrieved September 2, 2021, from https://developer.arm.com/documentation/ka002816/latest

Aruvian Research. (2019, August). Analyzing the Global Semiconductors Industry 2019. Research and Markets. Retrieved December 29, 2020, from www.researchandmarkets.com/reports/4825860/analyzing-the-global-semiconductors-industry-2019?utm_source=CI&utm_medium=PressRelease&utm_code=sx8523&utm_campaign=1286387%2B-%2BGlobal%2BSemiconductors%2BIndustry%2BReport%2B2019%3A%2BSales%2Bare%2BExpected%2Bto%2BKeep%2BGrowing%2Bto%2BCross%2BUS%2457 2%2BBillion%2Bby%2Bthe%2BEnd%2Bof%2B2022&utm_exec=chdo54prd

ASML. (2022). ASML EUV Lithography Systems. ASML. Retrieved January 17, 2022, from www.asml.com/en/products/euv-lithography-systems

Backer, K. D., Huang, R. J., Lertchaitawee, M., Mancini, M., & Tan, C. (2018, May 2). Taking the next leap forward in semiconductor yield improvement. McKinsey & Company. Retrieved July 27, 2021, from www.mckinsey.com/industries/semiconductors/our-insights/taking-the-next-leap-forward-in-semiconductor-yield-improvement

Baek, E., Das, N. R., Cannistraci, C. V., Rim, T., Bermúdez, G. S. C., Nych, K., Cho, H., Kim, K., Baek, C.-K., Makarov, D., Tetzlaff, R., Chua, L., Baraban, L., & Cuniberti, G. (2020, May 25). Intrinsic plasticity of silicon nanowire neu-rotransistors for dynamic memory and learning functions. Nature News. Retrieved September 2, 2021, from www.nature.com/articles/s41928-020-0412-1

Bartley, K. (2021, February 16). Big Data Statistics: How Much Data is There in the world? Rivery. Retrieved September 1, 2021, from https://rivery.io/blog/big-data-statistics-how-much-data-is-there-in-the-world/

Bauer, H., Burkacky, O., Kenevan, P., Mahindroo, A., & Patel, M. (2020, April 14). Coronavirus: Implications for the semiconductor industry. McKinsey & Company. Retrieved September 2, 2021, from www.mckinsey.com/indus-tries/semiconductors/our-insights/coronavirus-implications-for-the-semiconductor-industry

BBC. (n.d.). Architecture. BBC News. Retrieved September 2, 2021, from www.bbc.co.uk/bitesize/guides/zhppfcw/revision/3

BBC. (n.d.). What is electricity? BBC Bitesize. Retrieved September 2, 2021, from www.bbc.co.uk/bitesize/topics/zgy39j6/articles/z8mxgdm

Beaty, W. (1999). Electricity is Not a Form of Energy. amasci.com. Retrieved September 2, 2021, from http://amasci.com/miscon/energ1.html

Benchoff, B. (2019, November 7). Quantum Transistors: New Advances In Manufacturing Electronics. medium.com. Retrieved September 2, 2021, from https://medium.com/supplyframe-hardware/quantum-transistors-new-advances-in-manufacturing-electronics-63b1a53894e6

Bisht, H. S. (2022, January 13). Computer Organization: RISC and CISC. GeeksforGeeks. Retrieved July 12, 2022, from www.geeksforgeeks.org/computer-organization-risc-and-cisc/

Blaabjerg, F. (2018). Control of Power Electronic Converters and Systems: Volume 1. Elsevier Science.

Borth, D. E. (2018, August 28). Modem. Encyclopædia Britannica. Retrieved September 1, 2021, from www.britannica.com/technology/modem

Bourzac, K. (2019, February 19). Carbon nanotube computers face a make-or-break moment. C&EN. Retrieved September 2, 2021, from https://cen.acs.org/materials/electronic-materials/Carbon-nanotube-computers-face-makebreak/97/i8

Brant, T. (2020, November 11). Quantum Computing: A Bubble Ready to Burst? PCMAG. Retrieved September 2, 2021, from www.pcmag.com/news/quantum-computing-a-bubble-ready-to-burst

Brant, T. (2020, September 2). SSD vs. HDD: What's the Difference? PCMAG. Retrieved July 28, 2021, from www.pcmag.com/news/ssd-vs-hdd-whats-the-difference

Breed, G. (2010, July). Signal Integrity Basics: Digital Signals on Transmission Lines. High Frequencey Electronics. Retrieved July 27, 2021, from www.high-frequencyelectronics.com/Jul10/HFE0710_Tutorial.pdf

Brown, G. A., Zeitzoff, P. M., Bersuker, G., & Huff, H. R. (2004). Scaling CMOS Materials & devices. Materials Today, 7(1), 20–25. https://doi.org/10.1016/s1369-7021(03)00050-6

Cadence PCB Solutions. (2019). FPGA vs. ASIC: Differences and Choosing Best for Your Business. cadence.com. Retrieved July 28, 2021, from https://resources.pcb.cadence.com/blog/2019-fpga-vs-asic-differences-and-choosing-best-for-your-business

Calhoun, G. (2020, August 2). Intel, Nvidia, Et Al., And American Semiconductor Hegemony. Forbes. Retrieved September 2, 2021, from www.forbes.com/sites/georgecalhoun/2020/08/02/intel-nvidia-et-al-and-american-semiconductor-hegemony/?sh=72013a34c298

Caulfield, B. (2009, December 16). What's the Difference Between a CPU and a GPU? NVIDIA Blog. Retrieved July 28, 2021, from https://blogs.nvidia.com/blog/2009/12/16/whats-the-difference-between-a-cpu-and-a-gpu/

Chang, Y.-W., Cheng, K.-T., & Wang, L.-T. (2009). Electronic design automation: synthesis, verification, and test. Elsevier, Morgan Kaufmann.

Channel MOSFET Basics. Learning about Electronics. (2018). Retrieved March 29, 2021, from http://www.learningaboutelectronics.com/Articles/N-Channel-MOSFETs

Clarke, P. (2021, January 18). Semiconductor market shakes off 2020 Covid-19 gloom. eeNews Europe. Retrieved September 2, 2021, from www.eenewseurope.com/news/semiconductor-market-2020-covid-19

Cloudflare. (n.d.). What is the OSI Model?. Retrieved January 17, 2022, from www.cloudflare.com/learning/ddos/glossary/open-systems-interconnection-model-osi/

Columbus, L. (2020, January 19). Roundup Of Machine Learning Forecasts And Market Estimates, 2020. Forbes. Retrieved September 2, 2021, from www.forbes.com/sites/louiscolumbus/2020/01/19/roundup-of-machine-learning-forecasts-and-market-estimates-2020/?sh=5bd5326c5c02

Commscope. (2018). Understanding the RF path. commscope.com. Retrieved September 1, 2021, from www.commscope.com/globalassets/digizuite/3221-rf-path-ebook-eb-112900-en.pdf

Cross, T. (2016, February 25). After Moore's law | Technology Quarterly. The Economist. Retrieved April 3, 2021, from www.economist.com/technology-quarterly/2016-03-12/after-moores-law

Design And Reuse. (2021, January 13). Value of Semiconductor Industry M&A Agreements Sets Record in 2020. Retrieved January 17, 2022, from www.design-reuse.com/news/49290/2020-semiconductor-industry-merge-acquisition-agreements.html

Dsouza, J. (2020, April 25). What is a GPU and do you need one in Deep Learning? towardsdatascience.com. Retrieved July 28, 2021, from https://towardsdatascience.com/what-is-a-gpu-and-do-you-need-one-in-deep-learning-718b9597aa0d

EETimes. (2003, October 24). Maxim buys philips' fab in Texas for $40 million. EETimes. Retrieved July 27, 2021, from www.eetimes.com/maxim-buys-philips-fab-in-texas-for-40-million-2/

Electrical4U. (2020, October 23). Electric Potential. Retrieved February 20, 2022, from www.electrical4u.com/electric-potential/

Electronics Tutorials. (2021, July 19). Bipolar Transistor. electronicstutorials.com. Retrieved January 17, 2022, from www.electronics-tutorials.ws/transistor/tran_1.html

Electronics Tutorials. (2021, May 31). Electrical Energy and Power. Retrieved September 2, 2021, from www.electronics-tutorials.ws/dccircuits/electrical-energy.html

Emilio, M. D. P. (2020, January 6). Intel cryogenic chip for quantum computing. eetimes.com. Retrieved September 2, 2021, from www.eetimes.com/intel-cryogenic-chip-for-quantum-computing/

Encyclopædia Britannica, inc. (2021, February 26). electric charge. Encyclopædia Britannica. Retrieved September 2, 2021, from www.britannica.com/science/electric-charge

Encyclopædia Britannica. (n.d.). Central Processing Unit. Encyclopædia Britannica. Retrieved July 28, 2021, from www.britannica.com/technology/central-processing-unit

Encyclopædia Britannica. (n.d.). Hertz. Encyclopædia Britannica. Retrieved July 28, 2021, from www.britannica.com/science/hertz

Engheim, E. (2020, July 26). What does RISC and CISC mean in 2020? Medium. Retrieved September 2, 2021, from https://medium.com/swlh/what-does-risc-and-cisc-mean-in-2020-7b4d42c9a9de

Engheim, E. (2021, January 24). Why Pipeline a Microprocessor? Medium. Retrieved July 12, 2022, from https://erik-engheim.medium.com/microprocessor-pipelining-f63df4ee60cf

FCC. (2020, September 9). Fact Sheet - Facilitating 5G in the 3.45-3.55 GHz Band. fcc.gov. Retrieved September 1, 2021, from https://docs.fcc.gov/public/attachments/DOC-366780A1.pdf

Firesmith, D. (2017, August 21). Multicore Processing. cmu.edu. Retrieved July 28, 2021, from https://insights.sei.cmu.edu/sei_blog/2017/08/multicore-processing.html

Fisk, I. (2020, March 2). A Reckoning for Moore's Law. Simons Foundation. Retrieved September 2, 2021, from www.simonsfoundation.org/2020/03/02/a-reckoning-for-moores-law/#:~:text=Moore's%20law%20is%20the%20observation,was%20to%20wait%20two%20years.f

Fluke. (2021, May 9). What is resistance? Retrieved September 2, 2021, from www.fluke.com/en-us/learn/blog/electrical/what-is-resistance

Fortune Business Insights. (2021, May). The global semiconductor market is projected to grow from $452.25 billion in 2021 to $803.15 billion in 2028 at a CAGR of 8.6% in forecast period, 2021-2028... Read More at:- www.fortunebusinessinsights.com/semiconductor-market-102365. Retrieved September 2, 2021, from www.fortunebusinessinsights.com/semiconductor-market-102365

Foster, H. (2021, January 6). The 2020 Wilson Research Group Functional Verification Study. Retrieved January 17, 2022, from https://blogs.sw.siemens.com/verificationhorizons/2021/01/06/part-8-the-2020-wilson-research-group-functional-verification-study/

Fox, C. (2020, July 24). Intel's next-generation 7nm chips delayed until 2022. BBC News. Retrieved September 2, 2021, from www.bbc.com/news/technology-53525710#:~:text=Intel%20says%20the%20production%20of,current%2Dgeneration%20chips%20on%20sale.&text=In%20June%2C%20Apple%20said%20it,and%20design%20its%20own%20chips.

Fox, P. (n.d.). Central Processing Unit (CPU). Khan Academy. Retrieved July 28, 2021, from www.khanacademy.org/computing/computers-and-internet/xcae6f4a7ff015e7d:computers/xcae6f4a7ff015e7d:computer-components/a/central-processing-unit-cpu

Fox, P. (n.d.). Logic gates. Khan Academy. Retrieved April 3, 2021, from www.khanacademy.org/computing/computers-and-internet/xcae6f4a7ff015e7d:computers/xcae6f4a7ff015e7d:logic-gates-and-circuits/a/logic-gates

Frumusanu, A. (2020, August 24). TSMC details 3nm PROCESS TECHNOLOGY: Full Node scaling for 2H22 volume production. anandtech.com. Retrieved July 27, 2021, from www.anandtech.com/show/16024/tsmc-details-3nm-process-technology-details-full-node-scaling-for-2h22

Gallego, J. (2016, February 12). The Semiconductor Industry Is Anticipating The End of Moore's Law. Futurism. Retrieved April 3, 2021, from https://futurism.com/semiconductor-industry-anticipating-end-moores-law

GeeksforGeeks. (2020, July 28). Kernel in Operating System. GeeksforGeeks. Retrieved September 2, 2021, from www.geeksforgeeks.org/kernel-in-operating-system/

Gibney, E. (2019, October 23). Hello Quantum World! Google publishes landmark quantum supremacy claim. Nature News. Retrieved January 17, 2022, from www.nature.com/articles/d41586-019-03213-z

Gilleo, K., & Pham-Van-Diep, G. (2004). Step 10: ENCAPSULATION Materials, processes and equipment. Semiconductor Digest. Retrieved July 27, 2021, from https://sst.semiconductor-digest.com/2004/10/step-10-encapsulation-imaterials-processes-and-equipment-i/

GIS Geography. (2021, June 14). Passive vs Active Sensors in Remote Sensing. GIS Geography. Retrieved July 28, 2021, from https://gisgeography.com/passive-active-sensors-remote-sensing/#:~:text=Active%20sensors%20have%20its%20own,passive%20sensors%20measure%20this%20energy.

Gupta, D., & Franzon, P. (2020). Packaging Integration White Paper. IEEE. Retrieved July 27, 2021, from https://irds.ieee.org/images/files/pdf/2020/2020IRDS_PI.pdf

Hameed, T., & Airaad, S. (2019, January 25). NORTH AND SOUTH BRIDGES OF A MOTHERBOARD: EXPLAINED. Tech.78. Retrieved July 28, 2021, from https://srgtech78.wordpress.com/2019/01/25/north-and-south-bridges-of-a-motherboard-explained/

Hashagen, U., Van Der Spiegel, J., Tau, J. F., Ala'ilima, T. F., & Ang, L. P. (2002). The ENIAC—history, operation and reconstruction in VLSI. In The First Computers: History and Architectures (1st ed.). essay, MIT Press.

Hill, M., Christie, D., Patterson, D., Yi, J., Chiou, D., & Sendag, R. (2016). PROPRIETARY VERSUS OPEN INSTRUCTION SETS. Wisc.edu. Retrieved July 12, 2022, from https://research.cs.wisc.edu/multifacet/papers/ieeemicro16_card_isa.pdf.

Hoerni, J. A. (1962, March 20). Method of manufacturing semiconductor devices.

Holt, R. (n.d.). Schematic vs. Netlist: A Guide to PCB Design Integration. Optimum Design Associates Blog. Retrieved April 3, 2021, from http://blog.optimumdesign.com/schematic-vs.-netlist-a-guide-to-pcb-deisgn-integration

Honsberg, C. B., & Bowden, S. G. (2019). Doping. Photovoltaics Education Website. Retrieved March 29, 2021, from www.pveducation.org/pvcdrom/pn-junctions/doping

Howe, D. (1994, December 16). clock. Free On-line Dictionary of Computing. Retrieved April 3, 2021, from https://foldoc.org/Clock

Human Brain Project. (n.d.). Neuromorphic Computing. Retrieved September 2, 2021, from www.humanbrainproject.eu/en/silicon-brains/

Hutson, M. (2021, August 20). The World's Largest Computer Chip. The New Yorker. Retrieved July 27, 2022, from www.newyorker.com/tech/annals-of-technology/the-worlds-largest-computer-chip

IBM. (n.d.). RISC Architecture. ibm.com. Retrieved July 12, 2022, from www.ibm.com/ibm/history/ibm100/us/en/icons/risc/

IBS. (n.d.). International Business Strategies, Inc. (IBS). Retrieved February 21, 2022, from www.ibs-inc.net/

IC Insights. (2021, January 12). Value of Semiconductor Industry M&A Agreements Sets Record in 2020. Retrieved September 2, 2021, from www.icinsights.com/news/bulletins/Value-Of-Semiconductor-Industry-MA-Agreements-Sets-Record-In-2020/

Imperva. (2020, June 10). OSI Model. Retrieved January 17, 2022, from www.imperva.com/learn/application-security/osi-model/

Integrated Circuit Engineering Corporation. (n.d.). Yield and Yield Management. smithsonianchips.si.edu. Retrieved July 27, 2021, from http://smithsonianchips.si.edu/ice/cd/CEICM/SECTION3.pdf

Intel Labs. (n.d.). Neuromorphic Computing. Intel. Retrieved September 2, 2021, from www.intel.com/content/www/us/en/research/neuromorphic-computing.html

Intel. (2018, April 18). Inside An Intel Chip Fab: One Of The Cleanest Conference Rooms On Earth. Intel Newsroom. Retrieved July 27, 2021, from https://newsroom.intel.com/news/intel-bunnies-arent-like-your-bunnies/#gs.rj6bun

Intel. (n.d.). What is CPU clock speed? Intel. Retrieved July 12, 2022, from www.intel.com/content/www/us/en/gaming/resources/cpu-clock-speed.html

Intersil. (n.d.). The Benefits of Power Modules vs. Discrete Regulators. Mouser. Retrieved July 28, 2021, from www.mouser.com/applications/benefits-modules-regulators-power/

IRDS (International Roadmap for Devices and Systems). (2020). IRDS Lithography. IEEE.org. Retrieved September 2, 2021, from https://irds.ieee.org/images/files/pdf/2020/2020IRDS_Litho.pdf

IRDS. (2020). International Roadmap for Devices and Systems. irds.ieee.org. Retrieved July 27, 2021, from https://irds.ieee.org/images/files/pdf/2020/2020IRDS_ES.pdf

ITU (International Telecommunication Union). (2011). All about Technology. Retrieved September 1, 2021, from www.itu.int/osg/spu/ni/3G/technology/

Jazaeri, F., Beckers, A., Tajalli, A., & Sallese, J.-M. (2019, August 7). A Review on Quantum Computing: From Qubits to Front-end Electronics and Cryogenic MOSFET Physics. IEEE Xplore. Retrieved September 2, 2021, from https://ieeexplore.ieee.org/abstract/document/8787164

Kay, R. (2003, November 17). Serial vs. Parallel Storage. Computerworld. Retrieved July 28, 2021, from www.computerworld.com/article/2574104/serial-vs--parallel-storage.html

Khillar, S. (2018, March 26). Difference between Von Neumann and Harvard architecture. Retrieved September 2, 2021, from http://www.difference-between.net/technology/difference-between-von-neumann-and-harvard-architecture/

Kilby, J. S. (1964, June 23). Miniaturized Electronic Circuits.

Kingatua, A. (2020, November 12). What Is a Graphene Field Effect Transistor (GFET)? Construction, Benefits, and Challenges. All About Circuits. Retrieved September 2, 2021, from www.allaboutcircuits.com/technical-articles/graphene-field-effect-transistor-gfet-construction-benefits-challenges/

Kitayama, K.-ichi, Notomi, M., Naruse, M., Inoue, K., Kawakami, S., & Uchida, A. (2019, September 24). Novel frontier of photonics for data processing-photonic accelerator. AIP Publishing. Retrieved September 2, 2021, from https://aip.scitation.org/doi/10.1063/1.5108912

Klein, M. (2017, August 17). What Is a "Chipset", and Why Should I Care? How-To Geek. Retrieved July 28, 2021, from www.howtogeek.com/287206/what-is-a-chipset-and-why-should-i-care/

Knerl, L. (2019, November 11). Microcontroller vs Microprocessor: What's the difference? hp.com. Retrieved July 28, 2021, from www.hp.com/us-en/shop/tech-takes/microcontroller-vs-microprocessor

Kubota, Y. (2019, October 25). China Sets Up New $29 Billion Semiconductor Fund. The Wall Street Journal. Retrieved September 2, 2021, from www.wsj.com/articles/china-sets-up-new-29-billion-semiconductor-fund-11572034480

Lapedus, M. (2019, December 18). The Race To Next-Gen 2.5D/3D Packages. Semiconductor Engineering. Retrieved July 27, 2021, from https://semiengineering.com/the-race-to-next-gen-2-5d-3d-packages/

Lapedus, M. (2019, June 24). 5nm vs. 3nm. Semiconductor Engineering. Retrieved September 2, 2021, from https://semiengineering.com/5nm-vs-3nm/

Lapedus, M. (2020, July 23). The Race To Much More Advanced Packaging. Semiconductor Engineering. Retrieved September 2, 2021, from https://semiengineering.com/the-race-to-much-more-advanced-packages/

Lapedus, M. (2021, January 25). New Transistor Structures At 3nm/2nm. Semiconductor Engineering. Retrieved September 2, 2021, from https://semiengineering.com/new-transistor-structures-at-3nm-2nm/

Lau, J. (2017, August 7). MCM, SIP, SoC, and HETEROGENEOUS Integration defined and explained. 3D InCites. Retrieved July 27, 2021, from www.3dincites.com/2017/08/mcm-sip-soc-and-heterogeneous-integration-defined-and-explained/

Lee, C. (2017, November 16). What's What In Advanced Packaging. Semiconductor Engineering. Retrieved July 27, 2021, from https://semiengineering.com/whats-what-in-advanced-packaging/

Lewis, J. A. (2019, January). Learning the Superior Techniques of the Barbarians - China's Pursuit of Semiconductor Independence. https://csis-website-prod.s3.amazonaws.com/s3fs-public/publication/190115_Lewis_Semiconductor_v6.pdf. Retrieved July 27, 2021, from https://csis-website-prod.s3.amazonaws.com/s3fs-public/publication/190115_Lewis_Semiconductor_v6.pdf

Linder, C. (2020, July 26). DNA Is Millions of Times More Efficient Than Your Computer's Hard Drive. Popular Mechanics. Retrieved September 2, 2021, from www.popularmechanics.com/science/a33327626/scientists-encoded-wizard-of-oz-in-dna/

Lowe, D. (n.d.). Radio Electronics: Transmitters and Receivers. dummies.com. Retrieved September 1, 2021, from www.dummies.com/programming/electronics/components/radio-electronics-transmitters-and-receivers/

Lucintel. (2021, August). Semiconductor Market Report: Trends, Forecast and Competitive Analysis. ReportLinker. Retrieved January 16, 2022, from www.reportlinker.com/p05817483/Semiconductor-Market-Report-Trends-Forecast-and-Competitive-Analysis.html?utm_source=GNW

Maity, A. (2022, January 21). Microarchitecture and Instruction Set Architecture. GeeksforGeeks. Retrieved July 12, 2022, from www.geeksforgeeks.org/microarchitecture-and-instruction-set-architecture/

Matheson, R. (2018, April 6). Photonic communication comes to computer chips. Phys.org. Retrieved September 2, 2021, from https://phys.org/news/2018-04-photonic-chips.html

Maxfield, M. (2014, June 23). ASIC, ASSP, SoC, FPGA – What's the Difference? EETimes. Retrieved July 28, 2021, from www.eetimes.com/asic-assp-soc-fpga-whats-the-difference/

McGregor, J. (2018, April 6). The Difference Between ARM, MIPS, x86, RISC-V And Others In Choosing A Processor Architecture. Forbes. Retrieved September 2, 2021, from www.forbes.com/sites/tiriasresearch/2018/04/05/what-you-need-to-know-about-processor-architectures/?sh=1ac78a504f57

McKinsey & Company. (2020, August 20). Semiconductor design and manu-facturing: Achieving leading-edge capabilities. McKinsey & Company. Retrieved September 2, 2021, from www.mckinsey.com/industries/advanced-electronics/our-insights/semiconductor-design-and-manufactur-ing-achieving-leading-edge-capabilities#:~:text=Designing%20 a%205%20nm%20chip,especially%20for%20leading%2Dedge%20 products.

Mehra, A. (2021). Market Leadership - FPGA Market. Retrieved January 16, 2022, from www.marketsandmarkets.com/ResearchInsight/fpga-market.asp

MEMS Journal. (2021). Retrieved September 1, 2021, from www.mems-journal.com/

Mims, C. (2020, September 19). Huang's Law Is the New Moore's Law, and Explains Why Nvidia Wants Arm. Retrieved September 2, 2021, from www.wsj.com/articles/huangs-law-is-the-new-moores-law-and-explains-why-nvidia-wants-arm-11600488001

Minzioni, P., Lacava, C., Tanabe, T., Dong, J., Hu, X., Csaba, G., Porod, W., Singh, G., Willner, A. E., Almaiman, A., Torres-Company, V., Schröder, J., Peacock, A. C., Strain, M. J., Parmigiani, F., Contestabile, G., Marpaung, D., Liu, Z., Bowers, J. E., ... Nunn, J. (2019, May 17). Iopscience. Journal of Optics. Retrieved September 2, 2021, from https://iopscience.iop.org/arti-cle/10.1088/2040-8986/ab0e66

Mitchell, G. (n.d.). How fast does electricity flow? sciencefocus.com. Retrieved September 2, 2021, from www.sciencefocus.com/science/how-fast-does-electricity-flow/

Mittal, A. (2020, August 2). What is Power Integrity and Power Distribution Network? Sierra Circuits. Retrieved July 28, 2021, from www.protoexpress.com/blog/power-integrity-pdn-and-decoupling-capacitors/

Moore, G. (1965). Cramming more components onto integrated circuits. Electronics, 38(8).

Mordor Intelligence. (2021). GLOBAL ELECTRONIC DESIGN AUTOMATION TOOLS (EDA) MARKET - GROWTH, TRENDS, COVID-19 IMPACT, AND FORECASTS. Retrieved January 17, 2022, from www.mordorintelligence.com/industry-reports/electronic-design-automation-eda-tools-market

Moyer, B. (2017, January 2). HBM vs. HMC. EEJournal. Retrieved July 28, 2021, from www.eejournal.com/article/20170102-hbm-hmc/

MPS. (n.d.). Analog Signals vs. Digital Signals. Monolithic Power Systems. Retrieved April 3, 2021, from www.monolithicpower.com/en/analog-vs-digital-signal

MPS. (n.d.). Analog Signals vs. Digital Signals. Monolithic Power. Retrieved July 27, 2021, from www.monolithicpower.com/en/analog-vs-digital-signal

MPS. (n.d.). Voltage Regulator Types and Working Principles. Monolithic Power. Retrieved July 28, 2021, from www.monolithicpower.com/en/voltage-regulator-types#:~:text=A%20voltage%20regulator%20is%20a,input%20voltage%20or%20load%20conditions.&text=While%20voltage%20regulators%20are%20most,DC%20power%20conversion%20as%20well.

MRSI. (n.d.). Die Bnding. MRSI Systems. Retrieved July 27, 2021, from https://mrsisystems.com/die-bonding/#:~:text=Die%20bonding%20is%20a%20manufacturing,die%20placement%20or%20die%20attach.&text=The%20die%20is%20placed%20into,placed%20into%20solder%20(eutectic).

Murata. (2010, December 15). Basic Facts about Inductors [Lesson 1] Overview of inductors - "How do inductors work?". Murata Manufacturing Articles. Retrieved March 29, 2021, from https://article.murata.com/en-us/article/basic-facts-about-inductors-lesson-1

Nair, R. (2015). Evolution of memory architecture. Proceedings of the IEEE, 103(8), 1331–1345. https://doi.org/10.1109/jproc.2015.2435018

NASA Hubble Site. (n.d.). The Electromagnetic Spectrum. HubbleSite.org. Retrieved July 28, 2021, from https://hubblesite.org/contents/articles/the-electromagnetic-spectrum

NASA. (2018, June 27). Introduction to Electromagnetic Spectrum. NASA. Retrieved September 1, 2021, from www.nasa.gov/directorates/heo/scan/spectrum/overview/index.html

Nave, R. (2000). Voltage. Retrieved September 2, 2021, from http://hyperphysics.phy-astr.gsu.edu/hbase/electric/elevol.html

Nenni, D., & McLellan, P. M. (2014). Fabless: The transformation of the semiconductor industry. SemiWiki.com Project.

New World Encyclopedia, C. (2014, April 17). Integrated circuit. Integrated circuit. Retrieved March 29, 2021, from www.newworldencyclopedia.org/entry/Integrated_circuit

Newhaven Display International. (n.d.). Serial vs Parallel Interface. Retrieved July 27, 2021, from www.newhavendisplay.com/app_notes/parallel-serial.pdf

Nobel Media. (2000, October 10). Prize Announcement. NobelPrize.org. Retrieved March 29, 2021, from www.nobelprize.org/prizes/physics/2000/popular-information/

Nobel Prize Outreach AB 2021. (n.d.). The Nobel Prize in Physics 1956. NobelPrize.org. Retrieved March 29, 2021, from www.nobelprize.org/prizes/physics/1956/summary/

Nussey, B. (2019, November 2). Understanding the basics of electricity by thinking of it as water. Freeing Energy. Retrieved September 2, 2021, from www.freeingenergy.com/understanding-the-basics-of-electricity-by-thinking-of-it-as-water/

NVIDIA. (2020). GPU-Accelerated Applications. GPU Applications Catalog. Retrieved July 27, 2021, from www.nvidia.com/content/dam/en-zz/Solutions/Data-Center/tesla-product-literature/gpu-applications-catalog.pdf

Patil, C. A. (2021, January 17). The FAB-LITE Semiconductor Fabrication Model. Retrieved September 2, 2021, from www.chetanpatil.in/the-fab-lite-semiconductor-fabrication-model/

Patterson, A. (2021, August 19). Samsung Considering 3 U.S. Fab Locations. EETimes. Retrieved December 23, 2021, from www.eetimes.com/samsung-considering-3-u-s-fab-locations).

PCMAG. (n.d.). Definition of bus. PCMAG. Retrieved July 28, 2021, from www.pcmag.com/encyclopedia/term/bus

PCMAG. (n.d.). Definition of GPU. PCMAG. Retrieved July 28, 2021, from www.pcmag.com/encyclopedia/term/gpu

Pedamkar, P. (n.d.). What is Assembly Language. EDUCBA. Retrieved July 12, 2022, from www.educba.com/what-is-assembly-language/

Photonics Leadership Group. (2020). Future horizons for photonics research 2030 and beyond. Retrieved July 27, 2021, from photonicsuk.org/wp-content/uploads/2020/09/Future-Horizons-for-Photonics-Research_PLG_2020_b.pdf

Pimentel, B. (2009, March 4). GlobalFoundries created from AMD spin-off. MarketWatch. Retrieved September 2, 2021, from www.marketwatch.com/story/globalfoundries-created-amd-spin-off-the

Platzer, M. D., Sargent, J. F., & Sutter, K. M. (2020). (rep.). Semiconductors: U.S. Industry, Global Competition, and Federal Policy. Congressional Research Service.

Platzer, M. D., Sargent, J. F., & Sutter, K. M., Semiconductors: U.S. Industry, Global Competition, and Federal Policy (2020). Washington, DC; Congressional Research Service.

Porter, J. (2021, May 19). Google wants to build a useful quantum computer by 2029. The Verge. Retrieved January 17, 2022, from www.theverge.com/2021/5/19/22443453/google-quantum-computer-2029-decade-commercial-useful-qubits-quantum-transistor

Precedence Research. (2021, November 23). Semiconductor production equipment market to hit USD 121.87 bn by 2030. GlobeNewswire News Room. Retrieved January 16, 2022, from www.globenewswire.com/news-release/2021/11/23/2340230/0/en/Semiconductor-Production-Equipment-Market-to-Hit-USD-121-87-Bn-by-2030.html

Printed-Circuit-Board Glossary Definition. Maxim Integrated - Analog, Linear, and Mixed-Signal Devices. (n.d.). Retrieved April 3, 2021, from www.maximintegrated.com/en/glossary/definitions.mvp/term/Printed-Circuit-Board/gpk/973#:~:text=A%20printed%20circuit%20board%2C%20or,a%20working%20circuit%20or%20assembly.

process technology. PCMAG. (n.d.). Retrieved July 27, 2021, from www.pcmag.com/encyclopedia/term/process-technology

PSD. (2013). Successful Semiconductor Fabless Conference. In Power Systems Design. Paris. Retrieved February 20, 2022, from www.powersystemsdesign.com/articles/power-electronics-and-the-fabless-business-model-will-be-explored-at-successful-semiconductor-fabless-2013-in-paris/8/4872.

Rai-Choudhury, P. (1997). Handbook of Microlithography, Micromachining, And Microfabrication. Volume 1: Microlithography (Vol. 1). SPIE.

Raza, M. (2018, June 29). OSI Model: The 7 Layers of Network Architecture. BMC Blogs. Retrieved January 17, 2022, from www.bmc.com/blogs/osi-model-7-layers/

Rice University. (2013). Circuits and Electricity. Retrieved September 2, 2021, from www.acaedu.net/cms/lib3/TX01001550/Centricity/Domain/389/5.6B%20Circuts%20and%20Electricity.pdf

Riordan, M. (1998, July 20). Junction transistors. Encyclopædia Britannica. Retrieved March 29, 2021, from www.britannica.com/technology/transistor/Junction-transistors

RTL (Register Transfer Level). Semiconductor Engineering. (2021, February 2). Retrieved April 3, 2021, from https://semiengineering.com/knowledge_centers/eda-design/definitions/register-transfer-level/

Rubin, S. M. (1993). Computer Aids for Vlsi Design. Addison-Wesley Publishing Company.

S&P Global. (2019). S&P Global Market Intelligence. Retrieved February 21, 2022, from www.spglobal.com/marketintelligence/en/

Saint, J. L., & Saint, C. (1999, July 26). Integrated circuit. Encyclopædia Britannica. Retrieved March 29, 2021, from www.britannica.com/technology/integrated-circuit

Samsung. (2020, February 20). Samsung Electronics Begins Mass Production at New EUV Manufacturing Line. Samsung Global Newsroom. Retrieved July 27,2021,fromhttps://news.samsung.com/global/samsung-electronics-begins-mass-production-at-new-euv-manufacturing-line

Samuel, M. K. (2018, January 5). EUV Lithography Finally Ready for Chip Manufacturing. IEEE Spectrum: Technology, Engineering, and Science News. Retrieved July 27, 2021, from https://spectrum.ieee.org/semiconductors/nanotechnology/euv-lithography-finally-ready-for-chip-manufacturing

Sand, N. J., & Aasvik, M. (2019, January 25). Physical Properties of a MOSFET. Norwegian Creations. Retrieved March 29, 2021, from www.norwegiancreations.com/2019/01/physical-properties-of-a-mosfet/

Sanghavi, A. (2010, May 21). What is formal verification? eetasia.com. Retrieved April 3, 2021, from www.scribd.com/document/46878179/Formal-Verification

Savage, N. (2020, September 4). Google's Quantum Computer Achieves Chemistry Milestone. Scientific American. Retrieved September 2, 2021, from www.scientificamerican.com/article/googles-quantum-computer-achieves-chemistry-milestone/

Schafer, R., & Buchalter, J. (2017). (rep.). Semiconductors: Technology and Market Primer 10.0. New York, NY: Oppenheimer Equity Research.

Science World. (n.d.). Current Electricity. Science World. Retrieved September 2, 2021, from www.scienceworld.ca/resource/current-electricity/

SCME (Southwest Center for Microsystems Education). (2017, May). History of MEMS. Retrieved September 1, 2021, from https://nanohub.org/resources/26535/download/App_Intro_PK10_PG.pdf

Semiconductor Industry Association. (2021). Retrieved March 29, 2021, from www.semiconductors.org/

Semiconductor Packaging Market by Type. Allied Market Research. (2021, June 21). Retrieved January 16, 2022, from www.alliedmarketresearch.com/semiconductor-packaging-market-A09496

Shamieh, C. (n.d.). The Power of Joule's Law in Electronics. dummies.com. Retrieved September 2, 2021, from www.dummies.com/programming/electronics/components/the-power-of-joules-law-in-electronics/

Shet, R. (2020, January 31). Memories in Digital Electronics – Classification and Characteristics. Technobyte. Retrieved July 28, 2021, from https://technobyte.org/memories-digital-electronics/

Shieber, J., & Coldewey, D. (2020, March 5). Rigetti Computing took a $71 million down round, because quantum computing is hard. TechCrunch. Retrieved September 2, 2021, from https://techcrunch.com/2020/03/05/rigetti-computing-took-a-71-million-down-round-because-quantum-computing-is-hard/

Shilov, A. (2021, October 7). Samsung to Mass Produce 2nm Chips in 2025. Tom's Hardware. Retrieved January 17, 2022, from www.tomshardware.com/news/samsung-foundry-to-produce-2nm-chips-in-2025

Shireen. (2019, June 20). What is an RF filter and Why is it so Important? Retrieved September 1, 2021, from www.shireeninc.com/what-is-an-rf-filter-and-why-is-it-so-important/

Shulaker, M. M., Hills, G., Patil, N., Wei, H., Chen, H.-Y., Wong, H.-S. P., & Mitra, S. (2013, September 25). Carbon nanotube computer. Nature News. Retrieved September 2, 2021, from www.nature.com/articles/nature12502

SIA (Semiconductor Industry Association). (2020, December 3). Global Semiconductor Sales Increase 6 Percent Year-to-Year in October; Annual Sales Projected to Increase 5.1 Percent in 2020. Semiconductor Industry Association. Retrieved September 2, 2021, from www.semiconductors.org/global-semiconductor-sales-increase-6-percent-year-to-year-in-october-annual-sales-projected-to-increase-5-1-percent-in-2020/

SIA Databook. (2020). 2020 Databook. semiconductors.org. Retrieved January 16, 2022, from www.semiconductors.org/data-resources/market-data/sia-databook/

SIA Databook. (2021). Semiconductor Industry Association (SIA) 2020 Databook. semiconductors.org. Retrieved September 2, 2021, from www.semiconductors.org/data-resources/market-data/sia-databook/

SIA End Use Survey. (2021). Semiconductor Industry Association (SIA) 2019 End Use Survey. semiconductors.org. Retrieved September 2, 2021, from www.semiconductors.org/data-resources/market-data/end-use-survey/

SIA Whitepaper. (2021, July). TAKING STOCK OF CHINA'S SEMICONDUCTOR INDUSTRY. semiconductors.org. Retrieved September 2, 2021, from www.semiconductors.org/wp-content/uploads/2021/07/Taking-Stock-of-China%E2%80%99s-Semiconductor-Industry_final.pdf

SIA WSTS (Semiconductor Industry Association and World Semiconductor Trade Statistics). (2021). Semiconductor Industry - Tables and Figures. Retrieved January 16, 2022.

SIA. (2021, May 19). SIA Factbook. Retrieved January 16, 2022, from www.semiconductors.org/wp-content/uploads/2021/05/2021-SIA-Fact-book-May-19-FINAL.pdf

Singer, P. (2020, February 8). Scaling the BEOL: A Toolbox Filled with New Processes, Boosters and Conductors. Semiconductor Digest. Retrieved July 27,2021,fromwww.semiconductor-digest.com/scaling-the-beol-a-toolbox-filled-with-new-processes-boosters-and-conductors/

STMicroelectronics. (2000). Introduction to Semiconductor Technology AN900 Application Note. st.com. Retrieved July 27, 2021, from www.st.com/resource/en/application_note/cd00003986-introduction-to-semi-conductor-technology-stmicroelectronics.pdf

systemverilog.io. (n.d.). Retrieved April 3, 2021, from www.systemverilog.io/gentle-introduction-to-formal-verification

Teach Computer Science. (2021, December 21). RISC and CISC Processors. Teach Computer Science. Retrieved July 12, 2022, from teachcomputer-science.com/risc-and-cisc-processors/

Teja, R. (2021, April 2). What is a Sensor? Different Types of Sensors and their Applications. Electronics Hub. Retrieved July 28, 2021, from www.elec-tronicshub.org/different-types-sensors/

Teja, R. (2021, April 28). Classification and Different Types of Transistors. Electronics Hub. Retrieved January 17, 2022, from www.electronicshub.org/transistors-classification-and-types/

Templeton, G. C. (2015, June 22). What is silicon, and why are computer chips made from it? ExtremeTech. Retrieved March 29, 2021, from www.extremetech.com/extreme/208501-what-is-silicon-and-why-are-computer-chips-made-from-it

Texas Instruments. (2018). POWER DISTRIBUTION FOR SOC AND FPGA APPLICATIONS. training.ti.com. Retrieved July 27, 2021, from https://training.ti.com/sites/default/files/docs/pmicvsdisc.pdf

Thornton, S. (2016, December 29). The Internal Processor Bus: data, address, and control bus. Microcontroller Tips. Retrieved July 28, 2021, from www.microcontrollertips.com/internal-processor-bus-data-address-control-bus-faq/

Thornton, S. (2018, January 9). Risc vs. cisc architectures: Which one is better? Microcontroller Tips. Retrieved September 2, 2021, from www.micro-controllertips.com/risc-vs-cisc-architectures-one-better/

#:~:text=RISC%2Dbased%20machines%20execute%20one,than%20one%20
cycle%20to%20execute.&text=The%20CISC%20architecture%20can%20
execute,at%20once%2C%20directly%20upon%20memory.

TIRIAS Research. (n.d.). High-Tech Experts - Research and Advisory. TIRIAS Research. Retrieved February 21, 2022, from www.tiriasresearch.com/

Trimberger, S. M. (2015). Three ages of FPGAs: A retrospective on the first thirty years of FPGA Technology. Proceedings of the IEEE, 103(3), 318–331. https://doi.org/10.1109/jproc.2015.2392104

Tsai, M.-Y., Hsu, C. H. J., & Wang, C. T. O. (2004). Investigation of thermome-chanical behaviors of flip chip bga packages during manufacturing process and thermal cycling. IEEE Transactions on Components and Packaging Technologies, 27(3), 568–576. https://doi.org/10.1109/tcapt.2004.831817

Tucker, J. H. (1994). Hardware Description Languages. The Role of Computers in Research and Development at Langley Research Center. https://doi.org/19950010062

Turley, J. L. (2002). The Essential Guide to Semiconductors. Pearson.

Tyson, J. (n.d.). How Computer Memory Works. HowStuffWorks. Retrieved July 28, 2021, from https://computer.howstuffworks.com/computer-memory4.htm

Tyson, M. (2021, August 19). Nvidia announces record quarterly revenue of $6.5 billion. HEXUS.net. Retrieved September 2, 2021, from https://m.hexus.net/business/news/general-business/148259-nvidia-announces-record-quarterly-revenue-65-billion/

U.S. Department of Energy. (n.d.). How Lithium-ion Batteries Work. Energy.gov. Retrieved April 24, 2022, from www.energy.gov/science/doe-explainsbatteries#:~:text=When%20the%20electrons%20move%20from,circuit%20and%20discharge%20the%20battery.

Vakil, B., & Linton, T. (2021, February 26). Why We're in the Midst of a Global Semiconductor Shortage. Harvard Business Review. Retrieved September 2, 2021,fromhttps://hbr.org/2021/02/why-were-in-the-midst-of-a-global-semiconductor-shortage

Valentine, C. (2019, October 25). Photolithography Basics. Inseto UK. Retrieved July 27, 2021, from www.inseto.co.uk/lithography-basics/

Varas, A., Varadarajan, R., Goodrich, J., & Yinug, F. (2020, September). Government Incentives and US Competitiveness in Semiconductor Manufacturing. semiconductors.org. Retrieved January 16, 2022, from www.semiconductors.org/wp-content/uploads/2020/09/Government-Incentives-and-US-Competitiveness-in-Semiconductor-Manufacturing-Sep-2020.pdf

Varas, A., Varadarajan, R., Goodrich, J., & Yinug, F. (2021, April). Strengthening the Global Semiconductor Supply Chain in an Uncertain Era. Retrieved September 2, 2021, from www.semiconductors.org/wp-content/uploads/2021/05/BCG-x-STA-Strengthening-the-Global-Semiconductor-Value-Chain-April-2021_1.pdf

Venture Outsource. (n.d.). Electronic product design automation software drives hardware product launch and EDA JOBS. VentureOutsource.com. Retrieved September 2, 2021, from www.ventureoutsource.com/contract-manufacturing/electronic-product-design-automation-software-controlling-hardware-product-launch/

VLSI Guide. (2018, July). Clock Tree Synthesis (CTS). vlsiguide.com. Retrieved April 3, 2021, from www.vlsiguide.com/2018/07/clock-tree-synthesis-cts.html

Voltage and Current. All About Circuits. (n.d.). Retrieved September 1, 2021, from www.allaboutcircuits.com/textbook/direct-current/chpt-1/voltage-current/

Vora, L. J. (2015). Evolution of Mobile Generation Technology: 1G to 5G and Review of Upcoming Wireless Technology 5G. International Journal of Modern Trends in Engineering and Research (IJMTER), 2(10), 281–290. Retrieved September 1, 2021, from www.ijmter.com/papers/volume-2/issue-10/evolution-of-mobile-generation-technology-1g-to-5g-and-review-of-5g.pdf.

Weisman, C. J. (2003). The Essential Guide to Rf and Wireless. Publishing House of Electronics Industry.

Whalen, J. (2021, June 14). Countries lavish subsidies and perks on semiconductor manufacturers as a global chip war heats up. The Washington Post. Retrieved September 2, 2021, from www.washingtonpost.com/technology/2021/06/14/global-subsidies-semiconductors-shortage/

Wile, B., Goss, J. C., & Roesner, W. (2005). Comprehensive functional verification the complete industry cycle. Elsevier/Morgan Kaufmann.

Williams, M. (2016, April 8). What Is The Electron Cloud Model? Universe Today. Retrieved September 2, 2021, from www.universetoday.com/38282/electron-cloud-model/

Wilson, T. V., & Johnson, R. (2005, July 20). How Motherboards Work. HowStuffWorks. Retrieved July 28, 2021, from https://computer.howstuffworks.com/motherboard4.htm

Wright, G. (2021, March 4). What is a base station? WhatIs.com. Retrieved September 1, 2021, from https://whatis.techtarget.com/definition/base-station

WSTS (World Semiconductor Trade Statistics). (2017, December 16). WSTS Product Classification 2018. Semiconductors.org. Retrieved September 1, 2021, from www.semiconductors.org/wp-content/uploads/2018/07/Product_Classification_2018.pdf

Xilinx. (n.d.). Emulation & Prototyping. Xilinx. Retrieved July 28, 2021, from www.xilinx.com/applications/emulation-prototyping.html

Yahoo! Finance. (2021, September 2). Synopsys, Inc. (SNPS) stock Price, NEWS, quote & history. Retrieved September 2, 2021, from https://finance.yahoo.com/quote/SNPS/

Ye, P. D., Ernst, T., & Khare, M. V. (2019, July 30). THE NANOSHEET TRANSISTOR IS THE NEXT (AND MAYBE LAST) STEP IN MOORE'S LAW. IEEE Spectrum. Retrieved September 2, 2021, from https://spectrum.ieee.org/semiconductors/devices/the-nanosheet-transistor-is-the-next-and-maybe-last-step-in-moores-law

Yellin, B. (2019). SAVING THE FUTURE OF MOORE'S LAW. Dell Technologies Proven Professional Knowledge Sharing.

Zhao, L. (2017, December 18). All About Interconnects. Semiconductor Engineering. Retrieved July 27, 2021, from https://semiengineering.com/all-about-interconnects/

Sources – Illustrations

A13ean. (2012). Autostep i-Line Stepper. photograph, Wikimedia Commons. Retrieved April 3, 2021, from https://commons.wikimedia.org/wiki/File:Autostep_i-line_stepper.jpg.

Aldrich, S. (2018). Physical Vapor Deposition (Pvd). Wikimedia Commons. Retrieved April 3, 2021, from https://commons.wikimedia.org/wiki/File:Physical_Vapor_Deposition_(PVD).jpg.

Alistair1978. (2020). 'Twin and Earth' electrical cable. photograph, Wikimedia Commons. Retrieved February 20, 2022, from https://commons.wikimedia.org/wiki/File:%27Twin_and_Earth%27_electrical_cable._BS_6004,_6mm%C2%B2.jpg.

AMD Newsroom. (2020, October 27). AMD to Acquire Xilinx, Creating the Industry's High Performance Computing Leader. Retrieved April 25, 2022, from www.amd.com/en/press-releases/2020-10-27-amd-to-acquire-xilinx-creating-the-industry-s-high-performance-computing

Analog Devices Newsroom. (2020, July 13). Analog Devices Announces Combination with Maxim Integrated, Strengthening Analog Semiconductor Leadership. Retrieved April 24, 2022, from www.analog.com/en/about-adi/news-room/press-releases/2020/7-13-2020-analog-devices-announces-combination-with-maxim-integrated.html

Argonne National Laboratory. (2008). Argonne's Tribology Lab Plasma-Assisted Chemical-Vapor Deposition. flickr. photograph. Retrieved April 2, 2021, from www.flickr.com/photos/35734278@N05/3469453524.

Ashri, S. (2014). Parallel and Serial Transmission. Wikibooks. Retrieved April 3, 2021, from https://commons.wikimedia.org/wiki/File:Parallel_and_Serial_Transmission.gif.

Bautista, D. (2015). Suny College of Nanoscale Science and Engineering's Michael Liehr, left, and Ibm's Bala Haranand look at wafer comprised of 7nm chips. photograph, Albany, NY; IBM. Retrieved April 3, 2021, from http://www-03.ibm.com/press/us/en/photo/47302.wss.

Bender, R., & Dummett, B. (2019, June 3). German Chip Maker Infineon Buys U.S. Rival in $9.4 Billion Deal. Retrieved April 24, 2022, from www.wsj.com/articles/infineon-to-buy-cypress-semiconductor-in-multibillion-dollar-deal-11559540811

Broadcom Inc. (2013, December 16). Avago Technologies to Acquire LSI Corporation for $6.6 Billion in Cash. GlobeNewswire News Room. Retrieved April 24, 2022, from www.globenewswire.com/news-release/2013/12/16/597048/10061554/en/Avago-Technologies-to-Acquire-LSI-Corporation-for-6-6-Billion-in-Cash.html

Broadcom Inc. (2015, May 28). Avago Technologies to Acquire Broadcom for $37 Billion. GlobeNewswire News Room. Retrieved April 24, 2022, from www.globenewswire.com/news-release/2015/05/28/739835/10136316/en/Avago-Technologies-to-Acquire-Broadcom-for-37-Billion.html

Brodkin, J. (2014, October 20). Struggling IBM pays $1.5 billion to dump its chipmaking business. Ars Technica. Retrieved April 24, 2022, from https://arstechnica.com/information-technology/2014/10/struggling-ibm-pays-1-5-billion-to-dump-its-chipmaking-business/

Business Wire. (2014, August 20). Infineon Technologies AG to Acquire International Rectifier Corporation for US-Dollar 40 per share, approximately US-Dollar 3 billion in cash. Retrieved April 24, 2022, from www.business-wire.com/news/home/20140820005867/en/Infineon-Technologies-AG-to-Acquire-International-Rectifier-Corporation-for-US-Dollar-40-per-share-approximately-US-Dollar-3-billion-in-cash

Business Wire. (2019, March 27). ON Semiconductor to Acquire Quantenna Communications. Retrieved April 24, 2022, from www.businesswire.com/news/home/20190327005791/en/ON-Semiconductor-to-Acquire-Quantenna-Communications

Clark, D. (2016, July 26). Analog Devices to Acquire Linear Technology for $14.8 Billion. Retrieved April 24, 2022, from www.wsj.com/articles/analog-devices-to-acquire-linear-technology-for-14-8-billion-1469563887

CNBC. (2015, December 7). NXP closes deal to buy Freescale and create top auto chipmaker. CNBC. Retrieved April 24, 2022, from www.cnbc.com/2015/12/07/nxp-closes-deal-to-buy-freescale-and-create-top-auto-chipmaker.html

Currier, N., & Ives, J. M. (2009, November 24). Franklin's Experiment, June 1752 [Benjamin Franklin flies kite during thunderstorm]. History.com. Retrieved February 20, 2022, from www.history.com/this-day-in-history/franklin-flies-kite-during-thunderstorm.

Davis, C. (2019). Google Data Center. Wikimedia Commons. photograph, Council Bluffs; flickr. Retrieved May 11, 2022, from https://commons.wikimedia.org/wiki/File:Google_Data_Center,_Council_Bluffs_Iowa_(49062863796).jpg.

Design & Reuse. (2016, September 13). Renesas to Acquire Intersil to Create the World's Leading Embedded Solution Provider. Retrieved April 24, 2022, from www.design-reuse.com/news/40504/renesas-intersil-acquisition.html

Design & Reuse. (2021, September 29). Chip M&A Deals Reach $22 Billion in First Eight Months of 2021. Retrieved April 24, 2022, from www.design-reuse.com/news/50674/2021-semiconductor-acquisition-agreements.html

Enricoros. (2007). SiliconCroda. Wikimedia Commons. Wikimedia Commons. Retrieved April 2, 2021, from https://commons.wikimedia.org/wiki/File:SiliconCroda.jpg.

EPS News. (2019, September 20). Semiconductor M&A Accelerates in 2019. Retrieved April 24, 2022, from https://epsnews.com/2019/09/20/semiconductor-ma-accelerates-in-2019/

Etherington, D. (2016, October 27). Qualcomm to acquire NXP Semiconductor for $47 billion. TechCrunch. Retrieved April 24, 2022, from https://techcrunch.com/2016/10/27/qualcomm-to-acquire-nxp-semiconductor-for-47-billion/

Gibbs, M., & Uberpenguin. (2006). Interconnects Under the Microscope. Wikimedia Commons. Retrieved April 3, 2021, from https://commons.wikimedia.org/wiki/File:80486DX2_200x.png.

Hertz, J. (2021, September 11). The Swiftly Changing Landscape of Semiconductor Companies: 2021 Acquisitions Update. All About Circuits. RetrievedApril24,2022,fromwww.allaboutcircuits.com/news/the-swiftly-changing-landscape-of-semiconductor-companies-2021-acquisitions-update/

Iam, M. (2017). Photolithography. Wikimedia Commons. Retrieved April 3, 2021, from https://commons.wikimedia.org/wiki/File:Photolithography.tif.

IBM Research. (2019). Ibm Quantum Computer. flickr. photograph. Retrieved April 3, 2021, from www.flickr.com/photos/ibm_research_zurich/50252942522/in/photolist-2jyFt2u-WAMVUZ-UwMT2P-xzowft-BJvjFa-25UdWHB-UTiVVw-Wga1Ro-WRucfA-2hbTfxm-2iwebnp-qLD1Nn-XurtEh-qA8nzH-2iGGkKs-U71Lj3-P2xPB7-241ciS4-GeeXn-VbbAYh-3762-232N7FT-26tLwDy-2gnoFkA-WGMXyd-ScbQFo-4f5LeC-2j5ZdY7-BQdkR9-WfbJ8N-frkgp-T6BLkS-QAoqhf-VuCZLF-2iVsyuN-GxAA54-79HDkv-pmK1t2-oDC7LA-2kw1A1c-dglNXi-24Ax4dj-2hEUhiK-23qF8wx-2hbT82V-2krQGy5-Eqbkev-fyDfcH-GxVKi8-2kupFSJ/.

IBM. (n.d.). Retrieved January 16, 2022, from ibm.com

IC Insights. (2021). The McClean Report 2021. Retrieved April 24, 2022, from www.icinsights.com/services/mcclean-report/

Ikeda, M. (2007). Rca '808' Power Vacuum Tube. Wikimedia Commons. Retrieved April 2, 2021, from https://commons.wikimedia.org/wiki/File:RCA_%E2%80%99808%E2%80%99_Power_Vacuum_Tube.jpg.

Intel Newsroom. (2016, September 22). Intel Acquisition of Altera. Intel Newsroom. Retrieved April 24, 2022, from https://newsroom.intel.com/press-kits/intel-acquisition-of-altera/#gs.xw7164

IntelFreePress. (2013). Mobile Device Sensors. flickr. Retrieved April 3, 2021, from www.flickr.com/photos/intelfreepress/7791649188/sizes/o/in/photostream/.

IQM Quantum Computers. (2020, August 21). IQM Quantum Computer in Espoo Finland. Wikimedia Commons. Retrieved January 16, 2022, from https://commons.wikimedia.org/wiki/File:IQM_Quantum_Computer_Espoo_Finland.jpg

Jacinsoncables. (2007). Core Round Jainson Cable. photograph, Wikimedia Commons. Retrieved February 20, 2022, from https://commons.wikimedia.org/wiki/File:3_Core_Round_Jainson_Cable.jpg.

James, L. (2021, February 9). Renesas Acquires Dialog Semiconductor in $6 Billion Deal. All About Circuits. Retrieved April 24, 2022, from www.all-aboutcircuits.com/news/renesas-acquires-dialog-semiconductor-in-6-billion-deal/

Kharpal, A. (2016, July 18). Japan's Softbank to buy chip-design powerhouse arm for $32 billion. CNBC. Retrieved April 24, 2022, from www.cnbc.com/2016/07/17/softbank-poised-to-take-uks-arm-for-234-billion.html

Kumar, V. (2022). Apple's Mesa Data Center. rankred.com. photograph, RankRed. Retrieved February 20, 2022, from www.rankred.com/largest-data-centers-in-the-world/.

Macera, F. (1998). Packaged Eniac-on-a-Chip. www.seas.upenn.edu. photograph, Philadelphia; Trustees University of Pennsylvania. Retrieved May 11, 2022, from www.seas.upenn.edu/~jan/pictures/eniacpictures/EniacChipPackaged.jpg.

Manners, D. (2015, January 5). RFMD and Triquint Complete Merger. Electronics Weekly. Retrieved April 24, 2022, from www.electronicsweekly.com/news/business/finance/rfmd-triquint-complete-merger-2015-01/

Marvell Newsroom. (2020, October 29). Marvell to Acquire Inphi - Accelerating Growth and Leadership in Cloud and 5G Infrastructure. Retrieved April 24, 2022, from www.marvell.com/company/newsroom/marvell-to-acquire-inphi-accelerating-growth-leadership-cloud-5g-infrastructure.html

Mineralogy Museum. (2017). Silicon Wafers. Wikimedia Commons. photograph, Munich. Retrieved April 2, 2021, from https://commons.wikimedia.org/wiki/File:Silicon_wafers.jpg.

NASA. (2010). Electromagnetic Spectrum. NASA Science. Retrieved April 3, 2021, from https://science.nasa.gov/ems/.

NNI. (n.d.). Size of the Nanoscale. National Nanotechnology Initiative. Retrieved July 27, 2022, from www.nano.gov/nanotech-101/what/nano-size

Nowicki, W. (2019). Computer System Bus. Wikimedia Commons. Retrieved April 3, 2021, from https://commons.wikimedia.org/wiki/File:Computer_system_bus.svg.

NVIDIA Newsroom. (2020, September 13). NVIDIA to Acquire Arm for $40 Billion, Creating World's Premier Computing Company for the Age of AI. Retrieved April 24, 2022, from https://nvidianews.nvidia.com/news/nvidia-to-acquire-arm-for-40-billion-creating-worlds-premier-computing-company-for-the-age-of-ai

NVIDIA Newsroom. (2019, March 19). NVIDIA to Acquire Mellanox for $6.9 Billion. Retrieved April 24, 2022, from https://nvidianews.nvidia.com/news/nvidia-to-acquire-mellanox-for-6-9-billion

Oyster, F. T. (2014). Chipset Schematic. Wikimedia Commons. Retrieved April 3, 2021, from https://commons.wikimedia.org/wiki/File:Chipset_schematic.svg.

Palladino, V. (2017, November 20). Marvell technology to buy Chipmaker Cavium for about $6 billion. Retrieved April 24, 2022, from https://arstechnica.com/information-technology/2017/11/marvell-technology-strikes-deal-to-buy-chipmaker-cavium-for-6-billion/

Paumier, G. (2007). Molecular-beam epitaxy system at Laas. gauillaume-paumier. photograph, Toulouse, France. Retrieved April 3, 2021, from https://guillaumepaumier.com/, CC-BY.

Peellden. (2011). Semiconductor Photomask. photograph, Wikimedia Commons. Retrieved April 3, 2021, from https://commons.wikimedia.org/wiki/File:Semiconductor_photomask.jpg.

Picker, L. (2016, January 20). Microchip Technology to Buy Atmel for Nearly $3.6 Billion. The New York Times. Retrieved April 24, 2022, from www.nytimes.com/2016/01/20/business/dealbook/microchip-technology-to-buy-atmel-for-nearly-3-6-billion.html

Potrowl, P. (2012). Clean Room. Wikimedia Commons. photograph, Villeneuve-d'Ascq, France. Retrieved April 3, 2021, from https://commons.wikimedia.org/wiki/File:Villeneuve-d%27Ascq_-_IEMN_clean_room_-_6.jpg.

Qorvo, Inc. (2014, February 24). RFMD and TriQuint to Combine, Creating a New Leader in RF Solutions. GlobeNewswire News Room. Retrieved April 24, 2022, from www.globenewswire.com/news-release/2014/02/24/612604/10069612/en/RFMD-and-TriQuint-to-Combine-Creating-a-New-Leader-in-RF-Solutions.html

Qualcomm Newsroom. (2021, January 13). Qualcomm to Acquire NUVIA. Retrieved April 24, 2022, from www.qualcomm.com/news/releases/2021/01/13/qualcomm-acquire-nuvia

Rao, L. (2011, April 4). Texas Instruments Acquires National Semiconductor for $6.5 Billion in Cash. TechCrunch. Retrieved April 24, 2022, from https://techcrunch.com/2011/04/04/texas-instruments-acquires-manufacturer-national-semiconductor-for-6-5-billion-in-cash/#:~:text=Texas%20Instruments%20has%20signed%20an,in%20six%20to%20nine%20months

Reinhold, A. (2020). Transistor Package and Schematic. Wikimedia Commons. Retrieved April 2, 2021, from https://commons.wikimedia.org/wiki/ File:Transistor_pakage.png.

Renesas. (2018, September 11). Renesas to Acquire Integrated Device Technology, to Enhance Global Leadership in Embedded Solutions. Renesas. Retrieved April 24, 2022, from www.renesas.com/us/en/about/press-room/renesas-acquire-integrated-device-technology-enhance-global-leadership-embedded-solutions

Ringle, H. (2016, September 19). ON Semiconductor completes its $2.4 billion acquisition of Fairchild. Bizjournals.com. Retrieved April 24, 2022, from www.bizjournals.com/phoenix/news/2016/09/19/on-semiconductor-completes-its-2-4-billion.html#:~:text=announced%20its%20 %242.4%20billion%20cash,10%20non%2Dmemory%20semiconductor%20 company.

Roser, M., & Ritchie, H. (2020). Moore's Law Transistor Count 1970-2020. Wikimedia Commons. Retrieved August 14, 2022, from https://commons. wikimedia.org/wiki/File:Moore%27s_Law_Transistor_ Count_1970-2020.png.

Sandia National Laboratories. (n.d.). MEMS Video & Image Gallery. Microsystems Engineering, Science and Applications (MESA). Retrieved August 14, 2022, from www.sandia.gov/mesa/mems-video-image-gallery/

Scoble, R. (2020). Microsoft Bing Maps' datacenter. photograph, Wikimedia Commons. Retrieved February 20, 2022, from https://commons.wikime-dia.org/wiki/File:Microsoft_Bing_Maps%27_datacenter_-_ Flickr_-_Robert_Scoble.jpg.

Semiconductor Digest. (2015). Western Digital announces acquisition of SanDisk. Semiconductor Digest. Retrieved April 24, 2022, from https:// sst.semiconductor-digest.com/2015/10/western-digital -announces-acquisition-of-sandisk/

Shigeru23. (2011). Wafer Die's Yield Model (10-20-40mm). Wikimedia Commons. Retrieved April 3, 2021, from https://commons.wikimedia. org/wiki/File:Wafer_die%27s_yield_model_(10-20-40mm).PNG.

Silicon Valley Business Journal. (2014, December 14). Cypress Semiconductor buys Spansion for about $1.6 billion. Bizjournals.com. Retrieved April 24, 2022, from www.bizjournals.com/sanjose/news/2014/12/01/cypress-semiconductor-buys-spansion-for-about-1-6.html

Silicon Wafer. (2010). Wikimedia Commons. photograph. Retrieved April 2, 2021, from https://commons.wikimedia.org/wiki/File:Silicon_ wafer.jpg.

SK hynix Newsroom. (2020, October 20). SK hynix to Acquire Intel NAND Memory Business. Retrieved April 24, 2022, from https://news.skhynix.com/sk-hynix-to-acquire-intel-nand-memory-business/

Stahlkocher. (2004). Silicon Ingot. Wikimedia Commons. photograph. Retrieved April 2, 2021, from https://commons.wikimedia.org/wiki/File:Monokristalines_Silizium_f%C3%BCr_die_Waferherstellung.jpg.

STAMPRUS. (1959). Stamp 1959 Cpa 2326 Soviet Union. Catalogue of postage stamps of Russia and the USSR. photograph. Retrieved April 2, 2021, from https://commons.wikimedia.org/wiki/File:The_Soviet_Union_1959_CPA_2326_stamp_(Przewalski%27s_horse)_Counter_sheet_(pane)_cancelled.jpg.

TronicsZone. (2017). Pcb Design. photograph. Retrieved April 2, 2021, from https://commons.wikimedia.org/wiki/File:PCB_design.jpg.

Twisp. (2008). Flip Chip. Wikimedia Commons. Retrieved April 3, 2021, from https://commons.wikimedia.org/wiki/File:Flip_chip_flipped.svg.

U.S. Army. (1947). Eniac. Historical Monograph: Electronic Computers Within the Ordnance Corps. photograph, Philadelphia. Retrieved April 2, 2021, from https://commons.wikimedia.org/wiki/File:Eniac.jpg.

Usher, O. (2013). Cleanroom - Photolithography Lab. flickr. photograph, London, England; UCL Mathematical & Physical Sciences. Retrieved April 3, 2021, from www.flickr.com/photos/uclmaps/9148360385/.

Ziegler, C. (2011, January 5). Qualcomm snaps up Atheros for $3.1 billion. Engadget. Retrieved April 24, 2022, from www.engadget.com/2011-01-05-qualcomm-snaps-up-atheros-for-3-1-billion.html

Glossary

Term	Definition
2.5D Packaging	A packaging structure where die are connected to a shared substrate, called an interposer, which in turn is connected to a PCB.
2D Transistors	Transistors with a flat gate structure that borders the channel on only one side. Examples include BJT and MOSFET transistors.
3D Packaging	A packaging structure where die are stacked directly on top of one another.
3D Transistors	Transistors with raised gate structures that border the channel on three or four sides. Examples include FinFET and GAA Transistors.
Actuator	Device that converts electrical signal back into real world signals. Active actuators require external power sources, while passive actuators require no power to function.
Address Bus	A bus interface that helps a processor find specific data.
Alternating Current (AC)	Electric current that periodically reverses its direction. It is best suited for transporting power over great distances and is often used in utility grids.
Amperes (amp or A)	The base unit for electric current. It measures how many electrons flow past a given point in a single second.
Amplifier	An electronic component that increases signal strength.
Amplitude	The height of an analog "wave" signal.

(continued)

© Corey Richard 2023
C. Richard, *Understanding Semiconductors*, Maker Innovations Series,
https://doi.org/10.1007/978-1-4842-8847-4

Term	Definition
Analog Electronics	A field of electronics devoted to studying analog signals and the components that control and process them.
Analog Signals	Electromagnetic "wave" energy that can transmit information over empty space. Commonly classified by wavelength and frequency.
Analog-to-Digital (ADC)	A data converter that converts information encoded in analog signals into digital format.
AND Gate	A logic gate that requires two input conditions to be met before letting a signal pass through.
Anode	A negatively charged electrode comprising a material "with excess" electrons. It forms the negative side of a battery and donates electrons that flow through the circuit to a cathode on the other side.
Antenna	An electronic component that receives or transmits signals to other systems. Many antennas can act as both, alternating their function between transmitter and receiver.
Application Layer	Layer 7 in the OSI Model. It contains the user interface and describes what end users of a network actually see.
Application Specific Integrated Circuit (ASIC)	A type of logic device that is designed and optimized for a specific use in a single system.
Application Specific Standard Part (ASSP)	A type of logic device that is designed and integrated into a system the same way Application Specific Integrated Circuits (ASICs) are. The term "standard parts" here just means that the same part can be used in many different products.
Application Specific Standard Products (ASSPs)	Analog ICs designed for a specific application, similar to the Logic segment of the SIA Framework.
Arithmetic Logic Unit (ALU)	Part of a central processor that performs all the numerical and logic-based operations necessary to run software programs the processor was intended to deliver.
ARM Architecture	A popular licensed ISA.
Artificial Intelligence	A broad field dedicated to building computer systems that can perform "intelligent" tasks normally reserved for humans. Machine Learning and Deep Learning are types of Artificial Intelligence.
Assembly	The multi-step process for enclosing and sealing a completed integrated circuit or semiconductor device inside of an IC package.
Assembly Language	Low-level programming language used to directly communicate with a computer's hardware.

(continued)

Term	Definition
Atomic Layer Deposition (ALD)	A chemical deposition technique that is used to deposit thin films on the surface of silicon wafers during the semiconductor manufacturing process. A type of Chemical Vapor Deposition (CVD).
Backend Application Framework	Programming logic used by a software program to process data stored in a database for some useful purpose or end goal. The software back-end will usually connect with the software front-end to deliver useful output to the end user or users.
Back-End Design	A step in the semiconductor design flow after front-end design where a detailed list of instructions called a netlist is converted into a physical layout, which is tested and validated before sending to a semiconductor fab for manufacturing. Commonly known as Physical Design.
Back-End Manufacturing	The remaining stages in the semiconductor manufacturing process after wafer fabrication has been completed, including wafer bumping, wafer dicing, die bonding, external interconnect formation, encapsulation, sealing, and final testing.
Back-end of the Line (BEOL)	A part of the front-end manufacturing process where local and global interconnects form logic gates and connect wider system components. Also known as the "Post-Metal" part of the manufacturing process, since these interconnects are usually made from metals like copper or aluminum.
Back-End Validation	A stage in the back-end design process used to verify that a chip complies with all the rules of the chosen factory. Also known as Physical Verification or Back-End Verification.
Ball Grid Array (BGA)	A type of surface mount packaging technology that uses a grid of solder balls to connect a die-package assembly to a PCB.
Band Pass Filter	A filter that only lets signals in between two frequencies.
Band Reject Filter	A filter that only lets signals in outside of a range of frequencies.
Base	The middle part of a bipolar junction transistor that sits between the emitter and collector, similar to the gate in a MOSFET transistor.
Base Station	A wireless relay point that extends a service network to a specific area or coverage cell.

(continued)

Term	Definition
Battery	A power storage device that converts chemical energy stored in cells into electrical energy using electrochemical reactions.
Binary Computer Language	The pattern of "on" (1) and "off" (0) transistors that software developers use to communicate with computers.
Bipolar Junction Transistor (BJT)	A type of transistor that uses current to control the base. It has three parts – a base, emitter, and collector (similar to the source, gate, and drain in MOSFET transistors).
Bipolar Manufacturing	Specialized manufacturing technology used to fabricate specific types of integrated circuits and transistors.
Bit	The smallest unit of data that a computer can process. It can hold one of two values – on (1) or off (0) – and forms the basis of binary computer language.
Bit Rate	The number of bits that are processed over a given number of time. Often expressed in bits per second.
Block Diagram	A diagram that uses schematics and shapes to display the relationships between related objects in complex systems and processes. Commonly used in electrical engineering to depict circuits and other devices.
Boolean Logic	Mathematical logic that labels variables as either true or false. Common Boolean operators include "OR," "AND," and "NOT."
Booting Instructions	Specific compute instructions that tell a computer to turn on.
Burning (to memory)	The process by which programmable read only memory (PROM) is programmed with a set of data.
Bus-bar	The bundle of wires used to connect a processor with the various parts of an electronic system. The term was primarily used in the early days of personal computing.
Bus Interface	The physical wires through which data travels between the different components of a system or PCB.
Cache Memory	A type of RAM positioned most closely to the CPU. Cache has the greatest speed requirement of any memory type and typically stores instructions waiting to be executed. Also known as CPU Memory.
Capacitor	A device used to regulate voltage and store electrical energy.
Carbon Nanotubes	Structures made of rolled up graphene sheets that may serve as alternatives to silicon transistors in the not-so-distant future.
Carrier Signal	Analog "wave" signal used to encode and transport digital information wirelessly over significant distances.

(continued)

Term	Definition
Cathode	A positively charged electrode comprising a material "in need" of electrons. It forms the positive side of a battery and accepts electrons flowing through the circuit from an anode on the other side.
Central Processing Unit (CPU)	A type of logic device and microprocessor that serves as the main processing center for most sophisticated computing systems.
Channel	The opening across a transistor gate through which current can flow.
Chemical Energy	Energy stored in the bonds of chemical compounds that is released while undergoing a chemical reaction. Batteries convert stored chemical energy into electrical energy.
Chemical-Mechanical Planarization (CMP)	A type of removal process that uses a combination of chemical and mechanical force to smooth out the surface of a wafer.
Chemical Vapor Deposition (CVD)	A category of deposition techniques used for depositing thin films on the surface of silicon wafers during the semiconductor manufacturing process. CVD takes place at temperatures significantly higher than PVD and uses coating materials in solid form.
Chip-Scale Packaging	Integrated Circuit (IC) Packaging that begins the packaging process before the wafer has been diced, resulting in a smaller die-package area that is approximately the size of the chip itself. Also known as Wafer-Level Packaging.
Chipset	The configuration of bus interfaces and the microprocessor they connect with. Also known as Chipset Architecture.
Chip Tapeout	The process of creating and sending a GDS file to the foundry. Also called simply "Tapeout."
Circuit	A closed loop between any two differently charged bodies. In electronics, it most likely includes a power source that provides a current, power consuming components that use the current, and connecting wires that transport the current.
Circuit Node	Umbrella term for any individual element that an electrical signal can be sent to, whether that be interconnects, transistors, or other components that make up the circuit (not to be confused with manufacturing or process node).
Clean Room	Rooms in semiconductor fabs designed to house highly precise, ultrasensitive manufacturing processes. They often contain specialized air filtration systems that shrink the number of airborne particles to 1,000 times fewer than a sterile hospital operating room.

(continued)

Term	Definition
Clock Cycle	The amount of time between two pulses of a processor oscillator.
Clock Edge	The beginning and end points of a signal sent in a given clock cycle. Also known as Capture Edge.
Clock Frequency	The number of signal pulses per second generated by an oscillator used to synchronize the operations of a microprocessor. Measured in Hertz (Hz). Also known as clock rate or clock speed.
Clock-tree Synthesis (CTS)	A stage in the back-end design process where Physical Design Engineers make sure that the electrical signaling that delivers information around the circuit "clocks" evenly, or as intended, throughout the chip.
Cloud Computing	The use of pooled computing power stored in data centers and accessed via service networks.
CMOS (Complementary Metal-Oxide-Semiconductor)	Design methodology and manufacturing processes that can facilitate production of both p-channel and n-channel transistors. It can also be used to refer to the circuitry developed using CMOS processes.
Code Division Multiple Access (CDMA)	A multiple access standard technology that uses algorithms to code digitized voice bits or other data and transmit it across a wider channel (greater frequency range), which is then "de-coded" on the receiving end.
Collector	Where signal exits a bipolar junction transistor, similar to the drain in a MOSFET transistor.
Compiler	Device that translates high-level programming languages like Java and C# into machine-level language a computer can understand.
Complex Instruction Set Computing (CISC)	A type of ISA that uses lengthy, multi-clock cycle instructions.
Compute Function	The end task performed based on a given set of instructions.
Compute Instructions	Software code that tells a computer or processor to execute a specific task. Also called simply "Instructions."
Conductivity	The ease with which a material allows electric current to pass through it. The opposite of resistance.
Conductor	A material with high conductivity that allows electric current to pass through easily.
Control Bus	A bus interface that helps a processor control the operations of different parts of the system.
Control Unit	A part of the CPU that determines which instructions should be used.

(continued)

Term	Definition
Copper Hybrid Bonding	Die stacking technology that uses copper-to-copper interconnects to connect stacked die with greater interconnect density and lower resistance, enabling quicker data transfer and faster processing speeds than traditional Through Silicon Vias (TSVs).
Coverage Cell	Range of coverage for each base station. Cell types include Macro Cells, Micro Cells, Pico Cells, and In-Building Systems.
CPU Core	Individual microprocessors that make up a CPU, GPU, or other processor with multi-core architecture. Computing cores can be combined with other "core microprocessors" to tackle more complex tasks and run more taxing applications.
Critical Path	The longest path it takes for a signal to move through a circuit.
Crosstalk	A type of interference that occurs when energy from one signal inadvertently transfers to a neighboring transmission line.
Cryogenic Technology	Technology and equipment that allow cooling of materials to very low temperatures.
Current Leakage	Gradual unintended loss of electrical energy from a circuit. Also referred to as simply "Leakage."
Data Bus	A bus interface that transmits data to a microprocessor.
Data Center	Giant rooms or warehouses full of hundreds or thousands of servers used to store data, host applications, and boost capacity for consumers and businesses without the need to invest and manage all their own infrastructure.
Data Converter	Electronic device that can convert data into different signal types.
Data Transfer Rate (DTR)	The number of bits moved from one place to another over a given period of time. Usually expressed as bits per second.
DDR (Double Data Rate RAM)	A type of DRAM with greatly increased data transfer speed compared with earlier generations of DRAM.
Debugging	A method of fixing design problems identified during the verification process.
Deep learning	A specific kind of machine learning that uses algorithms to build brain-like neuron networks called artificial neural networks.
Demodulator	A device used to decode and break down a received analog carrier wave signal and convert it into a digital signal that a computer can understand. Opposite of a modulator.
Deposition	A collection of processes that add materials called thin films to the surface of wafers during semiconductor manufacturing.

(continued)

Term	Definition
Design Rule Checkers (DRC)	An EDA Tool used to verify that a chip design complies with all the rules of the chosen foundry.
Design Verification	A key step in the silicon design process whereby a front-end design undergoes one or more verification processes to ensure it will perform as intended. These processes can include formal verification, functional verification, and/or emulation.
Device Driver	A special computer program that operates a particular kind of device or module within a larger computer system. Examples include a printer driver, a graphics driver, a sound card driver, and a network card driver.
Die	A single integrated circuit. See Integrated Circuit.
Die Bonding	A set of processes whereby freshly cut die are attached to either a packaging substrate or directly to a PCB. Also known as "Die Attach."
Die Yield	A measurement of the number of functional die divided by the total number of potential die that make it to wafer probing.
Dielectric Loss	A type of loss interference that occurs due to issues with signal velocity.
Dielectric Materials	Materials used to insulate metal interconnects from one another and provide structural support throughout the circuit.
Die-Package Assembly	The combined structure of a die and the protective plastic or ceramic IC Package that encapsulates it.
Digital Electronics	A field of electronics devoted to studying digital signals and the components that control and process them.
Digital Signal Processor (DSP)	Processors used to process multimedia and real-world signals like audio, video, temperature, pressure, position, etc.
Digital Signal	Electric pulses that travel along transmission lines carrying information from place to place throughout an electrical system.
Digital-to-Analog (DAC)	A data converter that converts information encoded in digital signals into analog format.
Diode	A device that allows the flow of electricity in one direction. Less like a switch and more like a valve.
Direct Current (DC)	Electric current flowing in one direction only. It is best suited for powering lower-power end use applications like televisions and vacuum cleaners. Power adapters are needed to convert the alternating current (AC) power from a wall outlet to the direct current (DC) power needed to power household appliances.

(continued)

Term	Definition
Discrete Components	Independently manufactured base level functional components like transistors, resistors, capacitors, inductors, diodes, and others. Unlike functional components, which may be integrated onto a single substrate.
Distortion	A type of interference that occurs when the signal pattern is damaged or warped. In extreme cases, distortion can be so severe that incorrect data is delivered to the receiver.
Dopant	A chemical impurity added to a semiconductor to alter its electrical conductivity. Also called doping agent.
Doping	A technique in semiconductor manufacturing whereby chemical elements are added to a silicon wafer in order to give transistor sub-components special conductive properties that allow them to better control the flow of current.
Drain	Terminal through which current exits a transistor.
DRAM (Dynamic Random-Access Memory)	A type of RAM that functions as the CPU's short-term memory, allowing it to quickly access and process information. DRAM can hold more data than SRAM, but is slower overall.
Dry Etching	A type of removal process that uses plasma to wash away photoresist material that is no longer needed.
EDA (Electronic Design Automation)	A category of software tools used to design integrated circuits and other electronic systems. Also known as e-CAD or Electronic Computer Aided Design.
Electrical Energy	Energy drawn from the movement of electric charges.
Electrically Erasable Programmable Read-Only Memory (EEPROM)	Read only memory (ROM) that can be erased without a UV light tool, but can only be changed 1 byte at a time, making them relatively slow to erase and re-program.
Electrical Resistance	The difficulty with which a material allows electric current from passing through. Insulators have high resistance, while conductors have low resistance. The opposite of conductivity.
Electrical Signal	A series of electrical pulses that carry or encode information. In digital electronics, for example, binary computer sequences of 1's and 0's form a unique pattern that construes information from one part of the circuit to another. Also called Data Signal, or simply, Signal.

(continued)

Term	Definition
Electric Charge	A fundamental property of matter carried by subatomic particles like protons and electrons. The net ratio of protons to electrons determines an object's overall charge.
Electric Current	A stream of electrically charged particles like electrons moving in the same direction through space or a conductive material.
Electric Field	A physical field surrounding electrically charged particles that can exert force on other charged particles. Also referred to simply as "Field."
Electric Potential	A measurement of an object's charge condition at a given point in time. Positively charged objects are considered to have higher potential than those that are negatively charged. Closely related to Potential Difference, which measures the difference in electric charge between two separate objects.
Electricity	A form of energy or set of physical phenomena resulting from the movement of electric charge. It is not technically a "thing," but rather a term used to describe the relationship between charge and current.
Electrochemical Deposition (ECD)	A deposition technique for depositing thin films on the surface of silicon wafers during the semiconductor manufacturing process. It is used to produce thick metal layers on conductive substrates. Also called Electroplating.
Electrode	A conductor used to connect the metallic and non-metallic parts of a circuit. Examples include positively charged cathodes and negatively charged anodes that comprise each end of a battery.
Electromagnetic Force	One of the four fundamental forces of nature. It governs the interaction between electrically charged or magnetically polarized particles and is responsible for the attraction between opposite and rejection between similar charges.
Electromagnetic Interference (EMI)	Signal interference arising from random environmental disturbances.
Electromagnetics	A field that explores the physics and interaction of electric fields with one another.
Electromagnetic Spectrum	The broad range of analog signals classified by wavelength and frequency.
Electromotive Force (EMF or E)	The electric tension between two points of unequal charge measured in Volts (V). The greater the difference in charge between two points, the greater the voltage that exists between them. Akin to "electric water pressure" pushing current down a wire. Also called Voltage or Potential Difference.

(continued)

Term	Definition
Electron	A negatively charged subatomic particle that can exist freely or orbiting the nucleus of an atom.
Electron Beam (E-beam) Lithography	A special kind of lithographic technology that uses beams of electrons instead of light to etch patterns on a wafer's surface.
Electronic Numerical Integrator and Computer (ENIAC)	The first programmable, electronic, general-purpose digital computer. It was invented by J. Presper Eckert and John Mauchly at the University of Pennsylvania in 1946, and was basically a giant room full of vacuum tubes taking up almost 1,800 square feet and weighing nearly 50 tons (U.S. Army, 1947).
Electron Mobility	The natural ability of electrons to move through metals and semiconductors when acted on by an electric field.
Emitter	Where signal enters a bipolar junction transistor, similar to the source in a MOSFET transistor.
Emulation	A method of verification whereby an FPGA emulator is programmed with a new circuit design so it can be tested and observed in the real world.
Encapsulation	A process whereby Surface Mount Technology (SMT) is used to mount a die onto the IC Package enclosure and seal it using encapsulant compounds or molded underfills to form a completed die-package assembly.
Epoxy Die Attach	A common die bonding process that uses specialized resins as a connecting adhesive.
EPROM (Erasable Programmable Read-Only Memory)	Read only memory (ROM) that can be erased and re-written many times, but requires a restrictive process involving a specialized UV light tool to do so.
EUV Lithography	A special kind of lithographic technology that uses ultra violet light instead of more traditional light sources to etch patterns on a wafer's surface. It has a significantly smaller wavelength than alternative sources and can thus etch smaller feature sizes.
Fab	A semiconductor manufacturing plant where integrated circuits and other electronic devices are manufactured. Also called Foundries.
Fabless Design Companies	Semiconductor companies that design, but do not manufacture their own chips.
Fab-Lite Model	A semiconductor business model whereby an IDM like Intel or Samsung produces some of their own chips, while outsourcing manufacturing for a portion of their products.

(continued)

Term	Definition
Failure Analysis	The practice of monitoring production and systematically analyzing low performance or key failures in order to drive process improvements and boost yields.
Failure Analysis Engineer	Engineer who monitors production and systematically analyzes low performance or key failures in order to drive process improvements and boost yields.
Federal Communications Commission (FCC)	The government agency that strictly regulates who can use which frequency ranges (bands) for which types of communication, to prevent people from interfering with each other's signals.
Field Effect Transistor (FET)	A type of transistor that uses an electric field to control the gate. It has three parts – a source, a gate, and a drain.
Filter	An electronic component that lets signals with intended frequencies get into the system and keeps signals with unintended frequencies out.
FinFET Transistor (Fin-Shaped Transistor)	A type of field effect transistor with a raised gate structure covering the channel on three sides, giving the transistor greater control over the flow of current, consuming less power, and reducing the amount of current leakage.
Flip Chip Bonding	Process in Flip-Chip Packaging whereby die are flipped over and soldered to a ball grid array or directly to the PCB, forming interconnects within the chip's surface area and increasing the overall speed of the system.
Floor Planning	A stage in the back-end design process where Physical Design Engineers decide where each block or module should be located in the overall system.
Flywire Connection	Metal wire used to connect transistors to one another during the early evolution of the semiconductor industry.
Formal Verification	A method of verification that uses mathematical reasoning and proofs in lieu of a simulation to verify that an RTL design will perform its desired function.
Form Factor	Device size, shape, and area.
Foundry	A company that strictly performs semiconductor manufacturing. The term can also refer to the semiconductor manufacturing plants themselves. Also called Fabs.
FPGA (Field Programmable Gate Array)	Specialized integrated circuits that can be configured or **programmed** by a customer or designer after the chip has already been manufactured.
Frequency	The number of times an analog signal wave completes an up and down cycle, or repeats itself, over a fixed period.

(continued)

Term	Definition
Frequency Band	A given range of frequencies used for a specific purpose or application. Also known as Bandwidth or Channel.
Front-End Design	A step in the semiconductor design flow where system requirements are gathered and a detailed schematic is developed and verified before moving on to the back-end design process. Commonly referred to as RTL Design.
Front-End Manufacturing	The multi-step process prior to packaging and assembly whereby a circuit pattern is etched onto a silicon wafer and components are connected to one another through global and local interconnects. Also called Wafer Fabrication.
Front-end of the Line (FEOL)	A part of the front-end manufacturing process where transistors are directly etched into the wafer itself. Also known as the "Pre-Metal" part of the manufacturing process.
Front-Side Bus (FSB)	A bus interface that connects the CPU to the Northbridge, which connects to components that have the highest performance requirements, like memory and graphics modules.
Functional Components	Base level components like transistors and resistors that are integrated and manufactured on a single substrate. Unlike discrete components, which must be manufactured separately.
Functional Scaling	Performance improvements drawn from maximizing utilization within a given generation of chip technology, holding feature sizes and manufacturing process nodes equal.
Functional Verification	A type of verification that simulates front-end designs using SystemVerilog HDL code to verify the design will do what it is supposed to do in any possible condition.
Gain	When a signal gets bigger and more powerful after passing through an electronic component like an amplifier.
Gallium Arsenide (GaAs)	A type of semiconductor compound made from gallium and arsenide that is used to make electronic devices. Though fragile and more difficult to manufacture than silicon, it is commonly used for specialized applications like high-frequency signal processing in cell phones and light emitting diodes for lasers and lighting systems.
Gallium Nitride (GaN)	A type of semiconductor compound made from gallium and nitrogen that is used to make electronic devices. Though fragile and more difficult to manufacture than silicon, it is used for specialized applications like high-efficiency power transistors, RF components, lasers, photonics, and light emitting diodes.
Gate	The base of a transistor that sits between the source and drain. It protects the channel and decides whether to let a signal pass through.

(continued)

Term	Definition
Gate All Around (GAA) Transistor	A type of field effect transistor with a raised gate structure covering the channel on all four sides, giving the transistor greater control over the flow of current, consuming less power, and reducing the amount of current leakage.
Gate Length	The distance between the source and the drain inside a transistor.
GDS II (Graphic Data System)	A standardized format that is used to send a finished design to the fab at the end of the IC design cycle.
Geometric Scaling	Performance improvements drawn from shrinking feature sizes and transistor gate lengths across entire generations of integrated circuits.
Germanium	A type of semiconductor element used to make electronic devices (Ge32 on the periodic table). It was used to make transistors in the early days before being replaced by cheaper, higher-performance silicon transistors. It is still used for specific devices like high-frequency and high-power devices, as well as some audio electronics.
Global System for Mobile Communication (GSM)	The primary standard for communication networks globally. GSM is built using TDMA technology.
Graphene	An incredibly strong material with a thickness of only 1 atom. Graphene could potentially solve the quantum tunneling problems that silicon suffers from.
Graphics Processing Unit (GPU)	A special kind of processor best known for driving the graphics and 3D visual processing in electronic devices. Unlike CPUs, GPUs use parallel processing to perform calculations.
Hard Disk Drive (HDD)	Secondary memory built from a magnetic disk with a read/write arm that can store data indefinitely.
Hardware Abstraction Layer	A layer in our macro system stack that provides the software-to-hardware interface.
Hardware Accelerator	Specialized hardware module or circuitry optimized for specific computing tasks. Also known as simply "Accelerator."
Hardware Description Language (HDL)	Specialized computer "programming" languages used to describe the physical structure of ICs and electronic systems. VHDL, Verilog, and SystemVerilog are examples of widely used HDLs.
Hardware Layer	A layer in our macro system stack that includes the core processing hardware and circuitry that forms the base of an electronic system.

(continued)

Term	Definition
Harvard Architecture	A theoretical macroarchitecture that parses instructions and data into two separate memory banks, with a unique bus for each type of input.
Hertz (Hz)	The base unit for clock frequency. Equal to one clock cycle per second.
Heterogeneous Integration	A system integration strategy whereby numerous chips are integrated with one another either on the same board (PCB) or within the same package.
High Bandwidth Memory (HBM)	A 2.5D Memory Device structure that splits core logic into separate parts, stacking the memory die on top of one of them while leaving the other on its own.
High Pass Filter	A filter that only lets signals in above a certain frequency.
High Performance Computing (HPC)	The practice of using supercomputers or computer clusters to deliver greater processing speeds.
High-Level Synthesis (HLS)	A stage in the silicon design process whereby an RTL design written in an HDL like VHDL or Verilog is converted into a design netlist ready for back-end physical design. This is the stage that marks the end of front-end design and the beginning of back-end design.
Huang's Law	An observation by NVIDIA's CEO, Jensen Huang, that GPU AI Processing power has doubled every year since 2012.
Human brain project (HBP)	A widely recognized research project focused on building our understanding of neuroscience and computing.
Hybrid Memory Cube (HMC)	A 3D Memory Device structure where DRAM memory chips are vertically stacked on top of a logic device and connected to one another with a Through Silicon Via (TSV).
I/O Controller Hub (ICH)	The interface between Northbridge and Southbridge.
I/O Density	The concentration of I/O interconnects over a given amount of die surface area. Higher I/O densities reduce the amount of processing time it takes to move a signal, or information, from one part of an electronic system to another and can save valuable silicon real estate in stacked-die configurations.
IC Packaging	A special enclosure designed to protect the underlying circuit or semiconductor device. Typically made from plastic or ceramic materials.
III-V elements	Elements from group III and V in the periodic table. Such elements are particularly well suited for making semiconductors and electronic devices. Examples include silicon, germanium, and gallium arsenide.

(continued)

Term	Definition
Impurities	A chemical impurity added to a semiconductor to alter its electrical conductivity. Also called impurities.
Inductor	A device that uses magnetic fields to regulate voltage and control the flow of electricity. They are often found as discrete components in power supplies.
Inking	A process whereby defective die are often marked with a black dot so they can be tossed out or sold at a discounted price if still semi-functional.
Instruction Pipelining	A method of speeding up a task by breaking up a lengthy workflow into smaller constituent parallel tasks that can boost processing speed without requiring additional process flows.
Instruction Set Architecture (ISA)	Macroarchitecture that defines which types of instructions a given system must be able to perform.
Insulator	A material with low conductivity that prevents electric current from passing through easily.
Integrated Circuit (IC)	An electronic circuit formed from a bunch of transistors and other functional components fit together on a single block of substrate (semiconductor base material). Integrated circuits were invented by Jack Kilby at Texas Instruments and Robert Noyce at Fairchild Semiconductor in the 1960s.
Integrated Device Manufacturers (IDMs)	Semiconductor companies which design, manufacture, and sell their own integrated circuits.
Interconnects (I/O)	Connection points tying separate parts of the system to one another. Within a given IC, "pre-metal" local interconnects might help form logic gates and other core circuitry at the base of the circuit, while higher-level "post-metal" global interconnects connect broader parts of the chip to one another. System interconnects might connect an entire chip through the IC package to the rest of the system.
Interference	Physical disruptions that can degrade the accuracy of a signal that results in data loss, accuracy issues, or potential system failure. Common forms of interference include noise, crosstalk, distortion, and loss.
Interposer	An intermediate substrate that sits on top of a base substrate and serves as a connection between two or more die to one other and to the rest of the system.
Ion Implantation	A part of the doping process whereby dopants or impurities are shot under the surface of the wafer. Also known as "Ion Introduction."

(continued)

Term	Definition
Ionizing	Electromagnetic radiation with sufficient energy to detach electrons from atoms and molecules. This is the kind of dangerous radiation emitted by nuclear power plants and can be very dangerous.
Joule's Law	An equation describing the relationship between power, voltage, and current. It is named after English physicist James Prescott Joule, who discovered it in 1840. Power (P) = Voltage (E) x Current (I).
Kernel	A computer program at the core of a computer operating system that sits between the operating system and the hardware.
Kinetic Energy	A form of energy derived from motion, that is, motion energy.
Light Emitting Diode (LED)	A special kind of semiconductor device that emits light when electric current passes through it.
Line Yield	A measurement of the number of wafers that successfully make it to wafer probing without being thrown out. Also known as "Wafer Yield."
Logic Design Engineer	Engineer responsible for implementing the System Architect's vision by designing a circuit's core logic and functionality using register transfer level (RTL) design language.
Logic Design (RTL Design)	The basic circuitry design of a digital computer based on Boolean logic gates. Also known as RTL Design.
Logic Device	Integrated circuit that is custom designed for a specific application. The Logic IC segment in the SIA framework encompasses all non-micro component digital logic, including application specific ICs (ASICs), field programmable gate arrays (FPGAs), and more versatile, but application-specific, digital logic devices.
Logic Gate	Units made from transistors that apply Boolean logic to input data signals and block or release output signal to the next gate in the system. There are seven types of Logic gates in total – AND, OR, XOR, NOT, NAND, NOR, and XNOR.
Loss	A type of interference that occurs when energy is dispersed into the environment for a number of reasons. Three kinds of loss include Resistive Loss, Dielectric Loss, and Radiation Loss.
Low Pass Filter	A filter that only lets signals in below a certain frequency.
Machine Learning	A method of computation that uses algorithms to analyze and learn from patterns in data, improving the ability of the computer to adapt and improve. It is part of the broader field of Artificial Intelligence.

(continued)

Term	Definition
Macroarchitecture	High-level rules and structural guidelines used to define entire chip families. Describes the way in which instructions are delivered from programmer to the computer. Also known as Instruction Set Architecture (ISA).
Matrix	A vast array of numbers used for machine learning computations.
Memory	A type of circuit whose primary function is to store data and information for use in processing centers of the larger system.
Memory Hierarchy	The sequential structure of memory organized by proximity to the core system processor. From closest to farthest, the memory hierarchy includes CPU registers, cache memory, RAM working memory, ROM long-term storage memory, and external interconnects like the mouse and keyboard.
Metal Oxide Semiconductor Field Effect Transistor (MOSFET)	A type of field effect transistor that uses voltage to control the gate. It has three parts – a source, a gate, and a drain.
Microarchitecture	Describes the way high-level macroarchitecture or a specific instruction set architecture (ISA) is actually implemented into the hardware itself.
Micro Components	All non-custom digital devices that can be plugged into another system and used for computation or signal processing, like generic digital subcomponents. Examples include microprocessors, microcontrollers, and digital signal processors (DSPs).
Microcontroller	A computer processor that performs specific functions and is integrated with memory and I/O connections all on one chip. Microcontrollers are smaller and less powerful than microprocessors and can serve as plug-and-play computing power for simple operations.
Micro-Electro-Mechanical System (MEMS)	Tiny mechanical device that operates gears or levers at a microscopic scale and is manufactured using semiconductor fabrication techniques.
Micron	One millionth of a meter.
Microprocessor (MPU)	A computer processor that performs a general computing function and requires an external bus to connect to memory and other peripheral components.
Microwaves	A special set of analog "wave" signals that sit between a range of frequencies on the electromagnetic spectrum. Microwaves have higher frequencies than radio waves, but smaller frequencies than infrared and visible light.

(continued)

Term	Definition
Middleware Layer	A layer in our macro system stack that contains the back-end application framework and software logic powering a given software program.
Mixed-Signal Device	Electronic device that contains both digital and analog circuitry.
Modem	A device with a modulator and a demodulator that can execute modulation and demodulation algorithms at the same time, allowing it to convert between analog-to-digital and digital-to-analog signals quickly.
Modulation	The process by which digital information is encoded into an analog carrier wave signal by altering its frequency or amplitude. Modulation is what allows digital information to be sent wirelessly.
Modulator	A device used to encode an analog carrier wave signal with digital information. Opposite of a Demodulator.
Molded Underfills	Special materials used to help encapsulate finished die in IC Packaging to form completed die-package assemblies.
Molecular Beam Epitaxy (MBE)	A physical deposition technique that used to deposit thin films on the surface of silicon wafers during the semiconductor manufacturing process. A type of Physical Vapor Deposition.
Monolithic Integration (Homogenous Integration)	A system integration strategy whereby numerous functional modules are included on a single integrated circuit, yielding a fully functional system called an SoC (System-on-Chip).
Moore's Law	The 1965 prediction by Intel's founder, Gordon Moore, that the number of transistors that could be fit on a microchip would double every two years at the same time that computer costs were halved.
Multi-Chip-Modules (MCM)	A type of packaging structure that integrates multiple die into a single package. While System-in-Packages (SiPs) integrate die both horizontally (2D) and vertically (2.5/3D), multichip modules have a 2D structure, with all modules connecting to the same underlying packaging substrate.
Multi-core Architecture	A processor structure that combines multiple computing cores to tackle more complex tasks and run more taxing applications.
Multiple Access Standard Technology	A type of technology that allows service providers to route multiple calls through the same base station, or across a given amount of bandwidth.
Multiplex	Simultaneous transmission of several messages or data signals using a single channel of communication or bandwidth.

(continued)

Term	Definition
NAND Flash Memory	A type of EEPROM that can erase information, write data in chunks (as opposed to 1 byte at a time) and works considerably faster than EPROM and is the primary type of ROM used to store data in electronic devices today.
Nanometer (nm)	The base unit for measuring feature sizes in microelectronics. Equal to one billionth of a meter.
Nanosheet Transistor	A type of GAA field effect transistor with a raised gate structure and wide "sheet-like" channels.
Nanowire Transistor	A type of GAA field effect transistor with a raised gate structure and thin "wire-like" channels.
Netlist	A detailed list of the electronic components in a circuit and all the nodes to which they are connected. It is derived from a front end design written in register transfer level (RTL) code and used to guide back-end physical design.
Neuromorphic Computing Technology	Technology that models biological processing centers like the nervous system in an effort to create a new computing paradigm.
Neurotransistor	Transistors that can simultaneously store and process information, while greatly improving processing speed, as well as exhibiting characteristics of plasticity and learning like that of a human brain.
Neutron	A neutral subatomic particle found in the nucleus of every atom along with protons. It contains about the same mass as its proton counterparts.
NMOS Transistor	A transistor made of a p-type semiconductor sandwiched between two n-type semiconductors.
Noise	A type of interference that occurs when energy that is not part of the desired signal interferes with the signal being transmitted.
Non-Volatile Memory	Memory that can store data without access to power. Non-Volatile Memories are used for permanent data storage.
Northbridge	A bus interface that connects the CPU to components that have the highest performance requirements, like memory and graphics modules via the Front-Side Bus (FSB).
N-Type Semiconductor	A block of semiconductor material that has undergone the doping process and now contains an extra electron.
Ohms (Ω)	The base unit for electrical resistance. It measures the amount of opposition to the flow of current in an electrical circuit.

(*continued*)

Term	Definition
Open Source	A publicly accessible standard or technology that does not require licensing fees to use in a unique product or service. In hardware, open source ISAs like RISC-V can be used as a base macroarchitecture that design teams could build a circuit around. In software, tools like GitHub provide easy access to open source software built by other users and Open Source software companies.
Open Systems Interconnection (OSI) Model	A conceptual framework used in connectivity and telecommunications to describe the inner workings of electronic devices and networking systems.
Optical Chips	Circuits that use light and photons as the main signal carrier between and within electronic devices.
Optical Interconnects	Interconnect technology used for chip-to-chip data transmission and communication. Could be a strong alternative to traditional copper wiring.
Optical Transceiver	Specific kind of photonic integrated circuit (PIC) used by data centers to transmit information more effectively and efficiently across greater distances than copper cabling.
Optoelectronics	Semiconductor devices that produce and receive light waves.
OR Gate	A logic gate that requires one of two input conditions to be met before letting a signal pass through.
OSAT (Outsourced Assembly, Test, and Packaging Suppliers)	Semiconductor companies that specialize in back-end manufacturing assembly, test, and packaging activities. They are largely based in East Asia due to significant labor cost advantages.
Oscillator	Any signal emitting device. In wireless electronics, oscillators are the source of RF wave signals used as a "carrier" for the information being transmitted.
OSI System Stack	Seven layers in the OSI model representing concentric layers of abstraction. From hardware to user, the stack layers include the Physical Layer, Data Link Layer, Network Layer, Transport Layer, Session Layer, Presentation Layer, and Application Layer.
Oxidation	Process whereby a wafer is heated in a furnace along with oxide gas in order to help deposit thin film material layers on its surface.
Package-Die Assembly	The final product resulting from the assembly process. It comprises a finished die encapsulated by an IC Package.
Pads	Designated areas on circuit boards or integrated circuits used for things like soldering, wire bonding, or chip mounting.

(continued)

Term	Definition
Parallel Interface	Interconnect that runs multiple wires between two components and transmits multiple bits at the same time. Examples include DDR (Double Data Rate Bus) and PCI (Peripheral Component Interface Bus).
Parallel Processing	A form of computation that breaks down more complex problems into smaller constituent parts.
Parametric Testing	A testing methodology that measures several key circuit parameters on a test circuit structure to ensure that the wafer fabrication process is performing as expected.
Parasitics	Unwanted interference from other components. Such problems can arise when components are clustered too closely together.
Patterning	A collection of processes that shape or alter the materials on the surface of wafers during semiconductor manufacturing.
Peripheral Buses	Lower performance non-Northbridge bus interfaces like Ethernet, USB, PCI, BIOS, etc.
Photolithography	A key manufacturing process that shines specialized energy sources like electron beams or ultraviolet light through a photomask or series of photomasks in order to imprint circuitry patterns on the surface of silicon wafers that constitute individual die. Photolithography processes are performed in an expensive machine called a stepper.
Photomask	A semi-transparent plate used in the lithography process to etch patterns and circuit features onto a wafer. A specialized light source is shone through the photomask, which acts like a stencil and reacts with the exposed photoresist that coats the surface below. Also known as simply "Mask."
Photonically Optimized Embedded Microprocessors (POEM) Project	A DARPA-funded project commercializing photonic chip technology.
Photonic Integrated Circuit (PIC)	A chip that performs optical functions in areas like fiber communications, optical sensing applications like LIDAR, etc.
Photoresist	A chemical used during photolithography that breaks down in reaction to light. When we target photoresist with a reactive light source, we can etch circuit patterns on the surface of a wafer in the shape of our photomask(s).

(continued)

Term	Definition
Physical Design	A multi-stage process taking a front-end design through the numerous stages of the back-end design process until it's ready for manufacturing.
Physical Design Engineer	Engineer responsible for taking a front-end design through the numerous stages of the back-end design process until it's ready for manufacturing.
Physical layer (PHY Layer)	Layer 1 in the OSI model and Layer 2 in our Macro System Stack. It is the layer at which the data itself (a string of 1's and 0's) is transmitted to the underlying processing hardware.
Physical Vapor Deposition (PVD)	A category of deposition techniques used for depositing thin films on the surface of silicon wafers during the semiconductor manufacturing process. PVD takes place at temperatures significantly lower than CVD and uses coating materials in gaseous form.
Place-and-Route	A stage in the back-end design process where Physical Design Engineers decide exactly where to put all the electronic components then integrate all the wiring required to connect them to one another.
Planar Manufacturing	A set of manufacturing methods and processes that allows companies to fabricate thousands of integrated circuits at the same time and on the same substrate (silicon wafer). Planar manufacturing was invented by Jean Hoerni at Fairchild Semiconductor in the 1960s.
Platform Layer	A layer in our macro system stack that contains the operating system supported by Kernel and Device Drivers.
PMOS Transistor	A transistor made of an n-type semiconductor sandwiched between two p-type semiconductors.
Post-Metal Cycling	A set of common deposition, patterning, removal, and physical property alteration processes used repeatedly during the back-end of the line (BEOL) portion of the wafer fabrication process whereby metallic interconnect materials, usually made from aluminum or copper, are deposited in layers separated by dielectric materials to form metal interconnects between individual components and broader system circuitry.
Potential Difference	The electric tension between two points of unequal charge measured in Volts (V). The greater the difference in charge between two points, the greater the voltage that exists between them. Akin to "electric water pressure" pushing current down a wire. Also called Voltage or Electromotive Force.

(continued)

Term	Definition
Power	The work done by an electric circuit when an electric current is converted into some useful form of energy.
Power Converter	A device that converts between Alternating Current (AC) and Direct Current (DC) or between currents of the same type for voltage regulation purposes.
Power Density	A measure of the amount of power output per unit volume. The measure is closely related to the amount of heat that a circuit can remove, which can limit processor performance at smaller transistor sizes.
Power Distribution Network (PDN)	A network of metal planes, voltage regulators, and power converters that transport charges and electric voltage from a power source to the different processing centers of an integrated circuit or electronic system.
Power Engineer	An engineer responsible for building a robust power distribution network, including voltage regulators, power converters, and planes to ensure power is delivered where it needs to be, while ensuring voltage is never too high or too low at any point in the system.
Power Integrity	A measure of the quality of voltage flow throughout a system.
Power Management Integrated Circuit (PMIC)	Type of integrated circuit that is responsible for regulating power and voltage in a system or device.
Power Management Unit (PMU)	A microcontroller that regulates the power and voltage within an electronic system.
Pre-Metal Cycling	A set of common deposition, patterning, removal, and physical property alteration processes that are used during the front-end of the line (FEOL) portion of the wafer fabrication process whereby transistors are directly etched into the wafer itself.
Primary Memory	The main working memory of the computer. Primary memories can be accessed more quickly by the processor but have limited capacity and are usually more expensive than secondary memories.
Printed Circuit Board (PCB)	A laminated board on which integrated circuits and other electronic components can be soldered and connected to one another that provides mechanical support to the overall system.
PROM (Programmable Read-Only Memory)	Read only memory (ROM) that can be programmed after manufacturing, but cannot be changed once programmed.
Proton	A positively charged subatomic particle found in the nucleus of every atom along with neutrons. It contains about the same mass as its neutron counterparts.

(continued)

Term	Definition
Pure-Play Foundries	Semiconductor companies that manufacture, but do not design their own chips.
P-Type Semiconductor	A block of semiconductor material that has undergone the doping process and now contains one fewer electron.
Quantum Computing	A field of computing and computing systems that harnesses the superposition of qubits in conjunction with a phenomenon called quantum entanglement, where two particles are tied to one another over a distance, to execute exponentially more complex calculations than modern computers can handle. Particularly well suited to applications in cryptography, machine learning, big data, medicine, and materials science.
Quantum Entanglement	A phenomenon where two particles are tied to one another over a distance. Entanglement is a key phenomenon used by quantum computers to execute exponentially more complex calculations than modern computers can handle.
Quantum Supremacy	A point in time when a quantum computer that functions according to the laws of quantum physics performs better at a given task than a classical computer that functions using classical physics like Isaac Newton's law of motion.
Quantum Transistor	Transistors that harness the power of quantum tunneling and entanglement to process and store information.
Quantum Tunneling	A quantum phenomena whereby an electron can disappear on one side of a physical barrier and turn up on the other.
Qubit	A quantum computational unit that can exist as a 0, 1, or a combination of both at any given time.
Radiation	The emission or transmission of energy in the form of electromagnetic waves.
Radiation Loss	A type of loss interference that occurs due to system sealing issues.
Radio Frequency (RF)	A special set of analog "wave" signals that sit between a range of frequencies on the electromagnetic spectrum. Commonly used for broadcasting, networking, and wireless communication.
Random Access Memory (RAM)	Memory that allows a processor to both read or "take" input data and write or "deliver" output data to memory. RAM is used as working memory for running programs and storing temporary data close to the CPU for quick access.
Rapid Thermal Annealing	A property alteration manufacturing process that helps activate dopants by heating silicon wafers to extremely high temperatures for a brief period of time.

(continued)

Term	Definition
Read Only Memory (ROM)	Non-volatile memory that can be programmed only once and cannot be easily repurposed. ROM is used for permanent data storage.
Receiver	A device that accepts or **receives** an electrical signal.
Reduced Instruction Set Computing (RISC)	A type of ISA that uses standard, shorter single-clock cycle instructions.
Reference Clock	A clock used by digital processors to coordinate processing done by different functional blocks and ensure proper timing across the system. Also called simply "Clock."
Register	The physical entry and exit point for data flow to and from a CPU to the rest of the system. Each CPU has a fixed number of registers through which data can flow, with typical register capacities measuring 8-, 16-, 32-, or 64-bits "wide."
Register Transfer Level (RTL)	A low-level design abstraction used to model digital circuit designs using registers and logic operators. Also known as Logic Design.
Removal Processes (for Manufacturing)	A collection of processes that remove materials called thin films from the surface of wafers during semiconductor manufacturing.
Resistive Loss	A type of loss interference that occurs due to transmission line conductivity issues.
Resistor	A device used to impede the flow of electricity through a circuit.
RF Integrated Circuit (RFIC)	A specific kind of circuit used to transmit and receive wireless RF signals.
Scribe Line	A space in between each die that provides space for sawing during wafer dicing at the end of wafer processing and the front-end manufacturing process.
Secondary Memory	Slower memory that can only be accessed through interconnects and intermediaries. Also known as Backup Memory or Auxiliary Memory.
Semiconductor	A material with moderate conductivity between that of an insulator and a conductor. A balanced conductivity profile makes semiconductors particularly well suited to controlling and manipulating current in electronic devices.
Semiconductor Industry Association (SIA)	A leading semiconductor trade association and lobbying group founded in 1977. They perform deep, wholistic industry analysis of key developments and trends.
Semiconductor IP Companies	Semiconductor companies that design and license common modules and cell libraries that can be used by circuit designers to generate even more complex designs.

(continued)

Term	Definition
Semiconductor Value Chain	The core sequence of value-added activities that result in a finished semiconductor product, from initial customer need through chip design, manufacturing, packaging, assembly, system integration, and final product delivery.
Sensor	Device that detects a real-world input like heat or pressure and converts it into electrical signals. Active sensors require external power sources, while passive sensors require no power to function.
Serial Interface	Interconnect that transmits and receives data between two components across a single wire one bit at a time, but at much higher speed than parallel interfaces. Examples include PCIe (PCI Express Bus), USB (Universal Serial Bus), SATA (Serial Advanced Technology Attachment Bus), and Ethernet Bus.
Serial Processing	A form of computation that runs through tasks very quickly, but can only complete instructions in order, one after the other.
Shuttle Run	A Foundry manufacturing run that produces the designs of multiple customers at the same time.
Signal Compression	Techniques and algorithms used by DSPs to shrink the amount of bandwidth required to send a given piece of information.
Signal Integrity Engineer	An engineer who conducts electromagnetic simulations and analysis to identify and resolve potential signal integrity issues before they arise.
Signal Integrity	A measure of the quality of an electrical signal.
Silica (Silicon Dioxide)	Compound that is melted down and shaped into cylindrical ingots that are subsequently sliced into thin, unfinished wafers.
Silicon	A type of semiconductor element used to make the vast majority of integrated circuits and electronic devices (Si14 on the periodic table). It is inexpensive and abundant, comprising roughly 30% of the Earth's crust.
Silicon Cycle	A semiconductor business cycle whose length is defined by the difference between a high and low point in industry revenues and company valuations. The term is used to describe the highly volatile nature of the semiconductor industry, with wide swings in annual revenues.
Silicon Germanium (SiGe)	A potential new channel material that could help mitigate electron mobility issues.
Solder Balls	Metallic balls that connect die to a substrate or PCB. Also called "Wafer Bumps."

(continued)

Term	Definition
Solid State Drive (SSD)	Secondary memory that uses interconnected NAND Flash memory chips instead of a magnetic disk and can store memory indefinitely.
Source	Terminal through which current enters a transistor.
Southbridge	A bus interface that connects the Northbridge to all the lower priority components and interfaces like Ethernet, USB, and other low-speed buses via I/O Controller Hub (ICH).
Spiking Neural Networks (SNN)	Neural networks that mimic the structure of neuron networks in human brains.
Sputtering Gas	Specialized gas used to knock atoms off the sputtering target in order to form thin films on a wafer's surface during the deposition process in semiconductor manufacturing.
Sputtering Target	A material used to create thin films on the surface of a wafer during deposition in semiconductor manufacturing. It is placed across from the wafer in a vacuum chamber and is targeted with sputtering gas, which knocks lose atoms from the Sputtering Target materials and onto the wafer surface.
SRAM (Static Random-Access Memory)	A type of RAM that functions as the CPU's short-term memory, allowing it to quickly access and process information. SRAM is faster than DRAM, but can hold less data.
Static Timing Analysis (STA)	A common simulation method to compute and verify the expected timing of digital circuits.
Stepper	A machine used to align photomask(s) over a wafer during the photolithography stage of the semiconductor manufacturing process.
Strain Engineering	A type of engineering in which the atoms in a given material are stretched apart from one another, allowing electrons to pass through more easily and reducing heat release from a circuit.
Strong Force	One of the four fundamental forces of nature. It is responsible for holding the neutrons and protons that comprise the nucleus together despite protons having similar charges.
Substrate	Widely defined as an underlying substance or base layer. In electronics, it usually refers to the semiconductor base material that constitute wafers used to manufacture integrated circuits, most commonly made from silicon.
Superposition	A property of quantum particles that enables them to exist in two states (in this case 0 and 1) at the same time.
Surface Mount Technology (SMT)	An assembly process whereby electronic components are attached to the surface of a PCB.

(continued)

Term	Definition
Synchronous Design	A design methodology that uses a common "clock" across all circuits so that all signals reach the relevant parts of the circuit at the right time.
System Architect	Tenured engineer responsible for developing a high-level idea of what chip their team is trying to design based on user requirements or market need and determine what technologies, materials, and components will be used to build it.
System Bus	A collection of three bus interfaces – the data bus, address bus, and control bus – that collectively control the flow of information to and from a CPU or microprocessor.
System Integration	The process of attaching a final circuit or die-package assembly into an end product or device.
System-in-Package (SiP)	A type of packaging structure that integrates multiple die into a single package. Unlike Multi-Chip-Modules (MCMs) that are limited to 2D structure with all die connecting to the same underlying substrate, System-in-Packages (SiP's) have both horizontal (2D) and vertical (2.5/3D) structures, with some die stacking on top of other die connected through silicon vias (TSVs) to the underlying substrate.
System Level Architecture	A high-level outline of a chip's intended purpose based on user requirements or market need and a rough blueprint of system modules, design technologies, materials, and components that will be used to build it.
System on Chip (SoC)	A type of integrated circuit (IC) that includes an entire system on a single substrate.
Systems Companies	End product companies like Apple or Google that have started designing their own custom processors in-house.
SystemVerilog	A hardware description language used for front-end design verification.
Technology Node (or Process Node or just Node)	A given generation of semiconductor manufacturing technology comprising improved equipment, new materials, and process improvements that enable chip makers to make chips with smaller transistors (measured in nm) than prior nodes.
Testbench	Specialized computer code used during FPGA or ASIC verification or simulation used to verify that the correct outputs are produced from a given set of inputs.
Thin Films	Layers of material added to the surface of a wafer during the deposition process in semiconductor manufacturing. They form the clay in which circuit patterns and features can be etched during later steps.

(continued)

Term	Definition
Through Silicon Via (TSV)	Vertical interconnects that tie together stacked die to one another and the substrate below.
Time Division Multiple Access (TDMA)	A multiple access standard technology that uses multiplexing to break up and deliver calls in synchronous chunks, maximizing utilization of existing bandwidth.
Tracks	Conductive paths on circuit boards used to connect electronic system components to one another.
Transfer Molding	A process that uses melted resin to encapsulate a completed die or other semiconductor components in an IC Package.
Transistor	Electronic switch that stops electricity from passing or allows current to flow through. Transistors are strung together to make logic gates and form the backbone of digital electronics.
Transmission Line	Metallic lines or traces that carry information from place to place throughout an electrical system.
Transmitter	A device that sends or **transmits** an electrical signal.
Ultraviolet Light Processing (UVP)	A property alteration manufacturing process that modified a wafer's electrical properties by exposing it to ultraviolet light.
User Interface	The connection point where the end user interacts with a given system.
UVM (Universal Verification Methodology)	A way of conducting verification in which Verification Engineers build a model of each system module, then compare outputs of the design against this model to determine if the circuit is behaving as expected.
Vacuum Chamber	A piece of equipment used to reduce the presence of contaminant particles during the deposition process in semiconductor manufacturing.
Vacuum Tube	A glass or metal enclosure containing electrodes that can control the flow of electrons. Vacuum tubes were used for early computing applications like the ENIAC in the 1940s, but due to their fragility were swiftly displaced with the advent of transistors. They are still used today in select applications like microwave ovens and audio equipment.
Validation Engineer	Engineer who uses EDA tools like design rule checkers (DRC) to validate that a chip is ready for manufacturing.
Verification Engineer	Engineer responsible for verifying front-end design will function as expected.
Verilog	A hardware description language used for front-end digital design. Similar to VHDL, but is newer and based on Ada and Pascal programming languages.

(continued)

Term	Definition
VHDL	A hardware description language used for front-end digital design. Similar to Verilog, but based on C programming language.
Via Structures	Vertically oriented metallic interconnects that tie together components at separate levels of the die surface.
VLSI (Very Large Scale Integration)	The process of designing integrated circuits with very high volumes of functional components (millions of transistors).
Volatile Memory	Memory that can store data only with access to power.
Volt	The base unit for voltage. It measures the amount of electrical pressure between two points due to the difference in electric potential that exists between them.
Voltage	The electric tension between two points of unequal charge measured in Volts (V). The greater the difference in charge between two points, the greater the voltage that exists between them. Akin to "electric water pressure" pushing current down a wire. Also called Electromotive Force or Potential Difference.
Voltage Regulator	A power supply component designed to maintain a steady supply of voltage across varying environmental changes and conditions. Examples include DC/DC converters, PMUs (power management units), Buck converters (a specific type of DC/DC converters), Boost and Flyback converters.
Von Neumann Architecture	A theoretical macroarchitecture with a single bus connecting the CPU with a single memory bank.
Wafer	A round, thin slice of semiconductor material used to manufacture sheets of integrated circuits most commonly made from silicon crystal. They typically have a hard cut edge for handling purposes during the manufacturing process.
Wafer Bumping	A back-end manufacturing process where the bare die is connected directly to other components via small metallic balls (or bumps) that are soldered directly onto the wafer. This step is only performed for select kinds of die-package assemblies.
Wafer Dicing	Back-end manufacturing process whereby individual die are cut from a finished wafer using a diamond saw before being sent to a back-end facility for packaging and assembly.
Wafer Fabrication	A complex set of manufacturing processes used to produce "sheets" of fully completed integrated circuits "printed" on flat, round silicon wafers at a semiconductor fab or foundry.

(continued)

Term	Definition
Wafer Level Packaging (WLP)	Integrated Circuit (IC) Packaging that begins the packaging process before the wafer has been diced, resulting in a smaller die-package area that is approximately the size of the chip itself. Also known as Chip-Scale Packaging (CSP).
Wafer Prober	A device used to electrically test wafer die before final packaging, assembly, and testing is done.
Wafer Probing	A late-stage front-end manufacturing process where a device called a wafer prober electrically tests wafer die before final packaging, assembly, and testing is done.
Wafer Run	A full run-through of the wafer manufacturing process in a fab or foundry, from wafer fabrication through to wafer dicing.
Wafer Testing	A testing methodology that ensures each individual die is defect free and fully functional. Wafer testing enables fabs to identify dysfunctional die for disposal, measure performance, and track recurring errors so that processes can be improved.
Watt (W)	The base unit for power. It measures the amount of work executed by an electronic circuit in which one amp is "pushed" by one volt.
Wavelength	The distance between two successive high or low points on a given wave of light, RF Signal, or other electromagnetic wave energy. In photolithography, light wavelengths constrain the pattern size engineers can etch into the surface of a wafer.
Wet Etching	A type of removal process that uses liquid chemicals to wash away photoresist material that is no longer needed.
Wire Bonding	Process whereby die are connected to the rest of the system through little wires that lead out to the periphery of the package, forming interconnects (I/0) with the rest of the system.
World Semiconductor Trade Statistics (WSTS)	A leading non-profit organization that compiles key revenue and product category sales data for the semiconductor industry.
Yield	A statistic used to measure the productive success of a specific set of manufacturing processes or wafer run. There are two types of yield, including Line Yield and Die Yield, which together measure end-to-end yield.
Yield Optimization	A critical set of practices, feedback mechanisms, and testing processes whose goal is to maximize yield, drive down unit manufacturing costs, and boost margins.

I

Index

© Corey Richard 2023
C. Richard, *Understanding Semiconductors,* Maker Innovations Series,
https://doi.org/10.1007/978-1-4842-8847-4

Printed in the United States
by Baker & Taylor Publisher Services